MARKETING
PUBLIC
TRANSIT

Praeger Series in Public and Non-Profit Sector Marketing
Steven E. Permut, General Editor
Yale University

Marketing Public Transit
A Strategic Approach
Christopher H. Lovelock, Gordon Lewin,
George S. Day, and John E.G. Bateson

A Theory of Political Choice Behavior
Bruce I. Newman and Jagdish N. Sheth

Political Marketing
An Approach to Campaign Strategy
Gary A. Mauser

The Marketing of Ideas and Social Issues
Seymour H. Fine

Government Marketing
Theory and Practice
edited by Michael P. Mokwa
and Steven E. Permut

Marketing the Arts
edited by Michael P. Mokwa
William M. Dawson and
E. Arthur Prieve

MARKETING PUBLIC TRANSIT

A Strategic Approach

**Christopher H. Lovelock,
Gordon Lewin,
George S. Day,
and John E. G. Bateson**

PRAEGER

New York
Westport, Connecticut
London

Library of Congress Cataloging-in-Publication Data

Marketing public transit.

(Praeger series in public and nonprofit sector
marketing)
  Includes index.
  1. Local transit—United States—Marketing.
I. Lovelock, Christopher H.   II. Series.
HE4456.M37   1987   388.4′068′8   87-11583
ISBN 0-275-92499-8 (alk. paper)

Library of Congress Catalog Card Number: 87-11583
ISBN: 0-275-92499-8

First published in 1987

Praeger Publishers, One Madison Avenue, New York, NY 10010
A division of Greenwood Press, Inc.

Printed in the United States of America

The paper used in this book complies with the
Permanent Paper Standard issued by the National
Information Standards Organization (Z39.48-1984).

10 9 8 7 6 5 4 3 2 1

To our children:

Timothy and Elizabeth Lovelock
David Lewin-Rowen
Sharon, Geoffrey, and Mark Day
Lorna and Jonathan Bateson

Contents

Preface: Marketing in an Era of Limited Resources

The fortunes of public transportation continue to rise and fall with the political, social, and economic currents running through society. In Canada, Europe, and other parts of the world, urban transit has long been regarded as a valuable public service managed and funded by governmental agencies. However, the public transportation industry in the United States has undergone radical transformation since the end of World War II, when a predominantly privately owned industry began a cycle of declining ridership, fare increases, and service reductions in response to suburban growth and a shift toward the use of automobiles.

The public takeover of a dying transit industry signalled a realization that transit did have an important role to play in urban communities. It became increasingly clear that not everyone could afford to or even should drive their own cars—particularly into downtown business districts. The growth in automobile use produced increasing traffic congestion, worsening air pollution, and declining central cities. The two major energy crises of the 1970s further emphasized the need for alternatives to the automobile.

Yet, declining oil prices in the 1980s combined with a political swing away from publicly supported enterprises left urban transit low on the priority list for federal expenditures. Public transportation managers and their boards of directors found themselves faced with the unenviable task of delivering a service without the same level of resources.

The role of public transit marketing has also changed through the years. Public managers who took control of private transit organizations in the late 1960s and early 1970s found that the marketing function was nearly nonexistent. Promotional activities had long since disappeared as these companies were becoming increasingly unprofitable.

Public transit managers faced a dilemma. They were given a mandate to increase service and ridership. Yet, in many cities "marketing" was considered to be an inappropriate task for the public sector and an unwise use of taxpayers' money. Marketing, equated solely with advertising, was something for the private sector.

Marketing slowly began to come into its own in the 1970s as transit authorities began to establish and fund marketing departments—due to pressures to increase ridership and in response to a vigorous technical assistance program by the Urban Mass Transportation Administration.

The role marketing plays in transit agencies varies dramatically from one urban area to another. In some transit systems, a marketing orientation begins at the level of the general manager and marketing issues are considered from the board of directors to line department heads. At the other extreme, public information and promotion is relegated to a marketing department with the limited functions of printing schedules and responding to press inquiries. The goal of this book is to examine the role marketing can play in assisting transit agencies to cope with providing a public service in a time of limited public resources. We have examined the state of the art of transit marketing in today's difficult environment and have drawn upon research studies, programs, and management practices in use in the United States and abroad. As this book explains, the marketing of transit services extends far beyond promotional activities. To sell transit, an agency must develop a user orientation, which means that marketing implications are an integral aspect of decisions ranging from service design and pricing to quality control and strategic planning.

Managing a public transit service is never considered to be an easy job and few tasks are as challenging as developing a marketing orientation in an organization dominated by an operations mentality. Yet, as transit managers begin to cope with delivering a service within greater constraints, the marketing field can provide a strategic approach to designing, structuring, operating, and promoting public transportation.

Acknowledgments

We wish to thank Charles Weinberg for his contributions to our understanding of marketing in the public sector and Peter Dimond for contributing his collection of transit marketing materials and documents. We also wish to acknowledge Larry Coffman, Harron Ellenson, and Ernest Deeb who gave us firsthand insights into the problems faced by transit marketing managers.

Part I
Why Market Public Transportation?

1

Introduction

NEWS ITEM: *Time* magazine features "Washington's gleaming Metro humming past the Capitol and on to Virginia" and "Houston's contraflow busways battling rush hour traffic."[1]

NEWS ITEM: The *Wall Street Journal* headlines a page one article on San Francisco's Muni: "Accidents and Scandals Plague Bus and Subway System; Worse than Earthquakes?" The Journal equates the hiring of a public relations consultant to rehabilitate the transit system's image to that of being "director of tourism for Beirut."[2]

WHY THIS BOOK?

Where is public transportation going in the United States? Which of the above news items more accurately reflects the trend in urban public transit? Does the image of sparkling new transit systems accurately describe the future of urban public transit? Or, do the older, decaying systems (some of which could be characterized as a marketing manager's nightmare) better evoke the reality of mass transit? Actually, the contradictory image of transit is in itself an important reality of the U.S. transit industry. It is an industry without an industry-wide "trend." This was not always the case.

After years of decline during the three decades following the end of World War II, many U.S. urban transit systems were in near collapse when public funding and takeovers saved a dying industry. Catalyzed by two national energy crises in the 1970s, billions of dollars of federal, state, and local aid have flowed to transit authorities for rebuilding and expanding transit systems and subsidizing fares.

In other countries, such as Canada, public commitment to transit during the postwar years remained at higher levels, resulting in higher ridership per capita. In contrast, by the 1970s, the United States was faced with using public funds in a catch-up job to upgrade and enhance public transportation services in the face of competition from the automobile.

A stated goal of most transit managers has been to maintain and increase ridership. The results have varied from city to city. This is due to the fact that urban transit is basically a local service run by a local (or regional) organization responsible to a local political system. The quality of transit management and marketing varies widely, as does the political and financial support for transit services.

Statistics reporting growth or decline in transit ridership on a national basis can be misleading. For instance, since the New York region accounts for over 40 percent of all transit riders in the United States, any change in New York skews national averages. The financial collapse of New York City in 1974 led to cutbacks in maintenance of one of the world's largest transit systems. Within a decade, service quality plummeted to disastrous levels. Ridership dropped by 11.5 percent from 1975–1983,[3] masking ridership gains of 8.5 percent in other cities. Thus, looking for national trends can be difficult when political and fiscal problems in New York (or a few large cities) can mask gains being made in other urban systems.

As this book goes to press, the major challenge facing transit managers in the second half of the 1980s is how to handle reductions in government commitment to the funding of public transportation. In the United States, the threat is primarily that "the federal money machine isn't paying out the way it used to."[4] In the United Kingdom, transit authorities have also faced similar problems with reduced funding from the central government.

Managers can respond to funding cuts by slashing budgets across the board for services, planning, and marketing. Alternatively, top management and board members can view the situation as an opportunity to review operations strategically from a marketing perspective and avoid falling into "the trap of thinking that the purpose of transit is 'to run buses' rather than provide a service people need."[5]

The goal of this book is to provide managers with a decision-making framework for planning, designing, and promoting public transportation—particularly in a time of limited resources. Since every transit system is different and local political environments vary from city to city (as well as from nation to nation), it is not possible to outline a specific "formula" for managing and marketing transit. Application of marketing techniques and methods must be tailored to each situation.[6] On the other hand, there is no evidence to suggest that each transit system faces a set of unique circumstances that preclude directly comparing experiences.

Our purpose is to provide planners, analysts, managers, and transit board members with a strategic approach—from a marketing perspective—on operating a transit system with a consumer orientation. Transit professionals who develop a clear strategic approach to their organizations and communities will be better able to navigate through an environment dominated by conflicting political, social, and financial demands.

Our focus will center on transit operations in the United States, but we will be using examples and insights from other countries as well. All transit operations—and the constituencies that they serve—can benefit from a strong marketing orientation, but the political environment of the United States does pose special difficulties for the managers of U.S. systems.

MARKETING TRANSIT IN A POLITICAL ENVIRONMENT

Much has been already been written about the growth of automobile usage and the resulting decline of public transit.[7] As urban transit systems reached the end of the product life-cycle, public takeovers and funding have given transit a second life in the form of municipal or regional governmental agencies (see Exhibit 1–1).

Transit concerns in the 1960s and 1970s

From the late 1960s through the 1970s a resurgence of interest in public transit resulted in considerable increases in federal funding for local transit systems.

Where did all of this interest come from? Public funding for transit was justified "partly by lack of space in large cities for unlimited use of cars and partly by the demands of people who have no car and depend entirely on public means of conveyance."[8] Based on concern for equity, public funding for transit has resulted in most transit systems offering discount fares to elderly and handicapped individuals. Public recognition of the problems faced by "captive riders"—those who could not afford to own a car—first surfaced in the United States through the 1965 McCone Commission report investigating the causes behind the Watts race riot in Los Angeles. The Commission concluded:

Our investigation has brought into clear focus the fact that the inadequate and costly public transportation currently existing throughout the Los Angeles area seriously restricts the residents of the disadvantaged areas such as south central Los Angeles. This lack of adequate transportation handicaps them in seeking and

Exhibit 1–1
Transit's Product Lifecycle

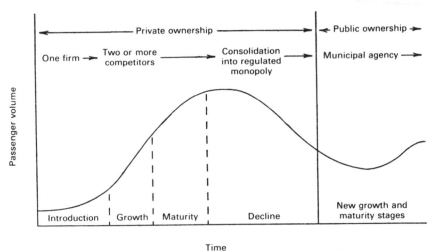

Time

Christopher H. Lovelock and Charles B. Weinberg, *Marketing for Public and Nonprofit Managers* (Copyright © by John Wiley & Sons, 1984), p. 304. Reprinted by permission.

holding jobs, attending schools, shopping, and in fulfilling other needs. It has had a major influence in creating a sense of isolation, with its resultant frustrations, among the residents of south central Los Angeles, particularly the Watts area. . . . Bus systems in the Los Angeles area have met increasing costs in operations by increasing fares and cutting back service. The consequence of these actions has been a transportation system which is prohibitively expensive and inadequate in service.[9]

Interest in public transit increased further as more and more people began to drive to work with the resulting increase in traffic congestion and travel time for drivers. Urban areas began to suffer from a glut of automobiles and a shortage of parking. Plans for additional new urban expressways triggered "highway revolts" by residents of neighborhoods slated for demolition and road construction. Land use patterns fostered by the automobile produced low density "suburban sprawl"—which was not conducive to transit service. Downtown business districts began to suffer from competition from suburban shopping centers.

The late 1960s and early 1970s also saw increased concern for air quality and the environment in general. Automobile emissions were documented to be one of the major causes of "smog." The disruptions and economic consequences of the energy crises of the 1970s further dramatized the need for alternatives to the private automobile. Thus, in addition to equity considerations, shift from the automobile became an important objective for public transportation. In this political environment, political support was strong for major investments in building new rapid transit systems, upgrading and expanding existing bus and rail systems, and making public subsidies available to support transit operations.

However, simply investing money in new facilities, equipment, and service does not suffice to achieve the objectives set for transit. Shiny new buses or rapid transit cars may look nice, but they make no contribution to improving the quality of life if they travel around empty. A key problem, then, for transit managers continues to be that of attracting (and retaining) riders. Management simply cannot afford to lose sight of the fact that unless public transit is well patronized, the benefits claimed for it will never be achieved.

At the same time, no manager can afford to increase the number of persons using a service without reference to cost factors. Financial constraints, political considerations, and basic economics require that operations be run efficiently and that the benefits derived from increased usage are not outweighed by the costs of attracting and serving these new patrons.

Developments in the 1980s

In the early 1980s, ridership and fiscal problems developed at a number of transit authorities. As prices began to decline at the gasoline pump, many transit agencies began to experience a loss of recently gained ridership. At the same time, the public became concerned with allegedly excessive taxation at all levels of government, and transit began to suffer from the budget cutter's ax. In contrast, ridership on Canadian systems has continued to grow following the 1979 energy crisis at over 6 percent per annum.[10] The reason, according to a *Wall Street Journal* report, was that:

Politics accounts for much of the contrast. While U.S. transit operators must contend with the prospect of progressive withdrawal of federal operating subsidies and reduced state and local grants, transit remains politically popular in Canada. "Every Toronto mayor in the last 10 years has won on a platform of better transit," says Stephen McLaughlin, the city's planning commissioner.

When transit fares are raised in Canada, however, officials say commuters don't complain much. [According to Alyre Cormier, executive director of the Canadian Urban Transit Association:] "If you offer a good level of service. . . . it's much easier to get fare improvements."[11]

The lessons for transit managers in the United States is that public support for transit is critical to the success of a transit organization in delivering a quality service; and that both tax-based funding and fare increases become more acceptable when service quality is high.

Building public support for transit

Public sector managers do not have the decision-making autonomy of their private sector counterparts. Transit managers must take into account a variety of political constituencies and governmental bodies in addition to transit riders. Since marketing concerns all aspects of a transit organization's relationship to its external environment, the marketing tasks of a transit manager assume far greater proportions than simply publicizing transit service.

Yet, this is not an impossible situation. Urban transit receives public support because a wide range of interest groups believe it is an important service. Transit organizations do have multiple constituencies. Support for transit can be found in neighborhoods, in retail business districts, and from employers, who benefit from the service. Environmental and "good government" groups, such as the League of Women Voters, are often involved in supporting public transit. At the national level, in the halls of Congress urban mayors have been a significant lobbying force for public transit.

Due to the visible role that public transit plays in a community, this book approaches transit marketing as multi-dimensional task. Successful transit marketing cannot be limited to a traditional role of advertising and publicity. In order to have the financial resources to provide the quality service that is needed to achieve increases in ridership and farebox revenue, transit managers must successfully market their organizations to a range of constituencies (including both riders and nonriders). This approach is the only viable way to build and maintain a political base of support in the community.

MARKETING WITHIN THE TRANSIT ORGANIZATION

As an academic discipline, marketing was traditionally concerned with issues concerning physical goods produced and marketed in the private sector. Not until the 1970s were significant efforts made to learn more about the application of marketing tools and techniques to service organizations in all three sectors of the economy—public, nonprofit, and private. As in many other service industries, marketing inputs to transit services were previously confined to advertising and promotional issues. Engineers and operations managers made the key decisions on service configurations, service features, and routes and schedules. Accountants and economists deliberated on pricing. A few of these individuals also possessed a strong customer orientation, but many did not.

The marketing mix for transit

Executing a marketing strategy requires the use of a broad array of marketing tools. Many people mistakenly equate marketing with the advertising and sales functions of an organization. In practice, marketing's scope is much broader. In order for an organization to sell its products or services to the public, decisions must be made in four broad areas, collectively referred to as the "marketing mix." These are:

1. *Product*—or service characteristics;
2. *Price*—both the amount and how it is to be paid;
3. *Communications*—which involves all messages between a transit organization and its prospective customers;
4. *Distribution*—where, when, and how the service is delivered to the public.

(Exhibit 1–2 provides examples of the marketing mix components in the context of a public transportation service.)

The marketing mix concept is valuable because it recognizes the interdependence of the different elements within a marketing program. A change (or failure) in any one ingredient can influence the effectiveness of the overall program. As in a cooking recipe, the different ingredients of the marketing mix need to be chosen to reinforce or interact with one another.

Marketing must be as concerned with service design and quality as it is involved in pricing decisions and communication programs. For example, advertising a transit service as clean, comfortable, and reliable will not have any credibility if, in fact, consumers experience a service with frequent delays and dirty, overcrowded buses. In such an unfortunate situation, managers who understand the interaction between different elements of the marketing mix will focus on improving service standards prior to initiating a promotional campaign emphasizing high standards.

Marketing and service quality

Managing and marketing transit services is not an easy task. Quality control is difficult because the service is continually on the move and most service personnel are not under the direct control of a supervisor or manager. When a customer buys a product in a supermarket, the product's manufacturer can guarantee with a certain degree of probability that the purchased item will meet certain performance standards as a result of quality control checks during production and distribution. If customers like the product but not the clerk at the checkout counter, they have the option of buying the same product from another store.

With public transit, the customer is purchasing a service—a trip from one point to another. In such an instance the product features are not only more numerous but also the responsibility of a single organization. A driver can be rude to a passenger, a bus can break down, or a service

Exhibit 1–2
The "Marketing Mix" for Transit

1. The Product
   - Vehicle Features (size, appearance, seating, ride quality, etc.).
   - Operating Characteristics (average speed, punctuality and reliability, schedule headways, quality of driving, crowding, nature of other passengers).
2. Pricing
   - Level of fare (cost per ride); availability of discounts and transfers.
   - Method of payment (cash, check, credit card).
   - Frequency of payment (every ride vs. periodic purchase of commuter cards or books of tickets).
3. Communications
   - Media advertising (papers, TV, radio).
   - Outdoor advertising (posters, billboards).
   - Direct mail.
   - Maps, brochures, signs, and timetables.
   - Telephone information service.
   - Drivers and other personnel.
4. Distribution
   - Location of routes and stops.
   - Location of information offices.
   - Location of fare payment.
   - Timing of service (hours of operation, schedules at specific locations, service connections to other systems and other transportation modes).

may be delayed in downtown traffic. It is much harder for management to be sure that these incidents will not happen, at least occasionally.

Since service quality can be a perennial problem for a transit agency, everyone working for a transit organization has an important marketing role. A bus driver is not only responsible for driving a vehicle, but is also representing the transit organization as a form of salesperson who can provide passengers with information and assistance. The maintenance staff not only fix engines and transmissions, but are ensuring reliable delivery of service. A planning department is not simply scheduling buses but perhaps working with local officials to develop a traffic mall and busways to reduce delays. Basically, a quality transit service depends upon a consumer orientation from top management to line operations. It has been said that in a transit organization, marketing is everyone's job.

The operation is the product

It would probably come as a great surprise to most transit operations managers to learn that they were themselves heavily involved in market-ing. Countless surveys have shown that travelers place importance on safety, reliability, comfort, convenience, and speed in addition to cost in making mode-of-transportation decisions. Success in delivering transit services that are competitive with the automobile depends on the operations departments delivering a carefully planned, quality service.

Transit organizations are faced with a reality that their operation, or service, is the product. Services have some important characteristics that distinguish them from physical goods and that make the marketing of consumer services a more complex problem than for consumer goods. The products can be manufactured in a factory, inspected for quality, stockpiled until needed, shipped to a possibly distant location, and displayed in a retail outlet. Sooner or later, assuming all goes well, a physical product will be purchased from the store by a customer and subsequently used at the purchaser's discretion.

A service, such as transit, is consumed as it is produced; so, unlike goods, transit services are time-bound as well as place-bound. The transit product consists of a ride between two points. Unless that ride is offered at times that are convenient to consumers and between origin and desti-nation points that are accessible, the transit system is unlikely to be the chosen mode. Of itself, the ride is ephemeral. There is nothing to show or to take home afterward. However, the equipment in which the trav-eler is conveyed, the driver and other personnel, the station or terminal facilities, the street furniture—all of these are highly tangible and may serve as important determinants of modal choice. Hence, the design of vehicles and other facilities as well as the appearance and behavior of transit employees may serve as determinants of modal choice.

UNDERSTANDING THE CONSUMER AND THE COMPETITION

Why do people ride public transportation? And more importantly, why is it so difficult to convince more people to leave their cars at home and take transit? These questions have perplexed transit operators, par-ticularly when they feel that they are providing a quality service.

Consumer research studies have found that people suffer from inertia and are reluctant to change established behavior without good reason. Travel behavior—and particularly daily commuting—consists of patterns that become deeply ingrained.

Consumer choice of transportation modes

Cost is one determinant of consumer modal choice. The average U.S. household spends $3,000/year to own and operate its automobiles, but only $225/year on public transportation.[12] Yet most car travelers belong to households that have already made a sizeable investment in purchasing a car. Transportation mode decisions tend to be based on out-of-pocket operating costs, which typically are perceived as small. Declining gasoline prices are reducing these costs, although downtown commuters are finding that parking costs in central business districts are continuing to climb.

Other factors, such as safety, reliability, time savings, convenience, and comfort, are very important components of a consumer's choice of travel mode. No matter how inexpensive a transit trip may be, ridership increases will not be achieved unless consumers can be satisfied on these other factors.

Before consumers can be expected to use public transit, they must 1) know that the service exists; 2) know how to use it; and 3) perceive it as equal to or better than car travel for a specific trip. In an interview in the *Wall Street Journal*, Richard Page, formerly chief administrator of the Urban Mass Transportation Administration (UMTA) and general manager of Washington's Metro, explains:

"We are in a competitive market" with the auto, he says. "Too often, we assume that transit's a good thing and if we have a nice bus and it arrives on time, people are going to ride it. We've got to get people aware of transit, help them know how to use the bus—and then make sure the bus doesn't get stuck in traffic."

"In many cases," Mr. Page adds, "we've still not done enough on public information—making it easier for the public to use the transit system." Transit managers need to emulate those systems that "have gotten fairly smart about marketing. They recognize that we don't have a captive audience."[13]

Countering the competition

Transit can (and must) capitalize on the fact that there are weaknesses in the competition's position: not all automobile drivers are very happy with their situation. This book suggests the use of targeted marketing strategies. For example, if automobile users only consider the full cost of car ownership at the time of purchasing a car, then transit marketing efforts need to target car buyers before they make an investment in a new car. If an urban area has frustrating and congested rush hours, then transit agencies can demonstrate that they have an alternative to the stress of commuting in bumper-to-bumper traffic. Perhaps it may be necessary to go so far as to publicize medical research studies that have linked the stress of commuting in heavy traffic to a range of health problems, ranging from high blood pressure and pulse rates to reduced mental capacity and malignant moods.[14]

The dispersion of work and residential locations to suburban areas (often outside of the reach of public transit)—makes a dramatic increase in transit's market share a long-term task. In the United States, transit accounts for only 6 percent of all commuter trips—yet transit still accounts for over 5,000,000 daily commuters. Based on the Canadian experience, it is possible to obtain annual increases in the use of public transportation, even without a major energy crisis.

All too often, public transit finds itself positioned in the marketplace by consumers as the low cost, low quality transportation service. Transit marketers need to counter the negative attitudes toward transit described, tongue in cheek, by one social commentator:

Maybe you hate mass transit. Maybe you associate mass transit with surly drivers; exhaust odors; dingy, ripped seats with slimy stuff spilled on them and sickening obscenities scrawled in plain view; filthy windows and paper-littered aisles; standing shoulder-to-shoulder with silent, embittered persons and hostile teenagers lugging big, ear-busting radios and tape decks; and sudden stops and lurches that send them all crashing and sprawling on top of you! Nightmares of sharp turns by a crazed driver—the mass sways, tilts, slides. You are swept away, pressed against disgusting surfaces by immense bodies—thrown into intimate physical contact with utter strangers who don't care that much for you, either!

Legitimate fears, obsessions. "Bus-riding is the ultimate test of democracy," someone once said. Maybe it was you.[15]

WHAT'S IN THIS BOOK

The ten remaining chapters of this book are divided into four parts. The next section, Part II, analyzes how consumers view public transportation. A careful understanding of consumer attitudes and behavior is necessary in order to develop strategies that can successfully increase transit ridership.

The first step in understanding consumer behavior is to realize that there are many different types of consumers—that mass transit riders are not a "mass market." The marketplace for transportation service is divided into a number of market segments, each with different characteristics and needs. In Chapter 2, we explain why market segmentation is an essential managerial strategy that recognizes the existence of different patterns of consumer demand in a market. The implication of market segmentation analysis is that cost-effective marketing programs must be targeted to specific groups.

In Chapter 3, we examine consumer decision making. Why do some people use public transit, while others insist on driving in spite of higher costs? Analysis of how consumers make transportation mode decisions can help transit managers plan services and develop promotional campaigns that address factors consumers themselves consider to be important.

Our discussion of market research in Chapter 4 addresses the issue of how a transit authority can obtain the information needed to develop marketing strategies that take into account market segmentation and consumer decision making. We suggest that market research is not an isolated technical task but an important part of the planning process that needs the involvement of transit management. Market research can be designed so that it is not a financial drain on the organization. The benefit of market research is that it provides managers with a basis for decision making beyond "gut feelings" and increases the confidence of decision makers who may see themselves taking risks when introducing new services or making changes to existing operations.

Part III focuses on the need for careful planning in a transit organization. In Chapter 5, we discuss the importance of strategic planning to marketing professionals in addressing and managing some of the issues, problems, and opportunities faced by urban transit agencies. At an organizational level, a strategic planning approach incorporates many of the elements of market planning but addresses a broad range of organizational issues.

Chapter 6 explains how a planning process can help marketing managers develop a logical marketing program and break away from the "crisis management" style of handling day-to-day problems. Planning can help managers develop a market strategy, make day-to-day decisions, allocate scarce resources, and introduce a basis for regular evaluation of performance.

Chapter 7 addresses a fundamental fact that faces all transit authorities: the operation is the product. Even the most operationally efficient service will not be used if it does not meet the needs of consumers. In this chapter, we discuss the important role of service planning and design in the marketing of public transportation.

Part IV focuses on the critical marketing task of managing demand for transit service. We discuss promotion in terms of demand management, rather than simply as "increasing ridership," because there are situations where increased usage is not desirable. For example, a transit system which operates at 100 percent capacity during rush hour will have a difficult time attracting new commuters at low cost. Promoting a rush hour service without additional capacity will not be successful unless new vehicles are added to the operation for a short period of the day—at times a costly and unrealistic plan. In this situation, a strategy for managing demand may entail convincing businesses to allow employees to commute before or after the rush hour. Another demand management strategy would be to target promotional programs to increasing off-peak use of transit—where excess capacity already exists.

In the private sector, pricing strategies are designed to cover costs and generate a profit. With its public subsidies, public transit pricing entails a different set of objectives for the transit organization. Pricing decisions involve allocation of costs between users and taxpayers (often with public debate) as well as determination of fare structures, distribution channels, and communication strategies. In Chapter 8, we discuss approaches to setting price, objectives of pricing, demand management pricing, and innovative fare collection programs such as monthly transit passes.

Chapter 9 focuses on marketing transit through use of "third parties"—intermediary organizations who benefit from transit service and are capable of influencing consumer behavior. Specific programs examined include employer sale (and subsidy) of transit passes, use of variable work hours, and joint promotions with retailers.

In Chapter 10, we discuss the role of communications in informing, persuading, and reminding the public about the availability of transit service. Many people make the mistake of equating communication and marketing. Communications is just one important element in the overall marketing mix. Communication programs include both those that take place through impersonal channels (TV, radio, or printed information) and personal channels such as a telephone information line. In this chapter, we explain why communications programs based on targeted strategies are most likely to succeed.

The last section of this book, Part V, is devoted to the role of marketing in the management of the transit organization. In Chapter 11, we explain how a centralized marketing department can actually be counter-productive to introducing marketing functions throughout the transit organization. In a service organization, almost every department has a responsibility for marketing. While developing a consumer orientation from top management to line departments is not a short-term task, we discuss strategies that can spread the marketing function throughout the organization.

NOTES

1. *Time* magazine, January 16, 1984, p. 19.
2. *Wall Street Journal*, June 20, 1984, p. 1.
3. Pickrell, Don H. "Federal operating assistance for urban mass transit: Assessing a decade of experience," unpublished paper presented at Transportation Research Board Annual Meeting (January 1986).
4. *Wall Street Journal*, August 22, 1985, p. 1.
5. Hemily, Brendon, and Michael D. Meyer. "Public transportation in the 1980s: Responding to pressures of fiscal austerity," unpublished paper presented at the Transportation Research Board Annual Meeting (January 1982).
6. For description of marketing techniques, see the Urban Mass Transportation Administration series, *The Transit Management Marketing Handbook* (1975); also see the UMTA's *Transit Marketing: A Review of State of the Art and Handbook of Current Practice* (1985).

7. See Jane Jacobs, *The Economy of Cities*; K. H. Schaeffer and Elliot Sclar, *Access for All: Transportation and Urban Growth*; and Wilfred Owen, *The Accessible City*.

8. Owen, *The Accessible City*, op. cit., p. 24.

9. McCone, John (Chairman). *Violence in the city—An end or a beginning?* A report by the Governor's Commission on the Los Angeles Riots (December 2, 1965), p. 65.

10. *Wall Street Journal*, December 31, 1981, p. 9.

11. Ibid., p. 9.

12. Consumer Expenditure Survey, cited in Peter Francese, "Most workers prefer solo drive, " in *The Patriot Ledger* (Quincy, Mass.), February 25, 1985, p. 16.

13. *Wall Street Journal*, July 19, 1983, p. 29.

14. *Washington Post*, Sunday, April 23, 1983, Section A, pp. 11–12.

15. Keillor, Garrison. "Your transit commission," in *Happy to Be Here* (New York: Penguin Books, 1983), p. 234–35.

Part II
The Consumers' View of Transit

2

Market Segmentation

"Mass transit" is an unfortunate term because it implies that transit ridership is a mass market of people with undifferentiated needs and characteristics. The term "transit riders" tends to evoke images of hapless commuters or the unfortunate poor and (perhaps) elderly.

In reality, the market for transit is made up of people of different ages, sexes, occupations, incomes, languages, races, and backgrounds. They travel for different purposes, with varying degrees of frequency, between different origins and destinations, and at different times of the day or week.

Market segmentation is an analytical tool for breaking down a roughly defined mass market into segments or subgroups. Market segmentation helps us to understand who really rides public transportation—and why. (For that matter, who doesn't ride public transportation—and why not.) Understanding the different types of people who ride transit (or quit riding, or never used transit) and their motivations can help managers make decisions ranging from pricing and service design to advertising messages.

Market segmentation provides managers with the background necessary to develop targeted marketing strategies and targeted campaigns. By utilizing market segmentation analysis, managers have the ability to target messages to specific audiences—which is far more effective than generalized appeals.

In a time of limited resources in most transit organizations, managers can obtain better value for the marketing dollar by targeting marketing campaigns carefully. By understanding market segmentation, transit managers can better choose between competing claims on a marketing department's limited budget.

THE CONCEPT OF MARKET SEGMENTATION

In evaluating a market and developing appropriate programs, there are three broad alternative approaches. The first is *market aggregation*: treating all consumers as similar and offering a standard product for everyone. Historically, mass transit has tended to fall into this category, under the assumption that everybody's urban travel needs could be satisfied by the same type of public transportation service. This has largely proved to be a fallacy.

Consider the scheduling implications of the different travel behavior of three commuter groups: 1) those who have regular daytime working hours; 2) those who have irregular hours, occasionally leaving work late at night; and 3) those who not only commute but also travel elsewhere during the business day. Unless the last two groups are assured of frequent, reliable service during off-peak hours, they are likely to rely on private cars instead of public transit.

At the opposite end of the scale is total *market disaggregation*: each consumer is treated uniquely. In the last analysis, each individual may be thought of as a separate market segment, on the grounds that each person is somewhat different from everybody else in personal characteristics, behavior patterns, needs, values, and attitudes. Total disaggregation of the population has particular appeal for modeling modal choice behavior. The best way to understand how travel decisions are made and how these decisions may be influenced is to study individual consumers. However, there are limits to how far disaggregation can be carried in planning and managing public transportation service.

With transportation systems developed to serve populations that can run into the millions, total disaggregation is simply not realistic. There are limits to the ability of transit managers to provide personalized service in buses designed to seat 50 people and trains that may carry as many as 1,500 travelers at one time.

Obviously, there has to be a happy medium between complete aggregation of the population on the one hand and total disaggregation on the other. This is the third strategy, *market segmentation*: grouping consumers into segments on the basis of intra-group similarities and inter-group differences.

Market segmentation may be viewed as a descriptive process in that it recognizes both individual differences and group similarities. Segments can be developed by dividing a large, amorphous group into smaller groups with certain characteristics in common. The concept of market segmentation is based on the propositions that 1) consumers are different; 2) differences in consumers are related to differences in market behavior; and 3) segments of consumers can be isolated within the overall market.

MARKET SEGMENTATION AS A STRATEGY

Market segmentation can be defined as a managerial strategy that recognizes the existence of different demand patterns in a market.

Management can select one of two different types of segmentation strategies: a *concentrated* strategy, focusing on only one segment within the population; or a *differentiated* strategy, selecting several segments to serve and developing tailored marketing programs for each. For example, a transit agency can focus solely on increasing commuter work trips or can develop separate strategies for commuters, the elderly, and the student/youth market.

Using market segmentation in the public sector

The mandate for public transit organizations is no longer one of maximizing financial profits for the carrier. Instead, deficit financing is provided in the hope of realizing social objectives that may benefit the whole community and/or specific disadvantaged groups.

In the private sector, market segments can be defined and targeted based on the potential profitability to the organization. For the transit manager, publicly defined objectives strongly influence development of a market segmentation strategy. Certain market segments become more important than others in terms of helping to achieve desired social and political benefits.

Although every transit operation is likely to have somewhat different priorities, the public objectives for transit tend to fall into three broad categories. The first objective concerns diversion of travelers from private automobiles to public transit. (A more limited goal is simply keeping current riders from abandoning transit for their cars.) The rationale for maintaining or increasing transit's market share is that transit mitigates traffic congestion and parking shortages in downtown areas and reduces air pollution and energy consumption.[1] Public transit is also viewed as an alternative to new highways and parking facilities.

The second objective is concerned with improving mobility for those who presently lack access to adequate private transportation, either because they do not own or have access to a car on a regular basis or because they are unable to drive.

The third objective entails retaining the support of the local community—residents, employers, and retailers. Their support is particularly important, since their taxes contribute to the operation of the transit system. If they perceive that transit is doing a poor job and is lightly patronized, they may generate pressure to curtail tax support of the system. Further, employers and retailers may fail to promote transit use to their employees and customers.

When the Orange County Transit District in Southern California conducted a county-wide monitoring study not only of current and prospective riders, but also of the general public, it found that many people were unaware of the district's successes, its ridership growth and other accomplishments. So a campaign was launched to educate taxpayers about the system's continuing success.[2]

Segmentation as the key to attainment of objectives

In order to achieve these objectives, one must define marketing goals in terms of encouraging ridership among specific segments of the population, rather than in vague terms of maximizing ridership for the overall system.

The following steps illustrate how a market segmentation analysis can fit within the context of a publicly defined objective.

Step 1: Define objectives and set priorities.

Example: Alleviate parking shortage in downtown area.

Step 2: Identify segments that are key to success.

Example: Drivers who compete for limited parking.

Step 3: Identify needs, characteristics, and present behavior patterns of key segments.

Examples: Employees who park all day;
           Shoppers who park for one to two hours.

Step 4: Further divide segments (where appropriate) into subsegments.

Example: Parking garage/lot users, on-street parkers, and illegal parkers.

Step 5: Develop marketing strategies targeted at each subsegment.

Example: Target employees at work place to use transit;
           Joint promotion of transit with retailers;
           Crackdown on illegal parking.

Step 6: Monitor results and evaluate relative success of each strategy.

Examples: Ridership counts on key bus lines;
           Revenue collection from parking tickets.

Step 7: Modify segmentation analysis or marketing strategy as needed.

Example: Offer discounted monthly transit passes through employers.

A marketing program derived directly from the public objective of solving a parking shortage would probably highlight a downtown parking problem to a general audience, producing the unintended result of discouraging shoppers from traveling downtown and diverting those trips to suburban malls. Instead, a market segmentation approach requires that the solution to a generalized public objective is defined in some detail by identifying specific submarkets and programs that will help to achieve the more generalized public objective.

APPROACHES TO SEGMENTING A MARKET

It can be said that there are as many ways to segment a market as there are to slice a pie. The task facing transportation planners and market analysts is to choose which variables are likely to aid in identifying key market segments. It is not always obvious which segmentation variables to use in a specific situation. Nor should a transit marketing analysis necessarily limit itself to use of just one variable (e.g., income). In most cases, the development of market segments involves the use of multiple dimensions.

Developing criteria for effective segmentation

In any situation, there is an almost infinite number of potential ways of segmenting the market. Which should the manager select? The following criteria offer useful guidelines for evaluating alternative segmentation schemes: size and importance of the segments, compatibility with the institutional mission, and accessibility of the chosen segments within the overall population.

Substantiality. The segments must be large enough and/or sufficiently important to merit the time and cost of separate attention. In the business sector, where the chief concern is to generate high market response relative to program cost, it is usually sufficient to define importance in terms of the size of the target market. This definition is inadequate in the public sector, where importance is sometimes defined by those who provide the organization's funding. For example, transit operators who receive federal funding are required to devote special attention to serving handicapped people. As a result, even though handicapped persons represent a very small market segment and the costs of serving them are extremely high, they have become an important market segment for public transportation.

It is difficult to tell how substantial a segment is unless there is some way of measuring its size. The procedure is usually fairly straightforward with such demographic variables as age, education, income, and so forth: these data, along with geographic population data, can be obtained from census and other government statistics. However, it is much more difficult to measure the size of market segments based on people's attitudes or intentions. For example, should a midday "shoppers' special" bus service be introduced in a suburban town that currently has no transit service outside commuting hours? A variety of techniques exist for gathering new data of this nature, but it should be recognized that the answers provided by surveys often prove misleading. Frequently, a search for details of actual consumer behavior in comparable situations provides more useful guidelines.

Compatibility. The skills and equipment required to serve a specific segment effectively must be compatible with the organization's mission and its resources. Private firms usually have some choice over the segments they serve. Public agencies, as we have already noted, are often mandated to serve a variety of segments with widely differing needs and are not always provided with sufficient funds to do so effectively.

The federal mandate for transit agencies to serve handicapped persons created considerable turmoil in the industry. Many transit agencies had to purchase lift equipped buses, to contract with private organizations (profit and nonprofit) to provide special services that managers felt they were not able to offer, and to redesign access to rapid transit stations. Transit managers' concern with federal mandates rests in the fear that the financial cost of gearing up to serve new market segments may result in reduced resources for improving service quality for the core segment.

Accessibility. Management must be able to identify market segments and develop strategies for reaching those segments. Two approaches can be used for targeted marketing efforts: *customer self-selection* and *controlled coverage*. In both instances the service is designed, priced, distributed, and promoted to a specific market segment. When the customer self-selection method is used, however, the service is marketed broadly, and it is expected that the target customers will self-select.

At first glance it would seem that no manager would ever want to use customer self-selection as a targeting approach over a more economical and targeted "controlled coverage" approach. Yet some benefits may make this strategy reasonable at times. Cost per reader/viewer/listener of a mass market medium can be economical. For example, one needs to compare costs of advertising in a metropolitan daily newspaper versus several less expensive neighborhood and community papers. Depending on the message and target market, a mass market vehicle can, paradoxically, be a better mechanism for reaching a specific audience.

An additional advantage to a customer self-selection approach is the opportunity to build primary demand by winning new consumers to the service who had not previously been strongly interested in it. At other times, a mass media approach may be the only viable alternative. During the 1984 Summer Olympics in Los Angeles, transportation officials used twice-daily television press conferences to dramatize the need for people to use public transportation and avoid congested areas. (The public responded so positively to the fear of freeway "gridlock" that traffic conditions actually improved for the two week Olympic games.)

In other cases, a carefully designed controlled coverage approach provides a more economical and effective means of reaching a targeted market, as the following example illustrates:

We had two very different campaigns to promote an existing route. One was the gold-plated Cadillac approach—a $1,200 actor's equity fee for professional actors, television, radio saturation, coin purses, bumper stickers, full-page ads in all the media. We had 3 months of cultivating awareness excitement, coffee, balloons, and then a free-ride coupon in the newspaper. The results were disappointing. The total cost was about $15,000 to $20,000. After doing some research, we found that we did not really get to the people who counted. We hit everybody but the people who really counted.

In the second campaign we tried to hit these people. We have enormous traffic jams coming up from the south, where we have the second Blue Dash system, so we printed a little brochure telling everything one needs to know about the Blue Dash. There was a full system map, timetable, and a free-ride coupon. We gave some high school students 5,000 of these to distribute in one week at the red light where all the roads came up from the south and there are traffic jams. Every time the traffic stopped the students invaded the highway (we got the troopers and the police on our side), and they gave one to every driver. The whole thing cost us about $1,000, and the results were very substantial. This shows that is not necessary to blitz the media in order to get results.[3]

The choice between customer self-selection and controlled coverage may vary by elements of the marketing mix. For example, a public transportation agency may advertise its services broadly to the community but, by its choice of routes and schedules, only distribute transit schedules to target market segments that are defined geographically and in terms of the timing of their travel demands.

Common bases for segmentation

The bases for segmenting a market can first be grouped into two broad categories: user identifiers and user responses.

User identifiers of relevance to transit marketers include familiar demographic and geographic variables such as age, gender, occupation, residence and work location, as used in many planning studies. Income may serve as a useful surrogate for car ownership and type of job held. Marketing professionals in the private sector also utilize "psychographic" variables such as personality and lifestyle in developing market segmentation profiles.

Benefit segmentation, another approach to identifying different categories of consumers, examines which benefits individuals are seeking by purchasing a product or service. Conversely, benefit segmentation also analyzes what costs consumers are seeking to avoid by making a particular purchase. This is particularly relevant to transit organizations where many riders will use transit in order to avoid the costs and hassles of driving and parking in congested cities.

User response bases include segmentation by product-related behavior (frequency of use, timing and location of use) and sensitivity to marketing variables (price and service change sensitivity, response to advertising, promotions, or consumer information).

Focusing only on user responses is generally not sufficient. Analytically, a marketer can group people by various combinations of identifier and response characteristics and then attempt to determine which combination of segmentation variables offers the greatest value in clustering individuals into categories that are distinctive and relevant for marketing purposes. In the last analysis, marketers are, of course, interested in how consumers behave (namely, response variables). But user identifiers are potentially valuable in terms of their ability to help explain—and even predict—consumer behavior.

Demographic and socioeconomic variables. These variables have the advantage of being relatively easy to recognize and measure. They form the basis for a great many census statistics and can often be readily linked to geographic variables. They are also readily and accurately obtainable from surveys.

Analysis of age and income is quite useful when examining groups who do not have access to a car and thus are "transit captives." The number of cars per household can also serve as a useful demographic indicator in identifying households with one car who may still have some travel needs that can be met by public transit.

It is questionable, however, whether demographics are a particularly useful predictor of modal choice behavior when the analysis is confined to those travelers who have a choice of modes. This does not mean, however, that demographics have no value in formulating marketing strategies for transit. For example, price sensitivity is related to income, raising the question of whether selective discounts can be given to those who need them.

Geographic variables. For transit organizations, geography often represents the most important enabling characteristic in defining target markets. If the bus does not go where you are going, then that trip will be made by another mode or not at all. At the opposite end of the spectrum from the captive transit ride is the captive auto rider who finds transit service inaccessible at either the origin or destination points. Thus, location of both origin and destination are very important determinants of whether or not people can or will use public transportation.

Many studies highlight the importance of location as a segmentation variable, indicating that transit's share of the travel market is a function of the accessibility of origins and destinations from stopping points on the transit route. For interurban rail or bus service, accessibility is perhaps best measured in terms of travel time to reach the transit system (which could be walking, auto, bicycle, or another transit mode).

The implications of location as a segmentation variable are threefold. First, if planners want people living or working in a particular geographic location to use transit, they must ensure that the transit service provides acceptable access to both their origin and principal destination locations.

The definition of "acceptable access" may vary according to topographic features (e.g., steep hills), local climatic conditions (frequency of rain, wind, extreme cold, etc.), street layout (lack of sidewalks or pedestrian crossings), road congestion, proximity of commuter parking to a transit stop, and age and physical conditions of travelers. The fact that a few hardy souls enjoy walking one mile to a train station in biting winter weather does not mean that numerous others will be prepared to join them.

Second, transit marketers are wasting time and money if they try to market their service for trips to travelers whose origins and/or destinations lie outside the transit envelope. For this reason, geographically specific media, such as direct mail or billboards, may often be a more cost-effective means of communicating with potential riders than area-wide media such as TV and radio. Another advantage of direct mail is that it can tailor information on routes, fares, and schedules to the needs of a specific location (e.g., residents of a local area or employees at a specific company).

Third, in evaluating the performance of a given transit system, attention should be focused on the share of the travel market gained by transit within its primary service area. Failure to win riders whose origins and/or destinations are not realistically accessible to transit service may be an indictment of the existing route structure, but it is hardly a reflection of the quality of service provided on present routes or of present pricing and communication strategies.

Benefit variables. One type of segmentation that is beginning to attract attention in the transit industry is benefit segmentation. Here the emphasis is on the benefits obtained by travelers from their chosen mode. Instead of segmenting the market according to *who* is traveling, how, when, where, and why they travel, the interest lies in grouping travelers according to their preferences for different modal attributes. In other words, it recognizes that the benefits that the user seeks from transportation will serve to determine mode choice and level of usage. Benefit segmentation also addresses the issue of costs that a consumer may wish to avoid by using a particular service. This approach is appealing in that it can help explain behavior rather than just describe it.

Transportation mode decision theory focuses on the perceived time and monetary costs to the consumer of transit trips versus automobile trips. The value of time has different, non-quantifiable attributes for different people. The benefit of having time to read rather than drive may be more important than saving 15 minutes commuting by car for some individuals. Conversely, some people will choose to drive on a congested highway with a train running down the median strip because they value the time to be by themselves.

The purpose of benefit segmentation is to group people according to the relative emphasis they place on the benefits and costs of alternative modes. In the New York City area, comfortable, nonstop commuter buses run parallel to subway routes in some instances; despite this competition and the fact that they charge much higher fares than the subway, these premium bus services have been very successful in attracting patrons. This example clearly documents that mass transit is not a "mass market." Within a public transit market, a successful transit operator found a market segment that was willing to pay a premium price for a premium service.

Psychographic variables. We use the term "psychographics" to refer to lifestyle issues, personal values, and personal traits such as self-confidence, aggressiveness, and conservatism. Psychic factors or personal values can be important in determining mode choice. Different people react differently to issues of crowding, cleanliness, and security fears. Some people define themselves very much in terms of the car they drive and place a high value on "personal mobility" and "freedom" afforded by the private automobile. People with similar values and self-perceptions can be grouped together.

A market segmentation study in the Boston area conducted an analysis of psychographic factors in choosing a travel mode for the Massachusetts Bay Transportation Authority. The study arrived at these conclusions:

We have defined three different population segments within the area served by the MBTA. One is very concerned about convenience and the social environment. A second has the problem of needing to save money but not wanting to be reminded about this need. The third also has money concerns but is impulsive enough to venture more from the home and needs to maximize the time spent away from home in enjoyment rather than in travel . . .

There is the need to acquaint the public with the fact that the "T" is something more than cheap transportation. In particular, it is important to position the "T" as a convenient facilitator of people's desires—a handy way to minimize travel time, enable the whole family to go along, and travel to virtually any desired location without attendant hassles (e.g., parking).[4]

Psychographics are particularly useful in formulating a communications strategy. The Boston study clearly indicates that while price is a major factor in transit use, people look for other attributes in mode choice (if nothing else, avoiding the hassles and costs of parking). Applying the psychographic analysis, we could predict that an advertising campaign relying solely on the theme of "Ride Transit: It's Cheap" is unlikely to be successful.

Knowledge and awareness levels. It may seem obvious that if consumers do not know about a service, it is doubtful that they will use it. Yet the detailed knowledge necessary actually to take a new transit service is surprisingly lacking in the population. We can segment both existing and prospective riders into groups based on their level of knowledge of a transit agency's services.[5] While nearly everyone in a major urban area may know of the existence of a bus and/or subway system, they may not have sufficient knowledge of the service to be able to use it themselves nor advise other prospective riders.

Segmenting by awareness level is very important when developing a targeted communication program so that potential users have enough information to actually make their trips without burdening them with levels of detail that make the possibility of making a transit trip too confusing to be worth the effort. One basic question that all transit managers should ask themselves is: if all prospective customers had perfect knowledge of our service, what would be the resultant impact on ridership?

Sensitivity to marketing variables. Consumers may also be segmented by their sensitivity or responsiveness to marketing variables. Price is often more important in one market than another and has led many transit authorities to charge differential fares based on zones, which recognizes a willingness to pay more for longer trips. Further, some consumers are more exposed to the mass media and more easily influenced by advertising, than are others.

Travel-related behavior as a basis for segmentation

Segmentation based on travel behavior can be used to delineate groups who use transit and those who don't. It can also be used to segment a spectrum of transit usage behavior—such as frequency of use, time of use, and trip purpose.

Some non-users may be more easily converted to transit use than others; some of those who only use public transportation occasionally may offer potential for more frequent use; and the heaviest users, transit's best customers, are the ones a system can least afford to lose. Conversely, those who receive free parking at work as a fringe benefit may be the hardest to convince to use public transit.

Car travel remains a competitive option for most of those riding transit by choice. Presumably they ride transit because it comes out better on balance than other alternatives. However, the margin of preference for transit may be small. In some transit systems, attitudinal surveys indicate that many existing regular transit riders are unhappy people, looking for the first opportunity to find an alternative way of traveling—or even of not having to make that particular journey at all. It's important to monitor the views of regular riders on a periodic basis to ensure that transit retains its overall competitive edge. Failure to keep in touch with these riders may mean that some of them are lost needlessly. Two approaches that have been used to categorize consumers according to transit usage behavior are detailed below.

Discretionary vs. nondiscretionary travel. Not all current riders make equal use of transit. In part this reflects occupational status: heavy riders are more likely to be commuters, traveling to and from their jobs or school each working day. Such trips are *nondiscretionary*—that is, they must be made between the same locations at a set time each day. That's why we get the peak-hour crunch. Several transit agencies have been working with planners and employers to encourage more use of staggered working hours and "flexitime" in an effort to spread the load over a greater time period. This strategy recognizes how the demand for travel is derived.

The fact that people only ride transit a few times a week does not necessarily mean that they only make that particular journey on the days when they ride transit. Some surveys have found a surprising amount of switching backwards and forwards between different modes, depending on the availability of a car ride, different arrival time requirements, etc.

For the most part, however, occasional riders tend to travel at off-peak hours and on weekends. Their trips are usually for shopping, entertainment, social and recreational purposes and are often *discretionary* in nature. For instance, a shopping trip need not necessarily be taken at a specific time or even on a specific day, and the urban shopper may have several alternative locations from which to choose. There are some differences by gender in the purposes and timing of off-peak travel, with women being more likely to to shopping trips and to travel during off-peak, daylight hours.

Heavy vs. light users. A high proportion of total product use is often accounted for by a relatively small proportion of customers. The bulk of passenger trips on public transportation vehicles are made by a core group of riders who commute to and from work each day at approximately the same time. Although in some cities a high proportion of residents and visitors may claim to have ridden the transit system in any given year, the great majority of these people are likely to have used it on only a few occasions.

A market research study in the Toronto area categorized respondents into four groups according to the frequency with which they used transit each week.[6] The following groups were studied separately when analyzing responses to the survey:

Group	Weekly Range of Trips
Nonriders	0
Light Riders	1–3
Medium Riders	4–9
Heavy Riders	10+

The study asked *light riders* why they didn't use transit more often. The most frequently cited reason, given by a quarter of all respondents in this category, was that it was faster by car. The need to use a car on the job was also cited. Asked if there were anything that the TTC could do to increase their riding, 24 percent said there was nothing, 20 percent proposed cheaper rates in off-peak hours, while many of the others suggested a need to overcome obstacles relating to inconvenience, lack of weather protection, and lack of accessibility.

Nonriders, of course, represent a major source of potential new business for transit. Many, however, are probably living and/or working too far from a transit stop for this mode to be a feasible alternative unless new routes are introduced (geographic segmentation). Others need the use of a car on their jobs. But in most cities, there are large numbers of current car drivers who *could* use transit. The question for planners and managers is, what will it take to attract them to transit?

A major barrier is that many nonriders have long since lost the habit of transit riding, while a large group have, regrettably, never developed it. Educational programs, particularly for those of school age, are one way of trying to combat such a problem; several transit authorities have made good progress in this direction (i.e., demographic segmentation).

Differing perceptions of transit versus automotive travel are marked between transit users and non-users. Non-users perceive transit as being much slower than car travel; for instance, 35 percent of the nonriders in Toronto cited this as a major reason for not using transit. A San Francisco Study found that transit users perceived buses to be as fast as cars for commute travel whereas non-users perceived cars as much faster.[7]

Too much generalization about nonriders may be unwise. There is evidence that the barriers to transit usage among current nonriders may be relatively more important in some cities than in others. A study in Baltimore showed significant concern among prospective riders to over-exposure to unsafe or unpleasant situations.[8] Security fears can also vary from one part of a metropolitan area to another and even from carrier to carrier and line to line.

Dealing with this personal security problem may require better policing, improved lighting, and an open architectural design, among other measures. However, it is possible that in some cities such fears may not be justified, in which case a communications effort may be needed to reassure potential riders of the security of the system. New rapid-transit rail systems, especially those with subway stations, have made special efforts to allay fears of personal danger and appear to have been successful in keeping vandalism and other crime to a minimum.

Trip purpose is another important base for segmenting a market. Many transit authorities have begun to look at markets other than the work trip. Transit agencies have initiated "shopper shuttles" to downtown areas (often with the cooperation of local merchants). San Francisco's BART has promoted shopping trips to increase ridership during the mid-day hours,[9] as has Long Beach (California) Transit (see Exhibit 2–1).

Some transit authorities have begun to market specifically to tourists

Exhibit 2-1
Promotional Brochure by Long Beach Transit

Ride Our Shopper Hopper
Long Beach Transit's Guide to Shopping

Long Beach Transit has over 150 ways to take you shopping and hopping in the Long Beach area.

We have routes leading to just about every shopping area you can think of.

Save yourself parking fees, gas and driving hassles. We'll give you a lift with time to relax, organize and think about what you need to buy.

Exact fare or proper identification if you're entitled to a reduced fare, is required upon boarding. Transfers are included.

It's so easy to ride the bus. Study this shopping guide, keep it and the next time you have to run to the store—make the run with us.

1 North Long Beach
Atlantic Ave. Between Market and Artesia
Take Long Beach Transit
Routes #2-5-6-7-10-15-16

2 Lakewood Center Mall
Lakewood at Del Amo
Take Long Beach Transit Routes #9-10-11-15

3 Bixby Knolls Shopping Center
San Antonio and Atlantic
Take Long Beach Transit Routes #5-6-7-10

4 Pacific Ave./Wrigley District
Pacific Ave. between
Willow and Pacific Coast Highway
Take Long Beach Transit Routes #1-4-13

5 Downtown Long Beach
All Long Beach Transit Routes except #10-15

6 Mary's Gate Village
Adjacent to the Queen Mary
Take Long Beach Transit Route #8

7 Ports O' Call Village
Los Angeles Harbor in San Pedro
Take Long Beach Transit Route #14

8 Los Cerritos Shopping Center
605 Freeway at South St.
Take Long Beach Transit Routes #1-16

9 Los Altos Shopping Center
Bellflower Blvd. and Stearns St.
Take Long Beach Transit Routes #1-9

10 Marina Pacifica Shopping Village
Pacific Coast Highway at 2nd St.
Take Long Beach Transit Routes #5-13-14

11 The Market Place
Pacific Coast Highway and Westminster Ave.
Take Long Beach Transit Routes #5-13-14

12 Belmont Shore/Naples Shopping District
2nd Street
Take Long Beach Transit Routes #5-8-13-14

13 Seaport Village
At the Long Beach Marina
Take Long Beach Transit Routes #5

14 Seal Beach Center/Old Town
Main St. and Pacific Coast Highway
Take Long Beach Transit Routes #5

A Good Run for Your Money
LONG BEACH TRANSIT

For more detailed information call 591-2301.
If our lines are busy, please bear with us and call again.

Source: Courtesy of Long Beach Transit.

and visitors for recreational travel. The Chicago Transit Authority operates a "Culture Bus" to museums and historic neighborhoods. In cooperation with local hotels, the Washington, D.C., Metro has been promoted with "Get-away Weekend" advertisements in the New York *Times* Sunday travel section. In Massachusetts, the MBTA has introduced special transit passes sold in bulk to convention groups visiting Boston.

Another approach is to market service for specific events, such as the Toronto Transit Commission's promotion of transit service to baseball games (see Exhibit 2–2).

RELATING TRANSIT OBJECTIVES TO SEGMENTATION VARIABLES

As previously discussed, two major public policy objectives for transit agencies are those centering on improving personal mobility and those relating to getting people out of their cars and into transit. We will now consider how strategies to implement objectives can be aided with the use of a market segmentation approach. The three objectives described below—mobility for elderly, pollution control, and reduced transit vandalism—are frequent issues in many transit organizations.

Improved mobility

Objectives relating to improvement of personal mobility tend to be keyed to the needs of several specific demographic segments who collectively constitute the group known as "captive" transit riders.

The captive group comprises those who can't drive or who do not have a car available to them (i.e., the elderly, the young, the handicapped, and the poor). Captive riders may also include secondary drivers in one-car families who are left without use of a car. These people ride transit because they have no alternative except for walking (if they are capable of this) or occasionally getting a ride from others (if riding in a car is physically feasible for them).

Frequently, transit-related legislation specifically singles out some of these segments for special attention. Among captive riders, the elderly and the handicapped have special needs that have been the subject of a number of government directives aimed at making it easier and safer for these people to use regular transit service. Even though some of these segments may be relatively very small and the costs of serving them relatively high (e.g., the handicapped), transit planners and managers must still cater to their needs.

Assuming that usable transit services are offered on routes meeting their travel needs, a major concern shared by most transit captives is likely to be cost. Although reduced fares are usually available for chil-

Exhibit 2–2
Advertising to Sports Fans by Toronto Transit Commission

Source: Toronto Transit Commission.

dren, the handicapped, and the elderly, there have been few moves in the direction of offering transit passes for the poor. Instead, many cities have opted for a low fare for everybody. This may be giving the service away too cheaply to middle and upper income people who are, perhaps, willing and able to pay more. The funds generated from higher fares for those able to pay them could be used to improve service quality and speed.

The following illustrates how strategies can be derived from a targeted objective:

Objective:	Improve mobility to the elderly in City X by increasing ridership among this segment by 10 percent over previous year's level.
Targeted Segments:	Persons aged 65 and over; All retired persons eligible for retirement benefits.
Possible Strategies:	From Census data, identify residential locations where elderly are concentrated. From surveys of elderly, interviews with appropriate agencies and representatives of senior groups, identify major destination points to which they travel (or would like to travel) and when. Review present services to see if they match key routes desired by elderly at times desired. Consider introducing new services during off-peak hours using equipment and drivers that are otherwise idle between peaks. Evaluate signs and informational materials for legibility by those with weak eyes. Evaluate suitability of equipment for use by frail older persons. Put most suitable equipment on key routes. Give special training to drivers on these routes. Review fare policies to see if suitable discounts can be/are being given. Clarify eligibility criteria, identification required. Publicize services/fares through media directed at elderly and through senior citizen organizations.

Modal shift

Objectives relating to modal shift are concerned with getting people out of their cars and into public transportation. At first sight, the target may appear to be simply all car-owning households. However, priorities need to be established in reaching people within this broad group if specific objectives are to be achieved. For instance, if our concern is with reducing energy consumption, then we might usefully attempt to group consumers according to quantity of gasoline they consume annually (presumably a function of miles driven, frequency of trips, and owner-ship of cars yielding poor gas mileage). If relieving congestion is our concern, then it makes sense to focus on people driving along specific routes during defined periods of the day or week. For environmental goals we could frame the following approach:

Objective:	Reduce pollution in City Y by increasing transit's share of commute-travel to specific percentage of all commuters in each of several designated corridors—producing a quantifiable reduction in vehicle miles traveled.
Target Segments:	Car drivers in corridors with densest traffic; Car drivers in locations with high congestion.
Possible Strategies:	Improve service frequency in dense, congested areas. Seek priority for transit vehicles and other measures to improve transit speed in key corridors. Use geographically specific media (billboards, direct mail, suburban newspapers, posters at retailers, employers) on key routes. Lobby for increased car parking rates at locations with high congestion.

Reduced vandalism

Transit vandalism is a continual and potentially expensive problem for transit agencies. One of the problems of even minor vandalism is that the damaged property or graffiti publicizes itself. As New York City found out in the 1970s, a graffiti problem can spread like a cancer if it is allowed to get out of control. A poorly designed communication program can exacerbate the problem by publicizing the problem to the general public (creating a marketing headache for transit managers). Thus a targeted marketing program is called for:

Objective:	Reduce reported incidence of vandalism to transit system in City Z by 15 percent over previous year's level.
Target Segments:	Parents, youths, and children living close to stations and routes where vandalism has occurred. Teachers in schools serving these areas.
Possible Strategies:	Increase surveillance in worst affected areas. Retraining of drivers/station personnel on affected routes to help them better handle aggression/conflict situations and improve communications with passengers.

Presentation of programs in selected schools designed to improve awareness of transit benefits and generate interest/pride in the system. Advertisements or press releases in selected neighborhood newspapers seeking cooperation of parents and other adults in combatting problems. Prompt repair/clearing of vandalized vehicles and facilities (especially on key routes).

CONCLUSION

Each of the segmentation approaches outlined in this chapter provides a different perspective on transit's present and potential markets. By focusing on the needs and behavior patterns of groups of individuals with certain characteristics in common, transit planners should better be able to develop strategies designed to achieve specific objectives in a cost-effective manner. Managers should be in a better position to set priorities and identify the best potential markets.

Transit's competitive position against the automobile may vary sharply for different segments. Intelligent segmentation analysis, particularly that which emphasizes benefits sought, may facilitate development and implementation of marketing strategies designed to improve transit's competitiveness for key segments.

The different types of segmentation discussed here should not necessarily be viewed as alternative approaches. In many instances, several forms of segmentation may be employed at once, either sequentially or concurrently. For example, special attention to specific demographic groups might be mandated by law, or attention focused on particular areas of a city that are accessible by existing transit services. Such variables may provide only the first cut, identifying one or more segments singled out for treatment. Subsequent analysis might seek to highlight the best prospects in the target group according to present usage behavior or benefits sought. Finally, alternative advertising strategies might be evaluated in the light of such segmentation variables as exposure to different types of media (e.g., newspaper reading habits, TV program viewing). Messages with a different content (or in different languages) might then be sent to different subsegments.

In summary, an organization can expect a number of benefits to result from a segmentation approach that meets the criteria listed above. These benefits include:

- a more precise definition of the market in terms of the needs of specific groups, why they behave as they do, and possible ways of influencing behavior;
- a better ability to identify competitive strengths and weaknesses, and opportunities for winning specific segments from the competition;

• more efficient allocation of limited resources to development of programs that will satisfy the needs of target segments;

• clarification of objectives and definition of performance standards.

NOTES

1. For a market segmentation approach to transportation energy planning, see Jeffrey Trombly, *Transportation Analysis Report* (Albany, N.Y.: N. Y. State Dept. of Transportation, January 1986); p. 57.

2. "Orange County takes mass transit to the public," *Passenger Transport* (January 6, 1986); p. 6.

3. Transportation Research Board. *Urban Transportation Economics*, Special Report 181 (Washington, D.C.: National Academy of Sciences, 1978); p. 187.

4. Research/Analysis Corporation. *A Segmentation Study on Transportation in the Boston Area*, conducted for the MBTA (1978), p. 13.

5. Robinson, Richard K. "Transit market segmentation: Research and applications," in *Marketing Public Transportation: Policies, Strategies and Research Needs for the 1980's*, Proceedings Series, edited by Richard K. Robinson and Christopher H. Lovelock (Chicago: American Marketing Association, 1981), p. 68.

6. Canadian Intermark. "A research survey on attitudes and uses by riders and non-riders of the Toronto Transit Commission," Project 256–76, Toronto Transit Commission (November, 1976).

7. Lovelock, Christopher. *Consumer Oriented Approaches to Marketing Urban Transit*, Ph.D. dissertation, Stanford University (Springfield, VA: National Technical Information Service: PB–220–781: 1973).

8. Grey Advertising. Transit marketing project, for the Urban Mass Transportation Administration (1976).

9. *Urban Transport News* 13, No. 24 (Nov. 25, 1985): 185.

3

Consumer Decision Making

Why do some commuters choose to ride public transportation while others drive alone in a car even though it is far more expensive? Analysis of how consumers make these transportation mode decisions can help a transit manager plan and promote services targeted to specific market segments, with a probability of success much higher than for a generalized promotional campaign.

THE DECISION TO TRY A NEW SERVICE

When faced with products or services that are new, consumers tend to move through several stages before deciding to make use of the service on a regular basis. The service may be new to a particular consumer, as opposed to being new on the marketplace (in which case they would be new to everybody). For a non-transit user to switch to transit involves a willingness to try a different experience and adopt new behavior patterns. The automobile user is already involved in a repetitive, or habitual, pattern and a switch to transit involves adopting a new daily behavior pattern. Changing a habit is not simple. It involves a number of steps, as the following story illustrates.

Jane Davidson takes the train

For the past four years, Jane Davidson had been driving from her home in the suburbs to the architectural firm downtown where she worked. She liked the convenience of her car, especially when she worked late or shopped after work. Occasionally, when she had to bring models and display materials home, she could load the car in the parking garage below the office and not have to carry the equipment too far. Lately, however, she had begun to notice the increasing parking rates downtown, and, although she did not keep track, she knew that auto insurance costs were rising. In addition, rush-hour traffic was frequently snarled and the 25 minute-drive home periodically turned into 50 minutes of what the local radio station called "stall and crawl."

Recently, the local transit service had been extended and had opened a new station near her home. Jane knew it was a 5 minute walk to the train station and a 20 minute ride to the downtown station across the street from her office. Service was frequent until 10 p.m., so she did not think she would ever have to wait for more than 10 minutes, but she wondered if she would ever get a seat. The train fare was $.75 each way, but she could buy a monthly pass for $25.

She really did not spend much time thinking about all this, but one morning when the radio reported an overturned truck blocking the freeway, she decided to take the train to work. The ride was comfortable, as she expected, but she could not get a seat in the middle of the rush hour. She did get to glance at the morning paper, however. Her ride home was just after the rush hour, so she had a chance to sit and relax. The next day it rained, and Jane drove her car again, but as time went on, she rode the train to work about half the time.

Let's examine the stages of Jane's decision making:

Problem recognition: The first stage of the decision process was for the consumer to recognize that she had a set of needs to be fulfilled. Jane Davidson recognized that parking and insurance fees were rising. She also did not enjoy her drive to work when traffic congestion was bad.

Awareness: The consumer has to become aware of an alternative, otherwise there is no solution for that individual. Perhaps advertising or news coverage of the new rapid transit extension first started Jane Davidson thinking about using the train. Alternatively, she may have heard about the service from a friend or fellow office worker who was using it.

Without awareness of a potential solution, the individual will treat a recognized problem, such as traffic congestion, as merely a "fact" of urban living. The psychology is similar to that of residents in snowbelt states complaining about cold weather in the winter. With weather, the choice is either to migrate south for the winter (impractical for most people) or to put up with cold weather as a fact of living in a northern climate—and complain about it! Without awareness of an alternative, the frustrated driver will take no action other than to complain about traffic conditions.

Knowledge and evaluation: Without detailed information, the consumer will not be able to evaluate the possibility of trying a new service. At some point, Jane Davidson had to obtain information on fares, routes, and travel times in order to make a decision—and she had to know how to get that information. She probably had to look up a phone number so she could call the transit authority for details of the service. With the requisite information, she could then evaluate rapid transit as an alternative to her regular commute.

Trial: Most people will not immediately switch from one mode to another. To guard against risk, the commuter will not immediately sell his or her car and buy a monthly transit pass. The automobile commuter will use the train, bus, or ferry on a experimental, or trial, basis. A transit authority may give away free coupons for rides in order to encourage trial behavior.

Jane's trial was a mixed experience. The trips were routine except that she was unable to get a seat on her way to work. In order to expect trial rides to result in ongoing purchases, the consumer is going to have to be satisfied by the initial experience.

Choice: Jane Davidson chose not to make a permanent commitment to either transit or to driving. Some days she would drive and others she would take the train. Her purchase decision was limited to paying a daily fare and not buying a monthly pass. Based on her daily circumstances, Jane Davidson will continue to evaluate which mode best meets her needs.

Confirmation: Upon deciding to use transit on a regular basis, the consumer may still be anxious for confirmation that the right choice was made. Expressions of appreciation by transit personnel akin to "Thanks for flying United" are possible strategies. If Jane were to receive positive confirmation of her decision to use the train, she would be more likely to begin using it more frequently until she reached the level of use where it was more economical for her to buy a monthly pass.

Consumers do not necessarily go through each of these decision stages in sequence for every product or service that is new to them. In some instances, particularly low value services where there is minimum social or personal risk, awareness and purchase may take place simultaneously without intervening stages. Thus, a visitor in a city might be walking to a destination, see a bus approaching with the name of the destination, and decide to take the bus on the spur of the moment. But commuters are likely to evaluate options more carefully, because they make daily repetitive purchases. Thus it is helpful for marketers to recognize the existence of these various stages, since different elements in the marketing mix may be appropriate at different stages, and for different consumers.

While the story of Jane Davidson illustrates the transportation mode decision process of a prospective transit user, planners and market analysts also need to consider the factors influencing the mode choice process of existing transit users who may be inclined to switch to car travel. By understanding impediments to continued transit use, transit authorities can develop strategies to retain existing ridership.

The consumer decision process

Understanding consumer decision making is particularly important for transportation planners and managers concerned with encouraging shifts in transportation choice from automobiles to transit. For car owners, transit usage may require changes in established behavior patterns, attitudes, and even in lifestyles. Essentially, non-transit users are being asked to adopt a "new" service with which they may be previously unfamiliar. A major challenge for transit managers is to understand why people with similar demographic backgrounds and traveling over the same routes often exhibit different modal choice behavior.

Let's examine the following model of a mode choice decision process:

Step 1: Decide to make trip (specify characteristics of trip).

Step 2: Form perception of travel needs (e.g., low cost, convenient).

Step 3: Form perceptions of alternative modes (e.g., transit unreliable). These perceptions are strongly influenced by personal values and attitudes.

Step 4: Seek additional information (e.g., call transit authority). Many consumers will simply bypass this step and proceed to Step 5 below.

Step 5: Match perceived needs against perception of each mode.

Step 6: Is there a match?

If no: Don't make trip, or change needs.

If yes: Select mode, make trip, update knowledge. This actual travel experience will serve to reinforce—or, at times, force—a reevaluation of personal values and attitudes. In either case, our actual experiences have a strong influence on future travel decisions.

This model helps us to recognize that individuals make choices based on *perceptions* of reality rather than on reality objective as defined by an expert (such as an engineer or operations analyst). Although the model shows a number of discrete stages in decision making, it should be recognized that the transportation choice for frequently-taken journeys may well become routine, so that only one mode is considered for evaluation.

To bring about the desired behavior change, transit marketers need to know about the criteria that people employ in making decisions relating to travel modes, as well as the relative importance of these criteria. Management also needs to know how consumers evaluate information in making these decisions. Since many consumers do not successfully obtain relevant information, transit managers have to find the most effective means of communicating with different market segments, together with the most appropriate appeals to employ in seeking to change the behavior of consumers.

Costs and benefits of using transit

The cost of owning and operating a car is quite expensive. According to Federal Highway Administration statistics, published in 1984, the owner of an intermediate-sized car driven 120,000 miles over a 12 year period can expect to spend approximately $33,400—or about 27.8 cents per mile.[1] It seems irrational that consumers will choose to drive when given the alternative to commute at low cost by public transportation. Yet automobile commuters tend to evaluate only the more obvious marginal costs of drivings when choosing a mode (e.g., gasoline and parking costs, but not necessarily maintenance, repairs, or tire replacements). In addition, there are other costs and benefits other than price to be considered when making a transportation mode decision.

These costs and benefits fall into five categories: sensory, psychic, place, time, and monetary. The following is a list of some of the costs and benefits that a passenger may confront when using public transit and that will affect a consumer's choice of transportation mode:

Sensory Benefits

Seating is comfortable.

Ride is smooth.

Vehicle noise is minimal.

Vehicle appearance is attractive.

Vehicle is air conditioned.

Weather protection is provided at stops.

Sensory Costs

Seating is uncomfortable.

Stops and starts are jerky.

Vehicle vibrates.

Vehicle is dirty.

Vehicle is overcrowded.

Vehicle is overheated/freezing.

Psychic Benefits

Driver is polite, helpful.

Feeling of personal safety.

Other passengers are pleasant.

Friends, colleagues, family approve of transit use.

Psychic Costs

Driver is rude, unhelpful.

Other passengers appear threatening or unsavory.

Bus is driven unsafely.

Fear of crime.

Friends, colleagues, family disparage transit use.

Offensive graffiti.

Worry about missing the bus.

Worry about consequences of late arrival.

Place Benefits

Stops are clearly marked and routes well described.

Stops are near home and destination.

Route is direct.

Monthly passes available at convenient locations.

Route is scenic.

Place Costs

Stops are hard to find, signs give no route information.

Stops are inconveniently located.

Route is indirect.

Monthly passes are hard to obtain.

Time Benefits

Time is saved on car maintenance and repair.

Opportunity to use travel time for reading, relaxing.

Transport runs at convenient time.

Short wait for transport.

Transport leaves on time.

Time Costs

Travel time from door to door is increased.

Time spent in traveling seen as a waste.

Time is spent waiting for delayed transport (also produces psychic cost).

Time is spent getting transit information, monthly passes.

Monetary Benefits

Employer sells monthly passes at a discount as a fringe benefit.

Rebates are received on car insurance for commuting by transit.

Transit pass holder receives discounts for events and with merchants.

Money saved by not having to drive to work.

Monetary Costs

All fares require payment in advance.

Actual costs of fares are significant for some market segments.

Costs and benefits should not be examined simply on an absolute basis. They should be studied relative to the characteristics of competing alternatives. If the dollar cost of bus travel is less than driving alone, the bus has a relative advantage over car travel. If bus travel is rated as somewhat comfortable but car travel and train travel are rated as very comfortable, the bus is at a relative disadvantage compared with either of these other modes. The question here would be how people with a choice between several competing transportation modes might trade off comfort versus price. Consumers also have to make tradeoffs on a range of variables including the ones listed above. A market research study may find that different market segments would, in fact, make different tradeoffs.

Incorporating nonmonetary costs into strategy

It is not difficult to see the need for managers to develop pricing strategies that take into account the monetary costs to consumers (and we discuss such strategies later in this book). Managers need to recognize, however, that the customer is likely to consider other costs in addition to financial expenditures.

Time costs are particularly important for a consumer service such as public transportation where scheduling (hours of service) and use of service (time on vehicle plus access time and wait time) assume major importance in consumer choices.

Travel is a derived demand; people travel to get to another location where they will do something else. Few travelers, other than vacationers and sightseers, would agree with Robert Louis Stevenson that "to travel hopefully is a better thing than to arrive." Transportation studies show that there is a negative relationship between level of demand and travel time on many routes, especially those widely used by business travelers. The shorter the trip time, the more people want to make the journey.

At issue for the transportation operator is the feasibility of increasing travel speed (reducing the time cost) to stimulate demand, and the level of additional capital and operating expenditures that would be incurred in doing so. Some transit authorities charge lower fares on slower services and premium fares on express services, so that travelers can trade off time and monetary costs.

Psychological studies of transportation behavior have shown that travelers perceive that while waiting for a transit vehicle, time passes from 1.5 to seven times more slowly than the time spent actually traveling in it.[2] Not knowing when a transit vehicle is likely to arrive, due to difficulties in maintaining a schedule, is likely to increase the perception of wait time for the passenger. In addition to tightly adhering to published schedules, possible strategies might include providing seating, shelters, and mounted transit information at bus stops so that travelers can study transit maps or just sit and read comfortably while they wait.

User perceptions of travel time can vary by trip purpose. A study by the Port Authority of New York and New Jersey found that travel time for airport trips is perceived differently than for commute trips and that travel to the airport is perceived differently than the return trip. The Port Authority also developed psychological profiles of how different travelers perceive and plan trips to airports.[3] (See Exhibit 3–1.)

GROUP INFLUENCES ON TRAVEL BEHAVIOR

Most people associate closely with others—families, friends, colleagues at work, etc. Other people can often influence a person's behavior in a variety of ways. In the case of group travel, if one person has a car and offers to drive, use of public transportation is unlikely unless another member of the group argues against car travel and can produce strong arguments in favor of transit.

Individual behavior can also be influenced by the values and attitudes of others and a desire to obtain approval for conforming with other people's behavior patterns. Consumer researchers often use the concept of opinion leadership to designate individuals whose opinions and behavior are valued (and emulated) by others.

Personal endorsements

Group influence is probably most important for the transit authority in areas where new services are being introduced. Nothing is more devastating than the negative personal endorsement. While consumers tend to remain silent about positive or neutral experiences, they are quite articulate (and repeatedly so) about negative experiences. The consumer experimenting with a new bus route is likely to tell friends and family about the "rude bus driver," or "filthy bus." Unhappy users will tell many more potential riders about their experiences than will satisfied consumers. The implication of word-of-mouth recommendation can be ascertained from a survey that asked consumers what most influences their buying decisions. Respondents said: company/product image, 38.6 percent; word-of-mouth recommendation, 37.4 percent; and advertising, only 20.5 percent.[4]

Exhibit 3–1
Express Bus Brochure by Southern California Rapid Transit District

Source: Courtesy of the Southern California Rapid Transit District.
In Los Angeles, the Rapid Transit District promotes its express bus service by advertising the nonmonetary benefit to riders of being able to use travel time productively. The design of the express bus and the promotion itself are clearly targeted to a group that has the option of driving to work.

The consequence for transit marketing managers is the importance of maintaining a courteous and efficient complaint hotline. In the private sector, consumer product companies are widely using "800" toll-free hotlines in order to forestall negative word-of-mouth campaigns. A common marketing theme for these telephone numbers is: "If you like our service, tell your friends; if you don't—tell us."

Since a bad experience has an impact far beyond the unhappy consumer, it pays for marketing managers to work with operating personnel in staff training to ensure courteous employee behavior when the inevitable breakdown or problem develops in actual operation. Monitoring complaint rates can assist in identifying problem employees or areas where operations management needs to focus effort.

Reference groups

An important influence on a person's attitudes and behavior is the reference group or groups to which he or she belongs, aspires to, or seeks to avoid. Face-to-face groups, such as family, friends, neighbors, and work associates, are often of primary importance, but the perceived values of other groups can be significant, too. For example, a young manager may stop riding mass transit because senior management uses automobiles. A study of motivational issues faced by bus travelers concluded, "Being a bus traveler is itself seen as low status compared to going by car. . . . "[5] While train travel is often seen as being somewhat higher status (in part because many commuter rail lines serve affluent suburbs), people do not generally self-identify as transit users, in the same way as, say, people identify with being owners of Cadillacs, Volvos, or even Volkswagens.

The implication for transit managers that it is sometimes important to sell transit not only to the targeted individual but also to the people and institutions who can influence that person. Companies that sell monthly transit passes to their employees send a message to employees that riding transit is a good activity (or why would the company devote resources to that purpose?).

Family members can also significantly influence an individual's behavior, even if the behavior only affects one person. Children can be important influencers in many situations (as most parents have experienced!). A transit agency can accomplish two objectives by operating an outreach program to local schools. First, the agency has an opportunity to introduce public transit use to a new generation of young people. Second, the agency has a convenient distribution channel for placing transit maps and schedules in the hands of parents through their children. An example is provided by the Transit Authority of Northern Kentucky, which distributes a transit education coloring book to school students (see Exhibit 3–2).

Exhibit 3–2
Transit Education Coloring Book

YOU CAN CALL THE TANK INFORMATION CENTER
AT 431-7000 AND FIND OUT HOW AND WHERE
AND WHEN YOU CAN CATCH THE COACH, AND
IF THEY FOUND YOUR LUNCH BOX ON ONE.

Source: Courtesy of the Transit Authority of Northern Kentucky.

INSIGHTS FROM CONSUMER RESEARCH

Faster service versus cheaper service

There is evidence from consumer research to suggest that, outside of the lower income groups, travelers are more sensitive to speed of service in their modal choice behavior than to the cost of service. For example, a study of commuters in Philadelphia found that 12 percent of auto users did not use transit because of high fares. This compared to 28 percent who felt the auto was faster and more convenient and 30 percent who viewed transit as either unreliable, overcrowded, or infrequently scheduled.[6]

The policy implications for transit managers are twofold. If the service is already speedy, this fact should be promoted—many auto users may be unaware of that fact. Route-by-route highlights are probably more meaningful than general statements. If the services are not competitive in speed, consider what can be done by way of 1) introducing new, premium-priced express services; and 2) speeding up existing services through introduction of new equipment, more frequent headways, introduction of exclusive bus lanes, or development of other traffic management systems giving priority to transit.

Faced with the alternative of slow services at cheap fares or faster services at higher fares, current car travelers are probably much more likely to see the latter as competitive with their automobiles. There is a potential bonus here for the transit manager in that faster service may make for more productive use of both labor and equipment.

Although speed is a critical variable, it is not the only one determining quality of service in the consumer's mind. Comfort, reliability, cleanliness, and personal security are important to consumers too. A number of transit systems around the country have demonstrated that good quality services targeted at suburban commuters can attract such individuals out of their cars while also commanding premium fares.

QUALITY OF SERVICE

The tangible characteristics and the ambiance of a service facility are important to the consumer for two major reasons. First, these characteristics contribute to the user's overall satisfaction with the service. This can happen even though the primary tangible characteristics may be secondary to the basic service. For example, most New York City subway cars are covered inside and out with graffiti, as are many of the stations. Although the graffiti may have no impact on the speed and reliability of service, they may well decrease total satisfaction on the part of the rider. Second, customers will tend to evaluate what they can't see (the service itself) by relying on tangible clues such as the condition of transit vehicles and stations, the demeanor and appearance of drivers and station staff, and the appearance of transit information aids such as maps and schedules.

The tangible aspects of the facility help attract the attention of prospective users, suggest the quality and the nature of the services offered, and provide support or evidence that promised benefits will be forthcoming. Conversely, a filthy vehicle may give the consumer a clue (warranted or otherwise) as to the safety and maintenance record of the operation. With no other basis of information, a prospective consumer will conclude that if "they" don't have time to clean the vehicle, the bus is unlikely to have received basic maintenance either. To prevent this assessment, even the lowest priced airline seeks to keep its fleet looking clean and shiny.

Reliability is key. Probably one of the most serious problems that can beset a transit authority is lack of reliability. Missed bus trips with results in delays getting to and from work are a very serious issue for commuters. A London Transport study concluded, "Emotional feelings are stronger and more negative traveling to and from work because bus unreliability upsets the working day and leisure time. It means leaving home earlier, maybe clocking in later and losing money, getting home later, etc., i.e. disturbs people's life-styles."[7]

Anecdotally, the following story by a newspaper reporter who was a dedicated transit user helps illustrate how important reliability is to the consumer:

For 11 years, I lived in Boston and Cambridge without a car. I can't say I was thrilled with that state of affairs every second. After all, I had to ride the Red Line. But I always preferred not having a car to the alternative. Wherever I went, I arrived without a two-ton thing I would have had to put somewhere before I could do anything. . . .

Then, the MBTA added a four-minute turnaround between Harvard and Porter squares and apologized for the inconvenience. No one ever explained how a four-minute turnaround increased the average trip time by about 40 minutes, but it happened. Last winter it took me an *average* of an hour and a half each way to get to and from work on the Red Line. Uncle.

I got a car. I had a baby and I got a car. They go together, especially in this city, because maybe a husband can wait an hour and a half every night for dinner, but a baby can't.[8]

The implication for a marketing department is significant. The quality of operations and changes in operations can have serious effects on transit ridership. Marketing managers must be in a position to work with operations personnel to articulate the importance of maintaining service standards in order to prevent the erosion of patronage.

The need to provide information. Several studies have highlighted a serious lack of awareness about transit service among infrequent riders and

non-riders. In a San Francisco survey, it was found that the less frequently people rode transit, the less they knew about the specifics of
particular services in their communities.[9]

In a Nashville study, potential riders were found to be poorly informed
about the availability of service and about routes and fares.[10] Obviously,
people can't be expected to use a system of which they are largely
ignorant. Even if they know that a service exists, they may be reluctant to
use it if they don't know where the stops are, how often the service runs,
how long the trip takes, how much it costs, and where to get off at the
destination end of the journey.

Good information is especially necessary when seeking to attract new
riders—whether new residents, visitors, or tourists—or to get existing
riders to make additional trips on new routes. Some transit properties
have made intensive efforts to improve bus-stop, station, and vehicle
signs; they have also developed improved maps, pocket schedules, and
telephone information services. Other systems, regretfully, still do a
substandard job in some of these areas.

A comprehensive consumer information system can affect a potential
rider's overall perception of the quality of a transit service since it is the
first contact a new rider will have with the operation. While a more
detailed discussion of consumer information aids occurs later in this
book, it is important to note that courteous telephone information personnel; an easy-to-read map, schedule, and guidebook; distinctive bus-
stop signs; and clearly marked buses all reinforce to the consumer that
the transit ride will be pleasant and without risk of getting lost.

CONCLUSION: STRATEGIC IMPLICATIONS FOR MARKETERS

Public transportation agencies are often faced with negative demand
where "a major part of a market dislikes the product (or service) and in
fact might even pay a price to avoid it."[11] The concept of negative demand helps explain why people make the seemingly irrational decision
of choosing to drive when faced with the lower cost alternative of public
transportation. In essence, many people are willing to pay the high price
of commuting and car ownership in order to avoid using public transportation. This obviously places a formidable hurdle in front of marketers of
public transportation.

Yet, all is not hopeless. With an understanding of how consumers
make decisions, realistic strategies and programs can be developed that
will have a high likelihood of success. The consumer evaluation process
has six strategic implications:

Information provisions: Non-transit users have a very poor knowledge of
actual public transportation services and even transit users themselves

may have little knowledge beyond the bus route or transit line that they use daily. Up-to-date information, which is easy to obtain and understand, is needed if consumers are going to try public transportation.

Quality image: The potential importance of physical facilities as an indicator of service quality suggests that transit agencies should manipulate these cues to their own advantage. Improving the physical image can provide tangible evidence that the service provides the appropriate atmosphere.

Retaining existing riders: Automobile owners who ride transit may view the transit authority as less than indispensable, since they are often in a position to abandon the transit system and drive their cars instead. Similarly, non-car owners may be able to find a car pool or even decide to walk or bicycle for short trips. Thus, transit marketing needs to be continually reinforcing positive images and messages in order to retain existing ridership.

Innovation: In order to increase ridership, transit agencies need to be experimenting with new services and promotional techniques. Whether it is offering free coupons for trial use, selling monthly passes, or providing new services, new ridership can only be attracted with an aggressive strategy.

Reducing perceived risks: For the non-transit user, using transit for the first time is perceived as risky. What if I get lost? Do I need exact change? Which is the right bus? What time does it arrive? These are all questions that face a potential transit user. As much as new users can easily be assured that their trip will be uneventful (i.e., good information, helpful employees), the more likely the consumer will try the service, be satisfied, and become a regular transit rider.

Implications of strong mode loyalty: The fact that car owners are often strongly loyal to use of their automobiles for almost all urban journeys creates special challenges for transit marketers. Marketing to automobile users needs to emphasize the attributes and strengths of public transit over the automobile under specific trip conditions.

NOTES

1. Federal Highway Administration. *Cost of Owning and Operating Automobiles and Vans, 1984* (Washington, D.C.: U.S. Department of Transportation, 1984).

2. Cherlow, Jay R. "Measuring the values of travel time savings," *Journal of Consumer Research*, 7 (March 1981): 360–71.

3. Selinger, Carl, and Christine Johnson. "User perceptions of airport landside transportation," unpublished paper presented at Transportation Research Board Annual Meeting (January 1986).

4. *Wall Street Journal*, August 12, 1985, p. 1.

5. London Transport. *Motivational Research into London Transport Bus Travel*, Project B415 (November, 1978), p. 4.

6. Zakaria, Thabet. "Employee transportation survey for central city Philadelphia," Delaware Valley Regional Planning Commission, unpublished paper presented at Transportation Research Board Annual Meeting (January 1986).

7. London Transport. *Motivational Research*, op. cit., p. 4.

8. Robb, Christina. "Turns for the worse," in the *Boston Globe Magazine*, Sunday, February 10, 1985, p. 33–34.

9. Lovelock, Christopher. *Consumer Oriented Approaches to Marketing Urban Transit*, Ph.D. dissertation, Stanford University (Springfield, VA: National Technical Information Service: PB–220–781: 1973).

10. Urban Mass Transportation Administration. *The Transit Marketing Project: Summary of Consumer Research*, Baltimore MTA and Nashville MTA (July 1976).

11. Kotler, Philip. *Principles of Marketing* (Englewood Cliffs, NJ: Prentice-Hall, 1986), p. 12.

4
Market Research

Successful marketing management requires a good understanding of the marketplace. In order to understand transportation markets, a transit organization must have accurate, timely information as well as a means to analyze and communicate this information to relevant decision makers. Thus, a market research capability is an important function for a marketing or planning department.

Still, it is important to recognize the limitations as well as potential rewards of research and to begin every investigation with a clear understanding of the organization's specific needs for information. Given the uncertain, dynamic, and competitive nature of the markets and publics with which most transit authorities must deal, no manager can hope to gain perfect understanding. The goal of marketing research is to reduce uncertainty to tolerable levels at a reasonable cost.

The purpose of this chapter is to provide managers with an overview of the market research process and the role of research within a public sector planning environment.

MARKET RESEARCH IN THE PLANNING PROCESS

The strategic planning process (discussed in Chapter 5) begins with an ongoing monitoring of the environment in which a transit system operates. Effective transportation requires a market research capability, to address the following questions:

- What are the characteristics of our market?
- What are the major trends influencing those characteristics?
- How is our system performing?

Most of the ongoing data collected by transit systems come from operations-oriented studies of peakloads, running times, origins and estimations, and revenue sources. They may be supplemented by data from secondary sources on population growth, vehicle registrations, building awards, and school plans in the area, but are generally inadequate to detect the reasons for changes or to forecast the seriousness of the impact. Few systems undertake periodic studies to identify changes in market segment characteristics, attitudes of riders and nonriders, and to track key variables influencing present and future performance.

Market research can help a manager *understand and define a problem* once it has been detected. A transit manager may notice a rise in complaint letters, an increase in vandalism, a falloff of patronage, or even an increase in press coverage—each may indicate problems that market research can help an organization understand.

Once the need for a change is recognized, market research can also help the manager *search for and evaluate alternative courses of action*. Although the process of generating alternatives can sometimes be relatively informal, much of the work done in this area is characterized by formal research procedures. Indeed, the careful gathering of descriptive data and the evaluation of specific alternatives through questionnaires and observational studies is the stereotypical conception of market research—and is probably the area where the most money is spent.

After a decision has been made and implemented, market research is often used to evaluate the results. The questions to be asked after a program has begun include:

- To what extent is it reaching its objectives?
- What other impacts, both anticipated and unanticipated, is the program making? .
- What accounts for deviation from the predicted results?

Performance monitoring is important not only because it can indicate a need for changes in a plan or its execution, but also because it enables managers and other personnel to learn from their mistakes—as well as their successes—and to redirect the organization accordingly.

In all but the smallest organizations, the marketing manager (or other senior executive) specifies the objectives of the research undertaking and expects others to assume responsibility for designing the research program, gathering the information, analyzing the data, and preparing a report. Because marketing research can become highly technical, there is often a temptation to delegate responsibility even further by assigning the entire project to internal experts or outside consultants. Such wholesale delegation may be unwise, since research specialists may make decisions that do not reflect the real concerns of management. Consequently, the manager commissioning the research must have sufficient knowledge of market research to be able to direct the project wisely and to maintain control of the research process at all times.

THE MARKET RESEARCH PROCESS

The process of market research can be broken down into the ten steps outlined below,[1] each of which is subsequently discussed in more depth.

1. Purpose of research: why is information to be gathered?
2. Statement of research objectives: what information is needed?
3. Review of existing data: what is already known?
4. Cost/benefit analysis: is the research worth the cost?
5. Research design: How are the data to be collected?
   a) exploratory
   b) descriptive
   c) causal
6. Methods of primary data collection:
   a) indirect communication
   b) direct observation
7. Research tactics: sampling procedures and instrument design.
   a) universe
   b) sample selection
   c) sample size
   d) instrument design
   e) pretesting
8. Field operations: collection of the data.
9. Data analysis.
10. Completing the project.
    a) interpreting the data
    b) recommendations
    c) report writing

Purpose of research: Why gather information

Since research is costly, the key questions to ask before beginning a proposed market research study are 1) "why is this information needed?" and 2) "what would be the implications of alternative findings from this research?" If none of the possible findings or outcomes is expected to have an impact on management decisions, then there is no point in conducting the research in the first place. Of course, not all discoveries will lead to changes. For example, if a survey of mass transit riders' opinions concerning transit information found that riders viewed printed transit schedules as clear and easy to understand, no changes would be needed in the current approach to presenting schedule information.

Several different types of studies can be conducted by a transit organization, depending on the purposes of the research. Six categories of study of are:

Descriptive studies. These generally concentrate on describing and analyzing the travel patterns of current riders and trends in patronage. This type of research is only useful for identification of the most obvious problems or opportunities (e.g., identifying problem of declining ridership). Instead, specific studies are usually necessary, focusing on the nature and seriousness of the problems affecting ridership, the reasons for these problems, and the nature of opportunities.

Problem detection studies. These may be used 1) to identify significant problems that need immediate attention, 2) to distinguish trends that will need to be anticipated, and 3) to help management appear to be responsive to public wishes and complaints. For example, BART conducted such a study and found that operations were considered unreliable, which changed the emphasis in operations from expanding service to improving existing service. A Denver RTD study found a large majority of those living within three blocks of a transit line felt they could not use it. A follow-up survey found they didn't know how to catch or ride a bus.[2]

Identifying potential riders. The key to identifying new riders is good segmentation research, for the reasons discussed in Chapter 2. The first step in this research is to identify the customer segments that are the most likely prospects for expanded use of transit. Equally important is the next step, determining the barriers to transit ridership for potential new riders.

One interview approach is to ask each target group what they want from each of the trips they take. For example, in the Baltimore and Nashville demonstration projects,[3] respondents were asked to rate the importance of such functional-related needs as "being able to come and go whenever you want," and "making the trip in comfort," as well as psychological benefits such as "arriving at work feeling fresh," and "traveling in a way that's accepted by people like yourself." Subsequently, respondents were asked to compare transit versus automobile for each of these considerations. With these results, it becomes possible to identify the areas of greatest dissatisfaction with mass transit, and those service elements that are important but not viewed as "deliverable" by the existing transit facilities.

A similar approach is to focus on operational characteristics of the system. Information on relative importance to the consumer can be combined with ratings of transit system performance for each characteristic. This approach can help decision makers by highlighting priorities for improving operations.

Identification and assessment of alternatives. The emphasis of research at this stage shifts to answering the question, "What can be done to bring about the desired improvement?" Research conducted for prior stages of marketing program development can usefully contribute to answering this question. In addition, a wide variety of exploratory techniques have been developed to gain insights into possible solutions to a problem. For example, interviews with small groups of riders, nonriders, or drivers can be used to obtain ideas for improvements in transit sign visibility, legibility, and comprehension.

Alternatives can be assessed by presenting them in surveys. For example, the Toronto Transit Commission found that nonriders in Toronto would be more likely to use the system if there were more service at night and on weekends, there were less crowding, and if transit passes and quantity discounts were available. This kind of research only indicates possible actions to pursue; whether the actions are feasible will require additional research.

Another approach is to present different service and price configurations and have survey respondents make choices between different alternatives. The task for the researcher is to analyze the tradeoffs made by different consumers. For example, the Long Island Railroad asked its riders how much more they would be willing to pay for improvements that would lead to a faster ride, a seat on the train, and new parking. Researchers found that getting a seat or having a parking space were worth over five times more to riders than a ten-minute savings in travel time.[4]

Testing and calibrating. As we enter this phase, the alternative strategies, policies, and services are few in number and may be operational. At this point, the research task is to test the marketable alternatives in the most realistic possible fashion. For communication programs, there are a variety of pretesting methods that ask whether the advertising message, brochure copy, and so on can be understood, believed, and will positively influence attitudes.

Alternative price levels or service packages can be treated as concepts to which prospective riders respond with expressions of interest. Under some circumstances the price and service levels can actually be manipulated in the context of a quasi-experimental design. This was done on a transit line serving Liverpool, England, by making an off-peak price reduction of 29 percent with minimal promotion at one station and similar reductions with medium intensity promotion at a second station, while monitoring a third station as a control for seasonal and cyclical changes in demand.

Performance evaluation. The evaluation phase brings the research cycle to a close and begins it anew. It is not sufficient to evaluate the effectiveness of a marketing program solely in terms of fare box counts, point-load counts, and so forth. While this information is important for assessing cost effectiveness, it is not adequate for determining what modifications are needed. For this, it is necessary to know whether and how much the marketing program has generated awareness, whether attitude changes have taken place on important attributes, and how different market segments responded. Such information serves as a valuable input to the development of further marketing programs.

Research objectives: What information is really needed?

A statement of research objectives should lead to a listing of specific information requirements. In other words, this stage involves going from the general to the particular. The person responsible for a marketing research project will often find that the manager has not thought through the specific information requirements. That manager will need to be "pushed" to make a careful statement about the information needed. Too often, at the end of a research project, managers complain that the research has not provided them with the information they really wanted. By that point, it is too late to redirect the focus of the study!

A useful first step is to state the information requirements in writing. These requirements can then be reviewed to see if they are specific enough to provide guidance to the research, set forth the issues to be investigated, and include all the relevant questions to be asked.

Some find it useful to determine information requirements by stating their beliefs about the market as a set of hypotheses. For example, a transit manager trying to determine a new fare structure may be interested in testing the hypothesis that reduced off-peak fares will increase ridership. The manager may also be interested in knowing at what level to price monthly transit passes. For the transit agency, data about price elasticity would be very important while information about service scheduling—while interesting—would not be necessary.

Another fruitful approach is to prepare samples of possible outcomes from the research project and see what other questions are raised. (The researcher may find it useful to simulate tables of results.)

Careful examination of sample output will also reveal whether the report contains data that are useful and can be eliminated from the study. It is often useful for a manager to determine beforehand what information would be needed if each of the alternatives being studied were adopted. The information may possibly be gathered initially at low cost, saving both time and money later.

Keeping costs down: Use of existing data

Before gathering new data to resolve a well-specified research problem, researchers should investigate the possibility of using data that already exists. Market researchers divide information into two classes, primary data and secondary data. Primary data constitute new information collected especially for the research project being undertaken; secondary data have been previously collected for other purposes.

People often underestimate the amount of secondary data available. A transit organization's own internal record keeping system, staff observations, and published analyses of travel behavior and decision making can provide a good deal of valuable marketing information not requiring field surveys. A good rule to follow is not to gather primary data until it becomes clear that no satisfactory secondary data are available.

Managers should look first to their existing information system, which summarizes basic ridership and fare data collected as part of ongoing operations. For those transit companies with complaint departments, keeping a log of the frequency of various types of complaints can serve as a form of problem or opportunity identification.

Secondary data collected by another organization, such as government statistics bureaus, can be valuable when used creatively. Denver has used data on the number of households in the standard census tracts to help identify saturated markets. By subtracting from this population data estimates of persons who wouldn't or couldn't use the bus, it was possible to establish when transit use along a route was already at a maximum. In San Francisco, it was found that 16 percent of the 232 Zip Codes in the service area accounted for 90 percent of BART's riders. The finding suggested that direct mail and newspaper inserts were the best way to reach most of the rapid transit system's market.[5]

Another source of data (and analysis) is to review prior urban travel consumer research. Literally hundreds of studies have been conducted in the past fifteen years on the general topic of urban travel behavior. Significant findings that are applicable to most urban areas include analysis of mode choice behavior, scheduling issues, consumer perceptions of wait time, and user frustration with transit information.[6] Using the results of prior research findings combined with local secondary data can often provide market research analysts with the basis for conducting a study without having to incur the expense of collecting primary data.

Value analysis: Is the research worth doing?

If primary data collection is required, we must compare the cost of the research to its value. While cost is easy to determine, value can be hard to calculate prior to conducting a survey. Thus, value can only be approximated.

Not all information is worth its cost, either because it is unlikely to have an impact on management decisions or because its anticipated cost exceeds its expected benefits. For example, one transit agency planned to undertake an expensive study of commuter traffic, but closer analysis of the situation revealed that the agency's major problems were lack of capacity and poor operating performance, not customer behavior. In other cases, an organization may not be able to afford a particular research project even if its cost is low relative to its value. Before devoting scarce resources to the design of an overly ambitious project, managers should develop a rough estimate of the size of the studies they can afford. In addition, the value and cost of alternative research designs should be estimated.

Before carrying out a research project, the manager should be satisfied that either 1) its cost is so low relative to the magnitude of the problem being studied that no formal analysis of the project's value is required, or 2) the expected value of the project exceeds its cost.

Few market research projects will produce findings conclusive enough to eliminate all doubt about the course of action to be taken. A good project is one that reduces uncertainty to a degree that allows a manager to make an informed decision—even if only to do more research.

At times, researchers are called on to gather market information on an issue that arouses strong opinions on opposite sides. Frequently, such views may be based on little or no acquaintance with reality ("I've made up my mind; don't bother me with facts"). In such situations the goal should not be to change anyone's opinion, but to make the participants in the debate take notice of the research. To achieve this goal, the research project must be truly relevant to the question that originally initiated it. Moreover, its reliability and accuracy must be such that the results cannot be dismissed out of hand. In hotly debated issues, this standard can be a very demanding one.

Research design

Research design, which provides the basic blueprint for carrying out the research project, involves both strategic and tactical decisions. The strategic decisions center on the choice of the research approach to be employed for obtaining the information. Tactical research design decisions include the specific data collection method, sampling procedures, and questionnaire format. Although the various decisions that make up the design stage are important in themselves, it is important to keep in mind that the process of design also involves ensuring that the parts fit together.

The need for quality research design is apparent from the results of a Transportation Research Board study of 41 transit marketing evaluations. The study concluded:

Most of the time, highly ineffective research designs are used. . . . Seldom do they constitute a legitimate test of the effectiveness of marketing activities. . . . Often transit managers are guilty of greatly over generalizing the results of research, when the design or methodology used does not even justify a test of the immediate or specific situation.[7]

The design of market research studies falls into three broad groupings:
1) exploratory; 2) descriptive; and 3) causal.

Exploratory studies: These studies are most often used in the problem-discovery and problem-identification phases of decision making.[8] Their purpose is to outline the dimension of a problem more clearly by helping researchers to become more familiar with it and to learn the vocabulary and perceptions of the users.

As one might imagine, exploratory studies are more informal and less rigidly controlled than standardized questionnaire interviews. Although only a small number of respondents are typically contacted, the interview is less structured and more intensive in order to discover opinions, issues, and problems, thereby providing greater understanding of the situation. With a focus-group interview, a small number of people (typically six to ten) are brought together to discuss a particular topic under the guidance of a skilled moderator. Group interaction is an important part of focus-group interviews. This can lead to more spontaneous and perhaps more honest comments.

Qualitative studies are compelling because they show real people talking in their own words. But caution is necessary. Analysis and interpretation of qualitative research is always difficult because of its reliance on subjective information. Further, it is unwise to generalize from the findings, since there is no assurance that one small group's opinions are representative of the entire marketplace (or even of a specific market segment). Focus group interviews can be invaluable, however, as a prelude to conducting a more scientific study. Managers and analysts must take care not just to search through the results to find data that support their prior beliefs when other interpretations are available—and perhaps more likely to be valid.

Descriptive studies: Unlike an exploratory study, a descriptive study must be based on a detailed research plan. Both the data-collection and the data-analysis strategies should be carefully thought out before the field research is begun.

Descriptive studies are used to portray accurately the attitudes, behavior, and other characteristics of persons, groups, or organizations and their frequency of occurrence. They are also used to determine the extent of association and to draw inferences about the relationships among variables. Although descriptive studies do not provide definitive proof of causal relationships, such proof is not always required to make inferences and to formulate predictions.

Causal Studies: Although descriptive research is often used to estimate relationships among variables and to make predictions, managers often want stronger evidence that a causal relationship exists in order to make inferences with confidence about the effect of one variable on another. How much will the new monthly transit pass increase patronage? How much did the fare increase reduce patronage? A snapshot survey cannot adequately address these questions, because all it can show is the existence of a relationship. But to say that a fare increase caused the number of riders to decline we must also be sure that the decline in ridership didn't start before the fare increase and that other reasons such as equipment shortages didn't also contribute to the decline.

Only a well conducted experiment can unambiguously address these issues. Although we can probably never prove that X causes Y, we can often build a very strong case. Causal studies often rely on experimental studies in a laboratory or in the field. An experimental approach often offers a chance to assess the impact of new programs at reasonable cost in money and time.

An example of an experimental approach is provided by a Southern California Rapid Transit District (SCRTD) study of use of free coupons to encourage ridership. SCRTD actually conducted three separate coupon promotions using direct mail, door hangers, and newspapers to determine which approach would be most cost effective for future marketing activities. (In the end, newspapers were found to be least effective.)[9]

Data collection

The two major methods of data collection are communications and observation. *Communications* requires the subject to participate in the research process whether this entails an interview or filling out a questionnaire. *Observation* involves only the recording of behavior. In some cases the subjects may not even by aware that they are being observed. One of the problems with surveys is that respondents may consciously or unconsciously alter their opinions or stated behavior because they are being asked questions. In many situations, it is preferable to simply observe their behavior unobtrusively.

In a study of fare collection devices, a transit authority might use a questionnaire approach to survey riders' views of new equipment. An observation approach would entail watching how people use the machines over time to determine how well people interacted with the equipment. The basic criteria in choosing between the two methods are 1) capability to provide the data, 2) time and cost, and 3) objectivity and accuracy. In the case of the fare collection equipment, a combination of both studies would probably provide the best documentation.

Survey administration

Telephone, personal interviews, and mail questionnaires designed for self-completion are the three major ways of collecting information. Cost is a key criterion in choosing among these methods. In general, mail is usually the cheapest of the three methods, followed by telephone and then personal interviews.

While mail questionnaires offer lower costs and more anonymity for respondents (when promised), there is the problem of low response rates. A 50 percent response to a new mail survey is often considered quite good, but it means that half the sample population failed to respond. If the views and behavior of nonrespondents are actually different from those of respondents, then the results obtained will be quite biased. Rarely can mail questionnaires be used to probe a subject in great depth. They are quite useful for a study of transportation behavior and mode choice split.

Although personal interviews are costly, they usually result in very high response rates. Conversations can go into a topic in greater depth. Interviews are required if many of the questions in a survey are conditional on a previous answer. Personal interviews would be necessary for obtaining feedback to a newly designed transit map or timetable.

Telephone interviews are less expensive and relatively quick to complete. They are often used in the last weeks of a political campaign. A major problem with telephones is bias. In many urban areas, bilingual interviewers will be necessary and there will be a tendency to underrepresent low income individuals. For a transit authority, telephone interviews would be helpful in determining response to new services or promotional campaigns.

A new technology for market research is the use of cable TV in cities with two-way systems. The Columbus Ohio Transit Authority (COTA) was the first transit system in the country to conduct a market research study, with instantaneous results for viewers, by using cable TV.[10]

An alternative approach was used by the Southern California Association of Governments following the 1984 Summer Olympics. The agency produced a series of television and radio programs with local stations that featured audience call-in at the end of each show. State of the art equipment was used to register high volume response as the audience would call different telephone numbers to register their responses.

The results of the call-in responses were compared to a random sample, which showed that the responses from call-ins were far more skewed—although the general direction was the same in four of the five questions.[11] While the potential exists for sampling error due to self-selection by respondents to media generated call-ins, the technique is a inexpensive method of gathering data and at the same time conducting a public relations exercise.

Analysis, interpretation, and presentation of the data

Data analysis often involves complex, sophisticated techniques. Many well conducted studies fail to make the most of the data that have been collected, often limiting analysis of the data to one variable at a time. When surveying the attitudes and travel behavior of a population, greater insights can usually be obtained by analyzing two or more variables simultaneously.

The reader should not reject data analysis just because it is complex; at times it can make a valuable contribution to understanding the phenomena underlying the data set. On the other hand, useful analysis techniques need not always be complicated. We will briefly discuss some basic concepts of data analysis, and refer the reader to the market-research texts we cited earlier for a more complete review.

In most cases, analysis of a single variable is concerned with measures of central tendency—the mean (or average value), median, and mode—and measures of variation in the range of observations. At times, only frequency of occurrence is tabulated (e.g., how many times a week respondents ride transit).

When two or more variables are examined simultaneously, the analyst usually tries to see if there is a degree of association between them. Often a simple cross-tabulation between two variables can provide useful insights into the data. For example, to what extent does transit usage vary by income or age or distance from a transit stop?

Although data analysis is one of the last steps in the market-research process, its impact appears much earlier. For example, the type of analysis to be done often influences the content and form of the questions. It is often a good idea to create dummy versions of the tables that are expected to appear in the final report and to make sure that the questions included (and their form) lend themselves to the sort of analysis required to complete those tables.

Interpretations of the data should be based on an analysis of what the survey actually discovered, not on what the manager and researcher hoped would be found. The limitations of the data must be recognized, too. Firm conclusions should not be drawn from results that are not statistically significant.

Effective communication of the findings to the users of the research is a vital component of the research process, embracing both the written report and the oral presentation (if any). Aaker and Day list five guidelines to making effective presentations:[12]

1. Communicate to a specific audience.
2. Structure the presentation.
3. Create audience interest.
4. Be specific and show data in visual form.
5. Address issues of validity and reliability.

The written report should include an executive summary that provides an overview of the key findings and conclusions and an introductory guide to the contents of each chapter or section. Graphs and charts are often an excellent way to communicate clearly a mass of data. Research design issues that could affect interpretation of the results, and thereby the conclusions drawn, should be clearly identified. The presentation should also provide some feel for the reliability of the results, particularly if the sample size was small.

MARKET RESEARCH IN A POLITICAL ENVIRONMENT

The failure to utilize market research is often based on a manager's intuitive feeling that he/she understands the market place, thus viewing marketing studies as a costly and time consuming effort that will only delay new projects. A study of eighteen major transit properties found that market research accounts for less than five percent of marketing budgets. Five of the eighteen properties spent nothing on market research over a three year period under study.[13]

The cost of failing to conduct market research was most dramatically experienced by a California system, the Santa Clara County Transit District, during conversion of a fixed-route bus system to Dial-a-Ride in late 1974. Decision makers felt that since it was difficult to encourage people to use transit, the district should design a premium quality, door-to-door service at a very low fare. To encourage ridership further, the district conducted a saturation media campaign prior to introducing service, to guarantee that the service was not underutilized. The end result was that "success" killed the service. So many people tried to use Dial-a-Ride that the communications system was unable to handle the excessive demand. The Dial-a-Ride service was eliminated within six months, after costly political and legal battles.

The lesson of the Santa Clara County case is that managers must rely on good planning supported by careful market research in making decisions. Decision makers in Santa Clara County tended to discount what research was available and relied on their own preconceptions. The Transit District had failed to survey its potential customers adequately to determine both their needs and the potential level of customer demand. By failing to conduct an experiment with a limited population group prior to introducing service to a population of over one million people, managers did not have the opportunity to evaluate results and make system modifications in an orderly manner. Failure became a highly visible event that quickly politicized the situation.

On a day-to-day basis, the findings of market research departments can also be particularly helpful to transit managers in discouraging transit boards, city councils, or other transit governing bodies from instituting or supporting politically motivated routes. Measurements, such as service standards, that permit clear comparisons of productivity among routes clearly indicate the cost of maintaining underproductive service; at least the tradeoffs are made distinct. In turn, these figures also provide ready answers that board members can use to fend off constituents who press for service to areas in which it is not economically justified.[14]

CONCLUSION

Market research is not a simple matter of asking questions. It is a process that provides a disciplined approach to data collection—a process designed to help a manager make decisions. Many market research projects are carried out in transit organizations, but because of weaknesses in planning, execution, analysis, and presentation, their findings often fail to influence policy. By following the market research process outlined in this chapter (or a carefully constructed variation of it), both managers and researchers are more likely to obtain findings that will be useful for decision making.

NOTES

1. Lovelock, Christopher H., and Charles B. Weinberg. *Marketing for Public and Nonprofit Managers* (New York: John Wiley & Sons, 1984), p. 129.

2. Transportation Research Board. *Urban Transportation Economics*, Special Report 181, (Washington, D.C.: National Academy of Sciences, 1978), p. 177.

3. *The Transit Marketing Project: Summary of Consumer Research, Baltimore MTA and Nashville MTA* (Urban Mass Transportation Administration, June 1976).

4. *The CRA Review* (Boston, MA: Charles River Associates, September 1985), p. 3.

5. Dunbar, Frederick, C., and Christopher H. Lovelock. "The state of the art in urban travel consumer research," in *Marketing Public Transportation: Policies, Strategies and Research Needs for the 1980's*, Proceedings Series, edited by R.K. Robinson and C. H. Lovelock (Chicago: American Marketing Association, 1981), p. 87.

6. Transportation Research Board. *Urban Transportation Economics*, op. cit., p. 180.

7. Transportation Research Board. *A Review of Transit Marketing Evaluation Practice*, Final Report, prepared for Urban Mass Transportation Administration (Washington, D.C.: May 1982), p. 17.

8. A more detailed discussion of the methods of exploratory research may be found in David A. Aaker and George S. Day, *Marketing Research*, 3rd ed. (New York: John Wiley & Sons, 1986). This section is partially based on that discussion.

9. Matosian, Jackline. "Effectiveness of different coupon delivery methods in building mass transit ridership," *Journal of Advertising Research*, 22, No. 3 (June/July, 1982): 54–56.

10. "Columbus conducts market research on TV," *Passenger Transport* (January 11, 1980): 1.

11. Rafiq, Timor, and Brad Williams. "Transportation: Tell us where to go: A

report on Televote '85," unpublished paper presented at Transportation Research Board Annual Meeting (January 1986).

12. Aaker and Day. *Marketing Research*, op. cit.

13. Booth, Rosemary. "Bus marketing costs: The experience of 18 section 15 reporters from 1981 to 1983," unpublished paper presented at Transportation Research Board Annual Meeting (January 1986).

14. Transportation Research Board. *Urban Transportation Economics*, op. cit. p. 179.

Part III
Planning: The Key to Successful Marketing

5

Strategic Planning

Introduction

Organizational planning in the private sector was significantly influenced in 1970 when the General Electric Company adopted a strategic business planning process. The concept created a link "between corporate and marketing strategy and the types of decisions that are involved in marketing strategy design."[1] The strategic planning approach incorporates many of the elements of market planning but addresses a broad range of organizational issues.

Governmental organizations, including some public transportation agencies,[2] have begun to develop strategic planning processes of their own. Given that transit managers typically find their days filled with short-run operating decisions, it is sometimes hard to see where the time can be found to disengage from immediate activities at hand and participate in a strategic review of the agency. Yet strategic planning has been described as "not an added management duty but a way of thinking about a business and how to run it."[3] For the transit managers, long-run growth and success depend on developing and implementing clear strategies to cope with the changing environment faced by their agencies.

Of importance to marketing professionals, strategic planning involves a review of the external environment in which the transit organization operates. The external environment consists of factors such as the agency's position in the market place; the importance of the competition; consumer and demographic trends; as well as political constraints and potential opportunities for the agency. Thus marketing managers have an important role to play in a strategic planning process.

Many transit agencies, both in the United State and abroad, have broadened their product line to include several different but interrelated types of service, such as:

- Transit services for the general public that receive government subsidies to cover shortfall between farebox revenues and operating expenses;
- Contract services to special needs groups (e.g., elderly or handicapped persons) where operating expenses are totally subsidized since no fees are charged;
- Vehicle leasing services, whereby vans or buses are leased to vanpool, buspool, and other groups for extended periods (typically one year);
- Brokerage service to plan, develop, and promote carpooling and private van/buspooling;
- Contract maintenance service.

Corporate planning activities by the transit agency should explicitly recognize the impact of supply and demand factors as they affect each of these service options.[4]

Types of plans

Normally, the marketing plan does not stand alone. The marketing issues and strategies that shape the marketing plan are an essential element of the long-range or strategic plan for the organization.[5] The strategic plan deals with all aspects of the environment—including political, financial, and personnel—and specifies the general direction for all functional departments in terms of objectives, goals, and investment priorities. A major distinguishing feature is the planning horizon: the *strategic plan* has a longer-range scope, from two to five years, while the *marketing program plan* will deal with the next one to two years and provide detailed action and budget steps for the coming year.

The marketing plan is also an element of the *annual transit operation plan*. The operating plan is the vehicle by which the individual program plans are integrated to ensure consistency. This is an important step in avoiding the not uncommon situation where operations are changed without adequate consultation or marketing input. A typical problem is the elimination of a bus route with no research into likely responses, leaving the marketing department to respond to the newspaper editorials, action lines, and complaint calls.

Finally, it has been argued that both the marketing plan and the strategic plan should take account of *community planning* by metropolitan planning organizations. Marketing plans can give definition to community plans by defining consumer transportation needs and options for meeting these needs. In addition, a marketing plan can help coordinate actions with a planning agency on staggered work hour promotions and other air quality programs.

The end result is that transit management planning can take and does take many forms. Figure 5–1 illustrates how a typical transit system could

Figure 5–1
Relationship of Transit Plans

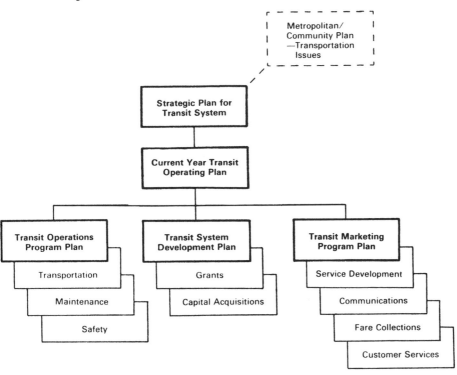

integrate its various planning activities.[6] Also shown in the exhibit are some of the supporting subprogram plans dealing with various aspects of the marketing mix.

WORKING IN THE PUBLIC SECTOR

The first task of a strategic planning process is to articulate the organization's mission and goals. In the private sector, management may be able to choose which markets it wishes to serve as well as define the actual products or services. For example, People Express, the no-frills airline (since merged into Continental Airlines) was able to develop a targeted definition of its users (discount travelers) just as the Hertz car rental company has chosen to focus on the business traveler. Both companies have also been able to mold their actual services to the target market. People Express charged extra for checked baggage and for food and beverage service; it ran an inexpensive operation suitable to a discount-seeking market, while Hertz offers a variety of premium services and vehicles to the business traveler.

Constraints on public sector managers

In contrast to their private-sector counterparts, public transportation managers have found that many of the fundamental market decisions have been made for them by the federal government, state legislatures, or local governments. For example, the federal government has told transit agencies that they must serve the handicapped-persons market and the elderly market. Since transit agencies are funded by governmental sources, managers must respond to those who provide financial support to the organization.

Some managers resent (and at times with good reason) the fact that their organizations must operate in a political environment. Yet public involvement is the cornerstone of democracy and with public funding comes involvement. From an historic viewpoint, urban public transportation was at the end of its product lifecycle when public funding converted regulated transportation monopolies into governmental operating agencies. Transit organizations are faced with a different external environment than was faced in the past—particularly since the influx of federal funds in the 1970s.

Constituencies for public transit

A strategic planning process can help transit managers work in a political environment. The political process is a two way street: agencies can respond to pressure but can also create—and do create—pressures of their own. The political constituencies who support public transportation need to be viewed as markets for the transit agency, even if these constituencies are not, in fact, direct users of a public transit agency's services.

Top level transit managers spend a good deal of time concerned with obtaining public finance to support their operations. They often face critics of public transit subsidies who believe that it is inequitable for nonusers to subsidize the trips of transit users. Yet it can be argued that the automobile driver benefits from the transit users' staying on transit, thereby not contributing to additional traffic congestion and competition for parking spaces. In essence, transit subsidies are a way for dedicated automobile users to pay transit users to keep their cars off the road. (It can also be argued that automobile users are subsidized by the provision of public-built and -maintained roads; while the federal highway system is supported by user fees, local road programs are often financed by general taxation and bonding.)

Downtown business executives and retailers are an example of a group who, in themselves, may not use transit, but their organizations benefit from public transit service to their locations. In a number of urban areas, business organizations have played a valuable role in assisting transit authorities, whether in the political/funding arena or encouraging businesses to promote transit use by employees. By conducting a benefit segmentation analysis, a strategic planning process will identify groups who do not use transit but may actually be constituencies of a transit agency.

A transit organization may have more latitude than is realized in developing its own mission statement and goals, and to some extent, defining markets and services. In Baltimore, the Metropolitan Transportation Agency (MTA) is funded by the state legislature, even though almost all service is provided in Baltimore and the immediate surrounding communities. Each year the MTA faced the same problem of many large urban systems: having to seek support from legislators whose constituents do not receive service. In the early 1980s, a new general manager articulated a mission for the MTA: to provide mobility for people (versus simply running buses). To build political support in areas where it was not financially feasible to run buses, the MTA decided to increase its support of ridesharing activities (carpool and vanpool formation) in suburban industrial parks and to provide assistance to small transit agencies in other areas of the state.[7]

Transit marketing managers typically face a more difficult task than their counterparts in profit-seeking firms, since they have to balance the time and effort required to attract public finance to the agency against demands of marketing directly to riders. There also must be a reasonable degree of compatibility between these two activities; otherwise one can easily lose credibility with either financial supporters or consumers. For example, a dramatic reduction in fares may attract some new riders, but alienate politicians who must raise taxes to pay the deficit. Conversely, a dramatic fare increase could reduce the need for public tax support, but could result in significant loss of ridership. A strategic planning process can help guide managers in developing policies and programs that are compatible with meeting the interests of these overlapping, but different, constituencies.

The reductions in the level of federal support for public transportation occurring in the 1980s have increased the need for a strategic planning process by transit organizations. Managers and local boards need to develop strategies for balancing transit budgets by increasing revenues from ridership, controlling operating costs, raising local tax contributions, or a combination of the above. Strategic planning provides a framework for making these difficult decisions.

The Utah Transit Authority, for example, initiated a strategic planning process with the objective of reducing "middle management's sense of risk in proposing new actions and making decisions with significant and positive long range effects, but less exciting results in the short term."[8] The planning process enabled the transit authority to decide on where to expand service and agree on disputed elderly/handicapped guidelines. With a broader statement of organizational mission (see Exhibit 5–1),

Exhibit 5–1
The UTA Mission Statement

The Old Plan

The mission of UTA is to provide safe, clean, efficient public transit service in the most cost-effective manner possible.

The New Plan

The mission of the UTA Transit Authority is to provide mobility as a public service to an increasingly diverse, dynamic and growing community, while maintaining responsible fiscal management of its resources. UTA recognizes that our people are the primary producers and deliverers of our product, that our efforts to plan, strategize and implement successful transit service is dependent on the initiative and creativity of each individual in the performance of his or her job, and that our service improves as our individual efforts improve. Therefore, it is the policy of the UTA to:

–Provide a range of innovative yet fiscally prudent transportation services.
–Work closely with the community, business, and public agencies for short-range and long-range needs and solutions.
–Pursue all revenue generating opportunities.
–Provide clear, safe, courteous and reliable service.
–Continue to serve the transportation disadvantaged and transit dependent.
–Be prepared to assist communities outside UTA district where sufficient demand, local support and funding are available.
–Provide a productive working environment.
–Provide training and education which mutually supports the goals of the UTA and its employees.

Utah Transit sought an agreement with ski resorts, which resulted in owner-subsidized service to ski areas.

Competition

An important task of a strategic planning process is to analyze the transit agency's current position in the marketplace; to understand the competition; and to track the agency's market share for various trips. Public transit agencies generally operate as a monopoly since they do not face competition from other transit organizations. However, transit faces intense generic competition from the automobile.

CHANGES IN URBAN DEVELOPMENT PATTERNS

Since the 1950s transit authorities have faced an uphill battle due to changes in urban development and demographics adversely affecting ridership. Until the post-World War II era, the growth patterns of American cities was heavily determined by the availability of public transportation, thus providing transit systems with a ready market. Transit managers have been well aware of the impact of the urban highway system in capturing significant transit ridership. Urban transit systems have attempted, with varying success, to maintain ridership for the central city work trips. Even where ridership stabilized (or grew slightly), transit systems were actually losing the battle for "market share" of trips to the central business district due to population and travel growth.

Even more alarming for transit authorities has been the dispersion of work sites outside the central city to low density suburban locations. The net result is a dramatic increase in suburb-to-suburb work trips—a travel pattern that public transit has been least able to serve effectively. Even in a city such as Boston, with a strong and growing central business district, the statistics are sobering. Between 1970 and 1980, suburb-to-central city commuting increased 12.5 percent. Public transit trips of these commuters increased 9.6 percent. While this is a positive trend, this figure still represented a loss of market share.

The major commuting change in Boston during the decade was a 24 percent growth of suburban residence–suburban worksite trips. For these trips, public transit use actually declined by 21 percent—resulting in transit's losing about half of its market share for these trips. While the suburban workforce is twice the size of the urban workforce, transit accounts for only 4.7 percent of trips.[9] A related problem is the lack of transportation for "reverse commuting" by inner city minority workers, necessary for securing employment in high-technology suburban industries.[10]

Over the past 15 years, car density in urban areas has increased while population density has decreased. These trends have occurred over a time period during which the United States experienced two dramatic energy crises.

Most urban areas in the United States are becoming less densely populated as people move from urban cores to the suburbs and country-side. Between 1970 and 1980, the number of persons per square mile fell in 88 percent of urbanized areas.

In most urban areas, however, car density is increasing. Between 1970 and 1980 the number of automobiles per square mile increased in 64 percent of urbanized areas, and if pickups are included, the share of areas with increasing car densities would be even higher. The growth of urban vehicles outpaced population and household growth in the 1970's.

Although the census may tell us that there are fewer people per square mile in urban areas, the statistics on cars confirm what we already know—urban areas are becoming more crowded. Someday, we may be able to quantify urban congestion by studying another density measure—cars per parking space.[11]

Demographic analysis is an important part of a strategic planning process. At the local level, it allows planners and managers to understand the forces at work that are shaping demand for the agency's services. While the national data may look discouraging, the authors of the census analysis cited above do mention a problem facing automobile users that could be used to the benefit of transit: a shortage of parking. A dictum of strategic planning may be that underneath most problems, there can be found an organizational opportunity.

OPPORTUNITY ANALYSIS: THE CHANGING ROLE OF TRANSIT

An important function of a strategic planning process is to look for opportunities that the organization can use to its benefit.

Raising parking costs

One opportunity that transit authorities can evaluate is the increasing cost of urban parking. If central city areas are going to experience a further shortage of parking, then the price for that parking will continue to increase. Parking price increases are an incentive to use public transportation—which provides the transit authority with a marketing opportunity.

In Boston, for example, daily parking rates doubled between 1980 and 1984.[12] Contributing to the parking shortage was an Environmental Protection Agency-mandated freeze on new parking construction, specifically to encourage the use of public transit as a means of improving air quality. In a strategic planning process, an agency can evaluate the impacts of external opportunities such as parking shortages and consider whether it wishes to become involved in activities such as encouraging parking management programs.

Increasing costs of car ownership

Another significant opportunity for transit authorities comes as a result of the rising costs of car ownership (which can run $2,000 to $3,000 per year, depending upon the type of car and distances traveled). For instance, the Baltimore Regional Planning Authority and the Los Angeles Regional Transit Authority have developed continuing marketing programs based on the high cost of owning and operating an automobile. This approach takes advantage of the fact that car ownership costs have exceeded the inflation rate. Auto owners are experiencing "sticker shock" when it comes time to purchase a new car. With the average age of a car having increased to eight years, about 12 percent of the population is in the new car market in a given year. This is an opportunity for transit agencies to market transit use as an alternative to purchasing a new car. For example, some two-car households may be able to get by without buying a new car if one household member is able to take transit to work. (This strategy also applies to those in the used car market.)

Transit and real estate development

Given the high cost of commuting, a number of real estate developers in urban areas across the United States have planned their projects so that they are accessible to public transportation and will often promote transit access as a benefit of moving to their property. The value of locating near transit is quite apparent from a study in Evanston (Illinois), a suburb of Chicago. This study found that proximity to public transportation was the most important reason for condominium purchasers buying a particular unit.[13] Transit marketers have a clear opportunity to work with their local real estate community to market use of public transportation.

Highway reconstruction

Another example of an external opportunity that transit authorities can evaluate is urban expressway reconstruction projects. Due to the deteriorating nature of the interstate system, Congress allocated additional gasoline tax money in 1983 to major repair projects, accompanied by some funds for public transit. Major repair projects on the urban sections of the highway system entail significant traffic disruption due to a reduction of road capacity. A shift of travel from automobile to transit is important in order to keep the remaining traffic moving during road work. In Boston, Pittsburgh, and Chicago, public transit agencies have had active marketing programs and/or service expansion to accommodate the public during highway reconstruction projects.

Strategic windows

In examining opportunities, the question of timing is central. Opportunities, even when long-term strategy is involved, are often available for only a short period of time. Some writers use the phrase *strategic window* to denote the time period during which an opportunity is available. The 1980/81 decisions concerning the building of a new rapid transit system in Vancouver, Canada, illustrate the concept well. With a World Fair scheduled for Vancouver in 1986, it was suggested that an important part of the fair could be a new rail transit system. This proposal seemed appropriate, since a Canadian company had developed new technology for a rapid transit system. If Vancouver could plan and build the new system in time to have it running as a demonstration project during Expo

'86, the Canadian federal government would finance a significant portion of the cost. This strategic window only opened after the new technology was developed and would close when it was no longer possible to complete the installation in time for the opening of the fair.

DEVELOPING A POSITIONING STRATEGY

A positioning analysis helps managers to understand how their organization and its products are serving market needs. In particular, positioning analysis allows managers to see how their organization is perceived relative to the competition and to determine how well it is meeting the demands of the market. At times, a transit organization may be providing a good level of service, but the competing road and parking system may also be operating extremely well due to lack of congestion. In other cases, users may not be aware that the agency provides service in a given market—a problem faced by some transit organizations. Management often has a biased view of the relative market positions held by the organization and its competition. Market research is required to determine whether management's perceptions are similar to those of current and prospective users.

Dimensions of transit performance

Another difficulty in understanding an organization's position is management's translation of performance characteristics into specific dimensions such as speed, safety, comfort, and reliability. For example, one transit agency improved its on-time record for commuter services from 70 to 90 percent of runs within 10 minutes of schedule and then tried to position itself as being high on the reliability dimension compared with cars. But commuters did not view "ten minutes late" as being "on time," particularly when the delays most frequently happened during the morning commute. Consequently, the transit service was not perceived as being reliable. Consumer analysis helps an organization to ascertain what its position really is, not what managers hope it is.

Target market segments

Positioning usually involves the choice of particular market segments, which implies that certain market segments will receive lesser emphasis or be ignored. At times transit agencies have found themselves relegated to a position of serving limited downtown commuting needs and providing service to those unable to afford an automobile.

While it can be legitimate to serve only some parts of a market while receiving financial support from the general public, regional transit agencies that rely on area-wide sales taxes may find themselves in a dilemma as a result. If the agency positions itself to meet the needs of suburban commuters, central city residents and their political leaders may complain about the sales tax. The reverse is likely to happen when the transit agency positions itself for the central city market. Unfortunately, it appears that the needs of the two segments are so different—in terms of pricing, type of buses used, and routings as well as overall image—that the choice of a position to occupy is a difficult task.

In Illinois, the formation of a Regional Transit Agency in the late 1970s resulted in a significant increase in service for many residents of the Chicago Metropolitan Area. Unfortunately, funding with a regional sales tax became politically untenable and the state legislature began funding allocations on an annual basis. After numerous funding crises with political fights between suburban and urban interests, the legislature restructured the RTA and mandated a fare recovery ratio and controls on union wages. Within the RTA itself, "political control has passed from the Chicago Democratic political machine, which generally favored a policy of high subsidies and low fares for social welfare reasons, to the more conservative Republican suburbs."[14]

Strategic planning can help an organization develop a rational approach to the varying demands placed on it by different constituencies. The Baltimore MTA's development of ridesharing services and provision of assistance to small transit authorities illustrates a strategy of developing different services for different markets as a method of broadening political support for the agency. In essence, Baltimore MTA is trying to reposition itself in the Maryland transportation marketplace. Repositioning strategies can involve communication programs, but can also include redefining the services an organization provides and even redefining the very structure of the organization.

Internal markets

An important role of strategic planning is to diagnose and analyze internal issues facing the organization. Public transit agencies are labor intensive organizations. In the United States, approximately 80 percent of transit operating costs are devoted to labor.

Employees as salespeople. The transit organization is almost always represented to the consumer by the frontline employee—such as the bus driver—and almost never by management. How that employee acts in public will strongly determine public perceptions of the organization. In essence, the attitude of the employee will give the customer a clue (warranted or not) as to the attitude of management. While frontline employees are not hired to be marketers, that is an important function of an employee who deals continually with the public.

Employees and customers. For the transit organization, a strategy of viewing the employee as an internal customer is an approach to improving the attitudes and behavior of employees, with a view to en-hancing service quality. Transit agencies may be able to adopt a com-munications strategy used by a number of airlines, which feature actual employees in paid advertising. The goal of this approach is not only to communicate a positive image of company personnel to potential cus-tomers but to reinforce that image with the employees themselves.

Seattle Metro recently initiated an annual "Driver Appreciation Day" to honor bus drivers publicly for their record of service and safety. Activities were held at Metro's five operating bases and received ex-tensive, favorable commentary in the media. Public surveys by Seattle Metro repeatedly show that the driver is the most appreciated aspect of Metro transit service.[15]

Quality circles. Some manufacturing companies in the United States have begun to adopt the Japanese "quality work circle" programs to their organizations as a means of improving productivity. Recently the San Francisco transit system, known as "Muni," has begun utilizing a quality circle program in several of its car barns. Quality circle programs can be helpful for both employees who interact with the public (e.g., drivers) as well as maintenance employees whose behind-the-scenes work is critical to a transit system's achieving vehicle reliability (an important consumer value).

DEFINING THE PRODUCT LINE

One of the ultimate goals of a strategic planning process is to review the organization's product line and to analyze its overall portfolio of services. Managers can evaluate which services need modification—or should be eliminated altogether. Equally important is an assessment of new products and services designed to meet the needs of identified market segments.

In the case of a transit service organization, product distinctions may be based as much on how customers use the product offering as on how it was created. For instance, urban public transportation agencies are in the business of moving people in transit vehicles. An operational defini-tion of the service might divide it into three products, categorized by type of vehicle—rail, bus, or ferry. This would not be a very useful way of defining the product line if research showed that many travelers used at least two modes—say, bus and train or bus and ferry—to complete a single journey.

Targeting services to customer needs

Of more interest to the transit marketer is who is actually using the service, when, where, and for what purpose. Looking at the business in terms of customer-use behavior may suggest opportunities for marketing the service to different segments in different ways. For instance, a delineation of different transportation offerings could be created by operational distinctions that are meaningful to travelers, such as express versus regular service. Further distinctions could be based on routes that serve key destinations: airport services, shoppers' shuttle, sight-seeing special. Still another point of differentiation might reflect timing and frequency of use, such as weekday commuting versus occasional midday, evening, or weekend travel. Finally, distinction could be made between different types of travelers, say, children, students, adults, and the elderly.

At what point do these distinctions lead to creation of a separate product? Splitting a broadly defined product into several more tightly defined products requires a degree of differentiation in the marketing programs. If a transit agency singles out express service for special marketing treatment, charging premium prices and promoting it separately from "regular" service, we can reasonably say that express service is now a separate product. The same would hold true for the airport service, shoppers' shuttle, and sight-seeing special, if tailored marketing programs were developed specially to boost ridership on any one of these.

In strategic planning, this product-line analysis relates directly to analysis of the organization's external environment. For example, an external analysis of travel patterns may reveal a significant increase in air travel—which results in a comparable increase in ground transportation needs to and from the local airport. A transit agency can analyze this growing need against its current line of airport service. A strategic planning process may identify organizational opportunities to develop new airport services designed to meet the needs of particular market segments.

With the dramatic changes in urban travel patterns, some prominent transit officials have raised questions about the product line traditionally offered by public transportation agencies. Milton Pikarsky, former chairman of the Chicago Regional Transportation Authority, considers public transit systems relying solely on fixed route bus and rail service as having effectively priced themselves out of many urban markets. Pikarsky sees a need for a less centralized network, utilizing vans, carpools, subscription buses, and taxis.[16]

Transit agencies as "brokers"

James Graebner, former director of the Santa Clara County (California) Transportation Agency, believes that "transportation systems should become transportation brokers. They should provide bus and rail service when it is appropriate and assist companies and agencies that are qualified to offer services such as ridesharing and vanpools." Graebner, who has served as president of the American Public Transit Association (an industry lobbying group), stated, "I think the industry, perhaps, needs to understand its role of evolving into a supermarket for transportation services."[17]

C. Kenneth Orski, a former policy administrator at the Urban Mass Transportation Administration, suggests that "we discard the obsolete idea that transit must remain the exclusive domain of public authorities." He cites the need for employer-provided transportation, shared-taxi services, express charter bus services, community "mini-bus" systems, and even neighborhood-based private automobile lease and rental agencies.[18]

There are examples of transit authorities broadening their product line. The Southeastern Michigan Transit Authority, which serves Metropolitan Detroit, has been actively involved in promoting vanpooling. The Golden Gate Transit District in Northern California actually operates subscription commuter club-style express buses to accommodate demand for premium quality services. The Tidewater Transit (Virginia) replaced poorly subscribed regular bus service in some suburbs with privately-run taxicabs and vans. Though still subsidized, the private operators—called "Maxi-Ride"—cost less and offer consumers more convenience.[19]

These new services are all responses to changing economics, demographics, and travel patterns. Strategic planning provides transit managers with a process to evaluate the transit organization's changing environment, to identify new markets, and to reevaluate services to better meet the needs of the public.

CONCLUSION

Strategic planning can provide a managerial framework for marketing transit in a changing environment. "It creates an actionable, strategic agenda rather than an 'ideal' agenda, which is more characteristic of fixed, long-range master plans. It helps an agency to initiate, not just to react."[20]

NOTES

1. Cravens, David W., Gerald E. Hills, and Robert B. Woodruff. *Marketing Decision Making: Concepts and Strategy* (Homewood, Ill: Richard D. Irwin, Inc., 1976), p. 321.

2. See Michael D. Meyer, "Strategic planning in response to environmental change," in *Transportation Quarterly*, 37, No. 2 (April 1983): 297–310, for a review of four transportation agency case studies of strategic planning.

3. Gray, Daniel H. "Uses and misuses of strategic planning," *Harvard Business Review* (January/February 1986): 89–97.

4. See Bruce Rubin and Wayne K. Talley, "A corporate planning model for a multiservice public transit firm," *Transportation Quarterly* (July 1985): 375–90.

5. Steiner, George A. *Strategic Planning: What Every Manager Must Know.* (New York: The Free Press, 1979).

6. Developed from *Transit Marketing Management Handbook,* Urban Mass Transportation Administration (1976), p. 2.

7. Wagner, David. Public address at American Public Transit Association, Annual Meeting, Boston (1982).

8. Hansen, Scott (UTA Board Member), in "Strategic planning at work: Look what happened at Utah Transit Authority," *Metro* (September/October 1985): 58.

9. Metropolitan Area Planning Council. *State of the Region* (Boston, 1985); as reported in *The Advisor* (newsletter of the MBTA Advisory Board), 3, no. 1 (February 1985): 4.

10. Gaffney, Dennis. "Affirmative action: Thomas Saltonstall moves against job discrimination in Boston," *The Tab* (March 28, 1984): 3.

11. Long, Larry, and Diana DeAre. "Where the cars are," *American Demographics* (December 1984).

12. Boston Air Pollution Control Board data, cited in the *Boston Globe,* March 1, 1985, p. 1.

13. *Condominium Conversions in the City of Evanston* (Evanston, Ill: Human Relations Commission, October 1978), p. 41.

14. Young, David. "Chicago: How one city coped with transit's rude reawakening," *Mass Transit* (September 1985): 16–17.

15. "Driver appreciation day salutes metro operators," *Passenger Transport* (January 27, 1986): 6.

16. Young, David. "Transit in transition: Major changes ahead?" *Mass Transit* (March 1983): 8.

17. Demoro, Harre W. "Graebner: Transit still on way up," *Mass Transit* (June 1983): 13.

18. Orski, C. Kenneth. "Rethinking transit," in *New York Times,* February 14, 1981.

19. "Resurgence of private participation in urban mass transit stirs debate," in *Wall Street Journal,* November 27, 1984, p. 31.

20. Stein-Hudson, Kathleen E., and Bruce D. McDowell. "Applying strategic planning in the transportation sector," *Transportation Research News* (July/August 1985): 22.

6

Planning the Marketing Program

INTRODUCTION

Some transit organizations do not have formal marketing plans. Managers often argue that they are too busy coping with day-to-day survival to have the time and resources required to formulate a plan. Other reasons given for not having a plan include claims that the market changes too quickly for a plan to have relevance or that the plan is only a written document that does not translate easily into action.

These objections merit some discussion. Developing a plan is a way to help an organization choose wisely among alternatives. Some people believe that they have an internalized plan "in their heads," but, in most cases, they are probably just deluding themselves. Of course, it is necessary to avoid plans that are mere paperwork. Plans must be based on a sound analysis of the external and internal environments that the transit organization confronts.

To be more than just words on paper, a management-approved plan must serve as the basis of resource allocation and performance evaluation. When managers see that resources follow plans and that results are monitored against planned targets, then plans are carefully constructed and become relevant.

What about the argument that plans become outdated too quickly? Plans actually help an organization to anticipate change and to generate questions requiring research. While there is always the possibility that an entirely unanticipated event may happen, in most cases careful analysis can identify trends and precursors. In other instances, the planning process can identify the major uncertainties so that contingency plans—for energy crises, transit strikes, funding shortfalls, weather emergencies, and so forth—can be constructed for alternative outcomes.

THE RATIONALE FOR PLANNING

A planned, systematic approach to the development of transit marketing programs is essential to the transit marketing manager for the following reasons:

- Scarce resources (time, money, and people) must be allocated to ensure maximum impact toward the achievement of the goals and objectives of the transit system.
- The plan provides a sensible basis for evaluating and improving the performance of the marketing unit.
- The individual elements that make up the overall marketing strategy need to be coordinated so that they don't work at cross purposes.
- The decisions and activities of the marketing unit must be integrated with other planning and operating decisions.

A well prepared marketing plan is even more important when the operations or overall system planning is inadequate, or the role of the marketing function is unclear. Such a plan is an excellent means by which the analyses, assumptions, strategy alternatives, and resource needs can be communicated to top management and line departments in the organization. Also, an approved plan provides the marketing unit with the formal authority needed to proceed with their programs and facilitates access to resources and coordination with other components of the organization.

BENEFITS OF PLANNING

Well-designed formal plans that guide management actions and resource allocations offer a number of benefits for the transit organization. Among these are the following:

1. *Coordination of the activities of many individuals whose actions are related over time.* Some decisions must be made before others or simultaneously with others. A marketing plan can be the means to coordinate decision making and subsequent activities.
2. *Setting a timetable.* A marketing plan anticipates the timing of needed activities and thus sets a timetable. It provides the basis for establishing a "critical path" time-line for the manager. Without a marketing plan, many necessary steps can become rushed and others—such as market research—neglected altogether.
3. *Better communication.* Because of the inevitable compartmentalization of management, it is essential that there be some integrating form of communication so that each manager will know, at least generally, what other managers are trying to achieve and how likely they are to accomplish their tasks. Communication is among the primary functions of a marketing plan and particularly

important in a transit organization where many operations managers will have a preconceived notion that marketing efforts are peripheral to the agency's primary activity—running vehicles.

4. *Identification of expected developments.* Many transit administrators could easily perceive the nature of future developments if they were to make a disciplined effort to look ahead. By forcing themselves to plan, managers often can place future events fairly accurately in time and can better understand their sequence and interrelationship.

5. *Preparation to meet changes when they occur.* Through planning, managers are forced to think through the actions they would take if certain events were to occur. Furthermore, the planning system can help to reduce irrational responses to unexpected events by outlining guidelines for thoughtful action in place of hasty and emotional reactions to surprises. In short, planning can help transit managers move from a crisis-management style to a more rational style.

6. *Focusing of efforts.* Managers generally have more problems and opportunities than they have resources available to devote to them. Successful planning systems provide a means for the organization to choose the problems and opportunities to which it may most effectively devote its limited resources. In addition, a well-designed planning process should result in a systematic procedure for generating and evaluating alternatives. Too often, administrators only consider one course of action. For every action undertaken, there is an "opportunity cost" of being unable to devote resources to another activity. A marketing plan helps the transit manager develop a clear set of priorities that can guide future decision making.

7. *Basis of a control system.* A marketing plan is not only a guide to action but also can be the basis of a control system. The marketing plan can be used to monitor deviations from assumptions that underlie the plan as well as results that do not meet targeted goals.

8. *Maintenance of organizational integrity.* By clearly specifying the strategies the organization will pursue and basing those choices in a thorough understanding of the organization's goals, marketing plans help prevent a series of ad hoc decisions that carry the organization farther and farther from its true concerns. This is particularly important for public transportation organizations that are continually beset by political pressures and demands. A planning process can accommodate the needs of the political environment without managers having to respond to day-to-day demands.

THE MARKETING PLAN AND PROCESS

It is almost an axiom that the primary benefits of planning come from involvement in the process, and not from the completed document. Planning is more a way of thinking than a set of forms or procedures. Thus, an important corollary is that planners do not plan, they help managers to plan. It has been observed that a persistent problem of public sector planning is that too much planning is done by planners without the acceptance of line management responsibility.[1] Without management commitment to the choices implied by the plan, there is not likely to be serious dedication to implementing the strategies. The steps of the planning process are summarized in Exhibit 6–1 and described in some detail below. However, there is no requirement that a written transit marketing plan follow a specific format. For illustrative purposes, we have included two recent transit marketing plans. The first, prepared for a suburban California transit system, Santa Monica Municipal Bus Lines (Appendix A), focuses on planning a communications program to reach specific market segments. In Appendix B we have reproduced the 1986 Marketing and Community Relations Plan of the Toronto Transit Commission, which operates bus and subway service in Canada's largest metropolitan area. This latter plan includes not only objectives and strategies for 1986 but also a review of 1985's objectives and activities, and (where documentable) the actual results achieved.

Situation analysis

The first step in the planning process is a thorough analysis of the internal and external environments of the transit market in order to lead to the specification of a set of problems (threats) and opportunities. The identification of threats and opportunities is the key output of the situational analysis. An external factor may be an increase in automobile prices (an opportunity) or a decrease in federal funding assistance (an external threat to the organization). Employees and their unions are a part of the internal environment of the organization and have a significant impact on marketing programs. For example, the transit consumer's satisfaction with a bus ride can be dependent on the courtesy and knowledge of the driver who is answering questions and collecting fares.

An analysis of the current situation begins with a compilation of all available facts about the system—services, revenues, programs, markets, and users. In many instances it is appropriate to combine the collection of marketing-related data in a broader *management audit*, consisting of three interrelated reviews of marketing, operations, and the external environment, each of which in turn may comprise separate sub-audits.[2]

The marketing-relevant information derived from this audit should be summarized in a Marketing Fact Book, which can be up-dated as new data are received. The analysis requires an understanding of the reasons for historical performance (for example, was the increased ridership in one period versus another due to a special information program or an equipment change) and the marketing problems and opportunities in light of current ridership and previous performance versus objectives.

A marketing problem is anything that inhibits the transit system from operating effectively. Such problems may be internal in nature (attributable to a fare increase, for example), or external (such as a declining

Exhibit 6–1
Marketing-Plan Format

EXECUTIVE SUMMARY

Situational Analysis (Where Are We Now?)
External
    Environment (political, regulatory, economic, social, technical, etc.)
    Consumers
    Employees
    Funders
    Distributors
    Competition
Internal
    Objectives
    Strengths and weaknesses

Problems and Opportunities
Momentum forecast
Identify gaps

Marketing Program Goals (Where Do We Want to Go?)
Specific (quantifiable)
Realistic (attainable)
Important
Prioritized

Marketing Strategies (How Are We Going to Get There?)
Positioning
    Target segments
    Competitive stance
    Usage incentive
Marketing mix
    Product
    Price
    Distribution
    Marketing communication
Contingency strategies

Marketing Budget (How Much and Where?)
Resources
    Money
    People
    Time
Amount and allocation

Marketing Action Plan
Detailed breakdown of activities for each goal or strategy
Responsibility by name
Activity schedule in milestone format
Tangible and intangible results from each activity

Monitoring System

economy). The Toronto Transit Commission (TTC) cited the following problems in a 1977 plan:[3]

1. Financial constraints on possibilities for system expansion. As a result it was seen as unlikely that the TTC would be able to tap potential markets in certain growth communities in the metropolitan area.
2. Slowing of metropolitan population growth.
3. Economic uncertainty and the sensitivity of ridership to changes in the local economy.
4. Crime on the subway (a survey found a substantial number of patrons concerned for their personal safety—especially at night and on the subway).
5. Present heavy system usage (by 75 percent of people in the metropolitan area over the age of 15 years) means that increases in ridership won't come easily.

A marketing *opportunity* is a favorable circumstance, which might contribute to the attraction of new riders or perhaps to slowing a decline in ridership. The same plan foresaw the following opportunities for the TTC:

1. Fare stability.
2. Opening of a new subway line (plus increased capacity on the existing main North–South line as consequence).
3. Rising gasoline prices.
4. Changing downtown shopping habits. If downtown evening shopping hours five days a week were to prove popular, there would be an opportunity to increase off-peak ridership.

However, it is very important to emphasize that problems and opportunities tend to change over time, reflecting a variety of social, economic, political, and technological developments—as well as internal changes within the organization itself. By 1986, for instance, the rise of gasoline prices had been reversed, and opportunities perceived by TTC in its 1986 plan included: 1) increasing dual usage of cars plus transit; 2) promoting rider and employee participation in maintaining a clean, safe transit environment; 3) new transit markets such as visitors to Toronto; 4) promoting specific routes with potential for ridership growth; and 5) perfecting processing of customer enquiries and complaints through the centralized customer communications system.[4]

This analysis of problems and opportunities needs to be supported by an understanding of the present strengths and weaknesses of the system and the conditions that led to past successes and failures.

A comprehensive situation analysis generates an enormous amount of data, which can easily obscure the purpose of the analysis. In order to summarize the implications of the data, many private sector firms develop a *momentum forecast*. This is a detailed forecast (perhaps by regions or routes) of key performance variables (ridership, share of trips, revenues and expenses, and resource requirements) that assumes no change in strategy or budget other than is necessary to adapt to foreseeable changes or events in the environment. Because it describes what would happen if the system adheres to the status quo, it is a useful benchmark for evaluating strategy changes.

Setting objectives and targets

Objectives are desired or needed results to be achieved in the future. Statements of objectives relate to such issues as the size of the profit (or in most cases the deficit and subsidy) and the level of ridership. The statements of objectives must also address the fundamental question of whether the emphasis is to be on diversion of travelers from private automobiles or improving mobility for those who presently lack access to adequate transportation.

Ideally, statements of objectives should be framed in such a way that they can be compared to the momentum forecast of key performance variables that was developed as part of the situation analysis. The size of the gap between the objectives and the momentum is a good indicator of the magnitude of the need for additional resources and changes in strategies. If the resources are not available because of a governmental financing formula, or if the feasible strategies are not likely to have the needed impact, then the objectives are unrealistic and need to be renegotiated.

Targets are specific, time-based points of measurement that the system intends to meet in the pursuit of its broad objectives. While an objective may sometimes change slowly, in an evolutionary manner, specific targets must be revised regularly with each review. But during the year they are adopted, they provide a very specific indication of the results that are expected from the marketing program effort.

In order to be useful, targets should be specific, and if possible, quantifiable. For example, the Toronto Transit Commission set a goal for 1986 of increasing off-peak ridership a net one percent to a total of 437 million rides with a corresponding net revenue increase of $3.1 million (Canadian). Other illustrative targets (not from the TTC plan) would be to decrease the cost per mile to the rider by ten percent during off-peak periods, or to improve the public image of the transit system by increasing "favorable" responses to a survey to 70 percent of all those interviewed.

When targets are realistic and attainable, they reflect resource limitations, political realities, and attainable program results. Targets should be challenging, but not set so high that they cannot be achieved. If these goals are achieved, the organization will enjoy a sense of accomplishment; if not, at least there should be a way of determining why not—an analysis that will be useful in determining objectives and setting targets for the next year.

Finally, all objectives should be tailored to the situation, ranked in order of priority. Objectives should be few in number so that they can serve as a useful focus and be ranked so that managers have guidance if it is necessary to make tradeoffs among alternative plans or tactics.

Formulating marketing strategies

A strategy is the specific approach that will be used to ensure orderly progression toward the goals and objectives and their component targets. In particular, a transit marketing strategy should include decision rules and guidelines within each of the following areas:

- Choice of target market.
- The benefits that need to be offered to the target market to encourage their patronage.
- The integrated combination of marketing decision variables (the marketing mix). This requires setting priorities for the allocation of resources to improving service characteristics, changing fare levels, and implementing communications programs.
- The relative level of spending effort.

Successful strategy development depends on a good information base developed as part of the situation analysis, and a conscious effort to consider a variety of alternatives before focusing on one approach. Superior strategies will relate closely to the analysis of problems and opportunities and the resulting goals. For example, one goal may be to "increase ridership among workers who commute in heavy numbers to an industrial park." To achieve this goal may mean working closely with employers (for staggered work hours), and/or revising the routing and scheduling to conform to the needs of the specific population segment employed in the industrial park.

A strategic problem faced by public transportation agencies is the need to raise money from people and organizations that do not use its services. Thus managers may need two distinct but interrelated marketing strategies: one for fund raising and one for user services. At times, marketing managers on either side may be constrained in what they do in order to coordinate efforts to to be consistent with each other's needs. In a bold move to increase ridership, the Southern California Rapid Transit District introduced a 25-cent flat fare on Sundays in the mid–1970s. The fare could only be offered in Los Angeles County because the Board of Supervisors in adjoining counties would not contribute the funds necessary to finance the program in their own communities. Ridership on Sundays in Los Angeles County increased by 19 percent during the 13 week trial period.[5]

Developing substrategies. Once the overall strategy has been formulated, there is a solid basis for preparing substrategies for an actual marketing effort. For example, an overall strategy could be to increase weekend ridership by increasing the awareness of area residents of transit routes and destinations as well as by developing new promotional tools. A substrategy would be to target selected segments with perhaps a weekend pass or student summer pass that would complement the lifestyles or needs of particular groups. Using market segmentation analysis to carefully target key groups is important in developing substrategies.

Marketing action plan. The marketing action plan is a detailed breakdown of the strategies that are intended to achieve each of the goals, plus an assignment of responsibilities by name of individual or office. This element of the plan indicates the tactics to be implemented. The activity schedule should be in "milestone" form, so that all concerned can know what actions have to be accomplished, by whom and by when, in order for the plan's goals to be accomplished on schedule.

Setting the marketing budget. The resources for implementation of the marketing plan must be allocated through the marketing budget. There are three critical resources in running an organization: money, people, and time. Because most public transit agencies rarely have enough money, people, or time, a central question in budgeting is how to use or allocate these scarce resources in the most efficient manner.

In allocating resources, management must consider the relationships among the different marketing elements as well as the relative cost effectiveness of making investments in each element. Unfortunately this ideal is hard to achieve if transit managers do not know how expenditures on a specific program or service improvement will affect ridership and revenues. Even when a favorable cost/benefit ratio can be documented, there may still not be adequate resources available because of funding restrictions.

Most transit marketing budgets are the end result of a series of negotiations that balance the resources needed to achieve desired goals with the resources available. For negotiations to be meaningful, the relevant goals may have to be modified. In the politicized, resource-constrained environment of transit management, the marketing planning process cannot be a neat, linear set of steps. As a result, marketing, planning, and budgeting are frequently shaped by factors beyond marketing considerations.

A frequently used approach to budgeting is simply to adopt a rule of thumb such as assigning a certain, very small percentage of operating revenues to marketing, or to match the budgeting experience of similar transit systems. Such rules of thumb are based on the implausible assumption that the budget proportions were properly established when previously employed and are still relevant for the present planning situation.

In general, transit marketing budgets are set at too low a level. Perhaps this is a consequence of past practices in the transit industry to reduce costs through curtailment of what were formerly considered nonessential support functions.[6] The *task budgeting* method of arriving at the marketing budget has much to recommend it because it relates planned expenditures to the tasks to be performed and the anticipated consequences of those actions. Alternative methods of budgeting may be workable, to the extent that judgments reflect management's experience with similar programs in similar circumstances, but they are obviously deficient when dealing with new programs targeted at unfamiliar market segments. In any event, for most systems, budget increases probably represent one of the most attractive short-run investments in increases in ridership and revenues.

Implementation

Planning without implementation is worth little.[7] Managers have a choice. They can either allow the elements of a marketing plan to emerge from "busywork" by a marketing staff or advertising agency distant from the strategic problems of the transit system; or they can insist that planning be an integral part of the process of establishing and implementing the future directions of a transit organization.

Although the introduction of marketing can benefit an organization greatly, it would be foolish to assume that adoption of a formal marketing program is a simple process. "Marketing" itself must be marketed, just as a new transit service needs to be promoted in order to secure its usage. Nor should the marketer assume that gaining acceptance of this function is an easy task.

Marketing is a complex management function that may pose considerable risk to administrators, especially those who manage bureaucratically and are set in their ways. Marketing is not always compatible with established procedures, yet sensitive marketing managers must still seek to establish harmonious relationships with other management functions (see Chapter 11, "Building a Marketing Orientation").

A critical task for newly appointed marketing managers in a transit organization that has previously lacked a formal marketing function is to choose appropriate early assignments. To build credibility, they should look for projects that will be seen as useful by managers in other parts of the organization. Further, these projects should have reasonable visibility and offer a high chance of success in a relatively short time frame. The implementers of marketing should recognize that initial projects are only trials; they must continue to develop the utilization of marketing until it is fully accepted as a vital, necessary organizational activity.

Evaluation of performance

Without a research and evaluation component, it is difficult to assess the impact of the marketing programs and to plan future programs. Decision makers want to see documentation of the results of successful programs as justification for expenditures in future years.

Performance evaluation in transit agencies needs two sets of indicators. One set should cover cost efficiency (labor, vehicle, fuel, maintenance, and service output). These performance indicators fall within the province of operations. Of concern to both marketing and operations are *service effectiveness* measurers designed to determine performance on such variables as:

- utilization of service;
- operating safety;
- revenue generation;
- operating subsidy per passenger.[8]

When evaluating actual performance against planned marketing targets, a greater level of specificity may be required than the generalized measures listed above. In particular, special studies may be required to obtain data to evaluate the effectiveness of specialized marketing programs directed at carefully defined market segments.

In Seattle, the Metro bus system's Marketing Plan one year proposed five major studies:

1. *Annual Attitude & Awareness Study*: to track changes in rider and nonrider usage and demographics, to further isolate and profile potential riders, and to clarify content of the most effective marketing messages.

2. *Monthly Pass Purchaser Study*: to assess possible changes in pass usage and buyer characteristics and to determine appropriate message content to market the pass to heavy-riding nonusers.

3. *Employer Program Survey*: to determine the impact of employer-subsidized passes and subscription bus service/passes on new and/or potential new riders.

4. *Service Planning Corridor Studies*: to assess the impact of service changes on attitudes and bus usage along specific route corridors, and to determine the importance of various service characteristics.

5. *Free Ticket Experiment*: to determine which of two recent studies more accurately profiled potential new riders, and then to gauge the effectiveness of free tickets as an incentive to begin riding the bus.[9]

CONCLUSION

A well-prepared marketing plan is an excellent means to communicate objectives, specific targets, and proposed strategies to top management.

The evaluation component of planning is critical for a marketing department in documenting its success and gaining credibility in the organization. In times of fiscal constraints, boards of directors are often likely to cut "management overhead" budgets before even evaluating operating departments or actual services. In this environment, it becomes all too easy to cut the budget of the marketing department. It is difficult to present the case that marketing plays an indispensable role in the organization unless there exists careful evaluation and documentation of successful projects.

Without a careful planning process, it is also difficult to rise above the "crisis management" style of "putting out fires" on a day-to-day basis. A successful planning function allows marketing managers to set the agenda for their departments and, to some extent, influence the agenda of the organization as a whole.

NOTES

1. Steiner, George A. *Strategic Planning: What Every Manager Must Know* (New York: The Free Press, 1979).

2. See Lawrence F. Cunningham and Kenneth N. Thompson, "The management audit in small public transit firms," *Transportation Quarterly* (July 1985): 345–64.

3. Toronto Transit Commission. *TTC Marketing Plan* (1977).

4. Toronto Transit Commission. *Marketing and Community Relations Plan* (1986). (See Appendix B to this book.)

5. See L. Frank Demmler and Christopher H. Lovelock, "Rapid transit in Los Angeles," in *Public and Nonprofit Marketing: Cases and Readings*, edited by C. H. Lovelock and C. B. Weinberg (New York: John Wiley & Sons, 1984).

6. Urban Mass Transportation Administration. *Transit Marketing Management Handbook* (1976).

7. Rothschild, William E. *Putting It All Together*, (New York: AMACOM 1976), p. 255.

8. Fielding, Gordon J., Timlynn T. Babitsky, and Mary E. Brenner. "Performance evaluation of bus transit," *Transportation Research* (February 1985): 73–82.

9. Municipality of Metropolitan Seattle. *Marketing Plan: Metro* (1979), p. 41.

7

The Role of Service Design

A major problem with the operations departments of many transit authorities is that they are not consumer-oriented. Procedures designed to maximize operation efficiency may be incompatible with traveler needs and preferences. In their search for operating efficiency and cost minimization, there is a risk that managers of service organizations may come to see consumers as a nuisance, a constraint, and even as a barrier to productivity.

The reductio ad absurdum of a mindset that stresses operating efficiency at the expense of the consumer is pungently illustrated in this newspaper report from the Midlands of England entitled "Get Rid of the People and the System Runs Fine":

Complaints from passengers wishing to use the Bagnalls to Greenfields bus service that "the drivers were speeding past queues of people with a smile and a wave of the hand" have been met by a statement pointing out that "it is impossible for the drivers to keep their timetable if they have to stop for passengers."[1]

Obviously, transit authorities are hard pressed to keep costs down, so tradeoffs have to be made between seeking operating efficiency and satisfying consumer preferences. However it is unwise to "average" consumer needs, since the urban travel market consists of several distinct segments with sharply different needs. In most successful companies, marketing considerations are equally important in service design and in the actual transit operation.

THE ROLE OF THE EMPLOYEE

No matter how fine the marketing effort, a transit authority without motivated employees will be unable to deliver a quality service to the public. If a marketing department produces timetables, but the drivers fail to distribute them to the riders, then the marketing department's efforts have failed. If an employee is rude to a new rider, marketing efforts to keep that rider on transit may be for naught. If equipment breaks down due to a poor maintenance operation then ridership will suffer.

Internal marketing

Since the product is the operation, marketing can only succeed if the transit service meets certain basic standards. Marketing professionals have often stated the necessity of a transit system's having a "consumer orientation" from the general manager on down to the line employees. Reaching this goal requires the development of an ongoing *internal marketing program* to determine employee attitudes, convince employees of the importance of their work, obtain their ideas and suggestions for improvement, and to make them feel involved in the delivery of the service. While there can be no substitute for good management structure, procedures, and accountability, there is considerable latitude in most organizations to develop employee involvement programs. In fact, employees who work with the public or in the shop can often contribute useful information and ideas to management for planning and improving services. Yet many transit authorities suffer problems of low employee morale and lack of motivation.

The Central New York Regional Transportation Authority developed an ambitious marketing program "to enhance both its employees' self image and the public's perception of the Centro person as a professional."[2] The campaign featured an advertising program based on the theme of "the Centro professionals, you can depend on them." The kickoff of the campaign featured a dinner honoring drivers and mechanics who had been cited individually in recent years for their performance. Centro also upgraded an ongoing Driver of the Month program based on employee safety and performance record from a $25 cash award to a banquet for winners and their families. Centro has also developed incentive programs with cash regards and drivers are asked to serve on committees that meet regularly with management representatives.[3]

According to a Transportation Research Board report, "Apparently, few—if any—transit agencies have undertaken formal employee attitude studies. Few, in fact, have any mechanism at all, other than the unions, for listening to what employees have to say about the system or about their own situations. A scattering of individual systems is turning, like Centro, to employee-management committees as a means of involving the employees in the system and working out mutual problems."[4]

Seattle Metro is a transit system that has actively involved and communicated with employees through an intra-agency monthly publication, a traditional in-house newsletter, and "Advance Flyer" notices posted on bulletin boards throughout the system. Employees have been allowed to help shape decisions on items such as the style and types of uniforms.[5] San Francisco Muni has also begun experimenting with employee "quality circles" at certain bus garages.

In the Netherlands, Amsterdam Transport has developed a program of employee participation and involvement. The rationale for these programs is best explained by the system's director of personnel and organizational development:

Our difficulty is that our people are spread out all over the city. Drivers not only work by themselves, but are constantly on the move. We cannot place supervisors all over the city telling them what to do. We have to teach them to accept responsibility. The drivers know better than anyone else what the public wants and needs. They are there on the scene after all.[6]

DIFFERENT PRODUCTS FOR DIFFERENT MARKETS

As noted earlier, the term "mass transit" tends to encourage managers to think of their customers as a mass market with undifferentiated needs. In Chapter 2, we described how the market for urban travel is divided into numerous segments, reflecting different travelers and types of trips.

Recognizing that there are different transit markets, many transit authorities now offer a range of different transit "products." Alternatives to the basic, local-stop transit service now include:

- Express service (bus or rail);
- Demand-activated service (often for elderly or handicapped persons);
- Shuttle services (for shoppers or around airports);
- Specialized services (airport expresses, sightseeing).

Express service

Speed of travel is known to be an important determinant of modal choice, and the demand for transit has been found to be travel-time elastic as well as price elastic. Speed is likely to be especially significant for nondiscretionary trips (e.g., commuting to work) by those who could use a car if they wished. Experience in New York and other cities suggests that people will pay premium fares for premium service.

Attempts to expedite rail service mainly involve elimination of stops. The criteria for skipping stops may reflect an emphasis on loading a train early in the route, leaving it to run full, nonstop, for the balance of journey to its terminus, with a following train taking care of passengers getting on and off at intermediate stations. Stop-skipping is also used to accelerate travel, with alternate trains stopping at alternate stations. This assumes little demand for travel between "odd" and "even" intermediate stations. Scheduling of express and stop-skipping trains is facilitated by provision of a third track. BART, in the San Francisco area, stops at all stations and has been criticized for emphasizing inter-station speed rather than providing for nonstop or limited-stop services.

Express buses fall into four broad categories: exclusive busways, exclusive bus lanes, freeway service, and limited stop service.

Exclusive busway service can be best described as a form of bus rapid transit. One of the best known examples is the eleven mile exclusive busway constructed alongside the San Bernardino Freeway southeast of Los Angeles, with a suburban terminus in El Monte and several station pull-off points. This busway has proven very popular in Los Angeles, saving peak-hour riders twenty minutes over car travelers on the congested freeway. Its advantage over rail is that, on leaving the busway, buses may disperse to multiple destinations.

One variation on the busway is the *transit mall* concept, where an entire city street is reserved for transit vehicles—usually in downtown areas. The transit mall facilitates loading and travel times in congested areas. Chicago and Portland, Oregon, are examples of cities that have reserved downtown streets for transit malls.

Exclusive bus lanes—in this case, lanes of an existing freeway are reserved for buses (and often for carpool and emergency vehicles). These restricted lanes give buses a highly visible advantage over traffic in adjacent congested auto lanes. There are 18 high occupancy vehicle lanes operating in the United States—eight of which were introduced since 1982.[7] While exclusive bus lanes have been successful on roads such as the Shirley Highway in Washington, D.C., political opposition forced highway officials to eliminate exclusive lanes reserved for carpools and buses in Los Angeles and Boston.

The Shirley Highway lanes were introduced at the time the road was opened, but in the other cities, an existing traffic lane in each direction on already congested roadways was converted to bus and carpool use. As a result, automobile drivers in Los Angeles and Boston felt that part of "their" road had been taken away, thus making the congestion problem more severe for them. These two experiments were cancelled before their effectiveness could be demonstrated.

Sometimes, where traffic volumes at certain times of day are highly skewed in one direction, contraflow bus lanes have been established. On an eight-lane expressway, for instance, where most traffic heads, say, southbound in the morning and northbound in the evening, two northbound lanes might be taken out of service in the morning, separated from the remaining lanes by a temporary median, and dedicated to buses running against the traffic flow on the lightly traveled lanes. In the evening, the process would be reversed. The Golden Gate Transit District in the San Francisco area has successfully developed both contraflow bus lanes and conventional bus lanes.[8]

Either type of exclusive bus lane requires much lower capital costs than construction of a busway, but involves heavy operating costs, including daily placement and removal of pylons alongside the segregated lanes and constant policing to prevent unauthorized use of the lanes by motorists. An important marketing consideration is that consumers may be reluctant to switch modes immediately, especially if they fear that an exclusive bus lane is only a temporary experiment. Lack of a heavy, initial surge in bus patronage may intensify political pressures for abandonment of the experiment, thus further discouraging the wait-and-see group.

Express service on freeways—in many cities, express buses now operate on freeways rather than exclusively on local city streets. This greatly speeds travel times providing the freeway itself is uncongested. In several instances, special pull-off points for buses have been constructed at underpasses, with a staircase to the pedestrian sidewalk on the overpass above.

Limited stop service is an approach involving running buses over routes served by traditional services, but restricting the number of stops, not unlike the skip-stop approach used for rail operations. To distinguish limited-stop buses from others, many transit authorities use such devices as flags, color coded headboards, or even special lights. Some express bus services, such as Calgary's "Blue Arrow," use a combination of the above approaches.

In addition to the benefits offered travelers through a service that is faster and more comfortable (less stopping and starting, use of smoother roads), express services may also yield productivity benefits for transit authorities. More passenger miles can be generated for the same labor cost, and both vehicle and driver may be able to make more round trips per day, thus helping to keep down staffing and vehicle requirements.

Demand-activated services

The advantage of the private car is that it operates at the owner's discretion. Taxis simulate these advantages, although sometimes there is a time delay in departure, and travel costs on a per trip basis are substantial in most cities. By contrast, traditional transit services run on fixed routes at fixed schedules.

The Dial-a-Bus concept has sought to meet consumer desires for door-to-door service, while trying to keep down costs by having travelers pool their rides with other people going in the same general direction. In theory, Dial-a-Bus looks promising, but in practice it has not always come up to the expectations of planners, operators, and consumers. Demand-activated services require the use of dispatchers and computerized equipment to optimize vehicle routing and utilization of a multi-vehicle fleet. The fewer the constraints on origins and destinations served, and the greater the carrying capacity of the vehicle, the more likely it is that there will be delays in pick-ups and that point-to-point travel times will be slow.

A number of demonstration projects have been sponsored in the United States and Canada in recent years. Although several have succeeded in working out initial bugs and in providing a service with which riders proved very satisfied, some well publicized operations have been discontinued due to excessive cost. Dial-a-Bus experiments suggest that approaches that have carefully defined target market segments are more successful and deserving of financial support than a generalized service.

A Dial-a-Bus service for elderly or handicapped persons in specialized small vehicles designed for handling a wheelchair is an example of a service that provides an important social purpose. Dial-a-Bus services that feed into interurban rail and express bus services may be costly of themselves but generate significant incremental revenues for the trunk-line operation by attracting transit travelers who formerly drove. In low density areas, demand-responsive services may be a cost-effective alternative to poorly patronized fixed-route services—particularly if contracted out to private operators—as demonstrated by the Tidewater (Virginia) Transit District.

Success factors—the most successful services seem to be those that encourage early reservations for single rides and regular bookings for trips made daily at the same time (e.g., multiple origins, single destination) rather than "many-to-many" service. Imposing these two constraints, of course, serves to make Dial-a-Bus service much less competitive with private cars for the unplanned random-point trips that cars can make so easily. Perhaps transit planners will need to recognize that there are trips for which public transportation, no matter how convenient and/or inexpensive, will be unable to compete with the automobile.

Nevertheless, some Dial-a-Ride services have managed to attract significant patronage. Calgary's DART system has had success with its service. Destinations that were particularly well patronized by DART included nursing homes and shopping centers.

An interesting contrast is provided by the experience of Santa Clara County's Dial-a-Ride program (discussed in more detail in Chapter 4). Its Dial-a-Ride program proved economically, operationally, and politically infeasible. Santa Clara County subsequently converted its bus fleet back to a fixed route system and entered into a contractual arrangement with local taxicab operators to provide demand-responsive, shared-ride taxi service focusing on specific population segments, such as elderly or handicapped persons, not adequately served by fixed route buses.

Downtown shuttle services

Some journeys require short linked trips between line-haul modes or a series of short "hops" within a geographically compact area. Shuttle services have been developed in many locations to provide frequently scheduled, tailored service that is realistically priced, given the nature of the trip and competing alternatives.

A number of cities have introduced downtown "shoppers' shuttles" to serve the central shopping area and link it with parking lots and/or line-haul transit terminals. Here, the competition is often walking (or not making the trip at all) and people tend to be price sensitive, so fares must be kept low. Seattle's "Magic Carpet" service is offered free within the core area and has succeeded in stimulating retail activity in the central business district. Some of these services use small, easily maneuverable buses or vans, which are equipped with space for shopping bags and parcels. Others simply rely on regular buses.

Airport travel

Airport shuttle services have to be designed to meet the needs of air travelers, who may be hurrying from one terminal to another, going to a remote parking lot, or transferring to a line-haul transit mode. Baggage space is especially important for such travelers, and the presence of baggage may also suggest a need for easy vehicle entry and exit. At international airports, it is important to provide information signs in multiple languages and/or easily recognized symbols.

With the dramatic growth in airline traffic over the past twenty years, ground transportation to airports has increased proportionately. Airports have become huge traffic generators, often second only to central business districts in total volume. Competing ground transportation modes to public transportation at an airport are renting a car, taking a cab (or perhaps a limousine), getting a ride from friends or family, or driving one's own car and parking in an expensive lot. To compete with these choices, transit services must provide comfort, baggage space, and reasonable frequency of service. These factors are likely to be more important than keeping fares low, although it would be a mistake to assume that all air travelers are well-to-do.

Following the earlier lead of Cleveland (which was the first U.S. city to extend its rapid transit line to the airport), Washington, Chicago, and Philadelphia have recently invested federal transit funds in building rail transit links to their respective airports. In New York, the MTA has heavily prompted its "Train to the Plane" to Kennedy International Airport. In Britain, London Transport has extended the Piccadilly tube (subway) line to Heathrow Airport. At Gatwick, London's other airport, the air terminal is constructed alongside a British Rail Station. Similar airport rail links exist in several other European cities.

However, for many cities, rail service to airports is not economically feasible. A promising alternative is to develop express bus services that provide a high quality trip at a premium price. These services may run directly to downtown or connect to the nearest rail or rapid transit station. Since air travelers are already paying a significant fare for their airline ticket, an extra dollar or more on a premium bus fare will not increase their overall travel cost significantly. Hence, premium bus services can be priced considerably higher than a conventional bus trip but still offer riders a significant savings over the cost of a taxicab ride. Some of these services are operated by public agencies, others by private carriers. In either case, the bus needs to be designed to accommodate significant amounts of baggage.

Sightseeing services

Many transit companies provide sightseeing services. These are attractive in that premium prices can be charged and most trips occur during the off-peak midday period or on weekends. To meet the needs of tourists such services require special routing and scheduling decisions. Tourists are also likely to be less price sensitive than typical transit users, but they may still be budget conscious. Tourists want a clean, comfortable bus with big, clean windows and a polite, knowledgeable driver to point out the sights with interesting commentary over a public address system. Clearly this type of service requires careful thought and preplanning, as well as special promotion. The Chicago Transit Authority operates "Culture Bus" routes that stop at museums as well as places of historic and ethnic interest. The tourist purchases a premium-priced ticket that is good for all day use on the route—allowing the passenger to board and disembark at various points of interest.

Cities offering ferry services for commuters may have an opportunity to promote those services to tourists during off-peak periods. Block bookings for parties may be promoted to tour organizers. To enhance the experience, it may be helpful to provide an on-board commentary, print special maps, inform prospective travelers about transit access to the ferry terminals, and even offer food and beverage service on board.

SCHEDULING AND ROUTING STRATEGIES

Scheduling

The timing of services is very important to travelers. For nondiscretionary trips especially, travelers need to have services scheduled at convenient times that will get them to their destinations in time to make appointments, job start times, and so on. Unreliable services, which often arrive late, can cause significant problems. On the other hand, nobody wants to get to a destination hours in advance of the needed time. Hence the transit operator needs to research starting and stopping times of major employers in order to determine optimum schedules for commuters. In the case of discretionary trips, travelers are more flexible and better able to organize their activities around the transit schedule.

An axiom on transit operations is that the less frequent the service, the longer the wait for another vehicle if the desired trip is missed. Researchers have found that travelers perceive time spent waiting as passing much more slowly and being more burdensome than time spent traveling in a vehicle.[9] Hence transit journeys that involve waiting for the vehicle to arrive lengthen the elapsed time of travel for door-to-door trips, both in an absolute and in a psychological sense. In some circumstances a frequent but slow service may be preferred to an infrequent express service, especially if the waiting location is exposed to the weather.

When scheduling services, tradeoffs may have to be made between operating efficiency and consumer convenience. For instance, optimum efficiency in vehicle utilization might call for scheduling a bus on a particular route every 24½ minutes. However, it is much more convenient for travelers if vehicles that operate on headways of 10 minutes or more are scheduled on "clock headways" (that is, every 10, 12, 15, 20, 30, or 60 minutes). In this way, vehicles come past a given stop at the same time each hour, which is much easier for travelers to remember than a schedule that apparently varies from one hour to another. This may be suboptimal for the operator, since it requires either adding extra vehicles and drivers or holding vehicles longer at terminals and turnaround points.

Routing

If transit is to serve the public, the routes must go to the places where people want to travel, assuming there are sufficient actual or potential travelers to make the service worthwhile. Routing must take account of geographic segmentation. Origin and destination studies will yield useful information on principal travel "corridors," but routing specifics must consider zones of accessibility to these corridors so that optimal decisions can be made on which streets to follow and where to locate transit stops. Not surprisingly, travel patterns change over time in response to changes in employment and residential patterns. Hence a route may need to be changed from time to time. Unlike rail, route changes are usually quite feasible with buses—although in some instances, long-established bus routes have been adhered to as rigidly as if the service ran on rails.

Fixed rail services can sometimes be made responsive to changed travel patterns by development of new feeder bus services. Commuter rail services, for example, were developed to bring suburban residents into downtown work locations. With the development of suburban office and industrial parks, significant new travel demand patterns are generated. Commuter rail services can develop "reverse commute" train trips by linking suburban work locations to train stops with connecting bus services (perhaps even offering one fare card for the complete trip). A reverse commute service to suburban areas can be targeted to central city residents and also provide job opportunities to lower income individuals. One of the innovations created by GO Transit in Ontario has been to run rail services through the center of Toronto, thus linking suburban cities on both sides of the metropolitan area with direct service.

Combining routing and scheduling strategies

Reflecting the fact that travelers' trip purposes vary by time of day and week, the geographic patterns of travel demands may vary too. Destinations such as shopping centers, recreation centers, and so on are not necessarily located in close proximity to major employment centers. So routes designed to serve commuters may be inappropriate for shoppers and other off-peak travelers.

This suggests a need to offer a somewhat different routing structure in off-peak periods than at the peaks. Some transit authorities now recognize that routing strategies cannot be divorced from scheduling strategies, and have revised their service offerings to meet travelers' changing needs over the course of each day.

DESIGN OF VEHICLES AND FACILITIES

Vehicle characteristics need to be tailored to the needs of different types of travelers. User needs many vary based on the type of trip planned and on personal characteristics of the potential rider.

Tailoring vehicle design to trip characteristics

Seating design and density on transit vehicles should logically reflect the length of journey that passengers are making, and the type of service being provided. For systems with high peak-to-base load ratios, it makes sense to have only a limited number of seats (sufficient to meet off-peak needs), thus leaving plenty of aisle room for peak hour standees.

Buses that are subject to vandalism (e.g., carrying lots of school children) may need to have vandal-proof seats and unbreakable windows. In San Diego some buses have been equipped with cameras, operated by the driver, to record acts of vandalism and harassment. They have proved to have excellent deterrent value and are popular with passengers.

By contrast, buses that run on express routes, seeking to appeal to car-owning suburbanites who will be paying premium fares, may need to be more comfortably equipped than a city bus. Features on many of Golden Gate Transit's buses include low density seating with headrests, reclining seats, individual reading lights, and overhead luggage racks.

Vehicles designed for use on routes traveled extensively by shoppers or by people connecting with intercity rail, bus, or airline services should logically include additional space for bags and packages, as well as wide entry and exit doors. Similar considerations apply to other transportation modes such as commuter trains, rapid transit vehicles, streetcars, and ferries. There have been important new developments in ferry design in recent years to improve both water speed and docking times. The Sea Bus in Vancouver, British Columbia, is an example of applying rapid transit design theories to waterborne vehicles.

One problem with having a fleet comprised of vehicles with different configurations is that it reduces operating flexibility. For instance, it would be inappropriate to put a high density urban bus on a route where passengers expected a comfortable commuter bus.

In the case of ferries, research shows that two major markets exist: commuters and pleasure travelers. Hence vehicle design features must be planned to accommodate both types of traveler.[10]

Provisions for elderly and handicapped persons

In the United States, federal regulations impose vehicle design standards to facilitate safe use by elderly and handicapped persons. Specifications include lower entrance steps, nonslip floors, and provision of grips and stanchions to hold on to. "Kneeling" buses have been produced to make it easier to board the bus. However, these innovations need to be combined with driver training, so that kneeling devices are properly used and elderly passengers are given time to reach a seat or grab a rail before the bus accelerates away from a bus stop.

Providing for the handicapped has caused some contention. To install wheelchair lifts in every bus would be prohibitively expensive relative to the number of handicapped persons who might use it. So the trend has been toward development of tailored services, using specialized vehicles, to serve this small but important segment. On the other hand, new rail systems such as BART and the Washington Metro have been designed (or redesigned) with wheelchair passengers in mind, and most of their stations incorporate elevators to bring passengers from street level to platform.

Stations, terminals, and street furniture

An understanding of market segments is useful in designing facilities for terminals, stations, shelters, and benches. Although it would be nice to install a bench and shelter at every bus stop, this approach may be economically infeasible. A review of traveler characteristics and travel patterns on a route-by-route basis may help in setting priorities. For instance, one report for a transit system in Santa Clara County, California (better known as "Silicon Valley"), proposed the following criteria for locating shelters and benches:

Shelters should be provided at well-patronized points:

- in exposed locations where no other shelter (e.g., a store front) may be available;
- at transfer points;
- in situations where people may have packages or goods that could be damaged by rain or wind;
- in locations patronized by the elderly and infirm, and by mothers with small children.

Benches should be provided in all shelters and also at locations:

- where waits may be lengthy;
- where people may be tired and carrying heavy packages;
- in residential areas, particularly those with large populations of old people, where it may be impractical to erect a shelter.[11]

The Santa Clara County Transit District eventually funded a $1 million bus stop improvement program. Shelters were installed at major intersections, hospitals, senior citizen houses, downtown areas, transportation hubs, park-and-ride lots, and transfer centers. According the project manager, determination of shelter locations was based "on the number of people waiting at bus stops and the length of time they have to wait. . . . Since half the shelters are placed on private property, any proposed location must be approved by the property owner and city in which it is located."[12] In St. Louis, a bus shelter program also focused on major employment and commercial centers. Both transit authorities considered recommendations from customers.[13] In some instances, shelters and benches have been installed and maintained by employers, colleges, or retailers served by the stop in question.

An important issue in station and terminal design is security, particularly for facilities in high crime areas. Good lighting, use of TV monitors, open areas, lack of hidden corners and winding corridors—all of these may contribute to a safer and more pleasant environment.

Passenger comfort while waiting can be enhanced by installation of seating, provision of food service or automatic dispensing machines, heating and cooling systems, washrooms, and a pleasant decor that is kept clean. When stations are cold, drafty, cheerless, dirty, badly lit, and generally uncomfortable, they discourage transit use—especially when the headways between trips are long.

Since rail or rapid transit stations have a major impact on the local community as well as on the travelers who use them, transit planners also need to consider the concern of local businesses and residents as these relate to design features.[14]

SERVICE AND INTERMODAL INTEGRATION

Many journeys involve changing transit vehicles, and virtually all involve use of two or more modes if one recognizes that walking is a mode in its own right. Apart from the need to ensure that transferring does not pose undue difficulties for transit captives such as the elderly or handicapped, attempts to market the system to those with access to a car require that transfers be convenient, simple, and punctual. We will review briefly four types of transfers: car/transit, bicycle/transit, walk/ transit, and transit/transit. In each instance, an understanding of consumer needs and preferences will help in designing and operating a transfer facility that minimizes the hassles often associated with such transfers.

Car/transit transfers

Access by car is widely used in suburban locations where a stop or station may be some distance geographically from residential neighborhoods, but only a few minutes' drive away. Understanding the demographics and type of trips being made from a defined geographic area can provide insights in determining potential interest in new parking facilities at a transit station. Analysis is obviously important for new facilities, but careful study of an existing station may show opportunities for improving facilities and increasing ridership.

With a park-and-ride facility, travelers drive to a parking lot, leave their cars, and ride the train, bus, or ferry. Successful marketing of parking facilities requires locating the lot close to the transit stop, proper lighting, and security. The availability of, and access to, such lots needs to be communicated to car drivers who are not currently using transit but are potential transit riders.

Pricing of parking requires transit authorities to balance a number of factors in establishing a parking fee policy. Some transit authorities prefer to provide free parking and to absorb the cost in transit ticket prices. While unfair to nonparkers, this strategy is responsive to the many suburbanites who expect parking to be free and dislike having to pay twice to be able to use transit. Excessive charges for parking may also result in commuters' cars clogging suburban streets as they search for free curbside parking. This practice not only reduces parking revenue but can create political problems for the transit authority within local communities.

On the other hand, free or nominal parking fees can generate excessive demand and reduce ridership on connecting bus routes. As parking prices in downtown areas have become quite expensive in many cities, suburbanites may be willing to tolerate modest fees at suburban stations. Decision analysis needs to rest on determining how much incremental ridership can be generated by absorbing the partial or entire cost of parking in the transit fare and whether increasing existing fares for this purpose would have any effect on current riders.

With a "kiss-and-ride" facility, the passenger is dropped off and picked up at the transit station by another person (usually a family member). If a large number of cars are involved, the traffic situation can quickly deteriorate. So it is necessary to design short-term waiting areas for cars dropping off and picking up passengers. Usually, these areas are located closer to the station entrance/exit than the all-day parking area. Proper signs are needed that drivers use the correct lanes and only wait in designated areas.

Pedestrian/transit interface

One often hears people complain about interminable walks at airports. In that instance, there may be few alternatives to flying. However confusing, badly lit, smelly connections that involve long walks and stair climbing, as well as being perceived as unsafe, are likely to act as a serious deterrent to transit use among those who have an alternative. Stations need to be designed to minimize such problems since they reduce transit's ability to compete effectively in the urban travel market. Poor connections are particularly discouraging to those traveling outside peak hours (especially at night when security may be a perceived problem), parents with small children, old people, the handicapped, and travelers carrying packages or bags. Peak hour travelers, by contrast, are more likely to be concerned about crowding in pedestrian access areas.

Bicycle/transit interface

A small but growing number of people bicycle to a transit stop and park their bikes there. The high cost of sports bikes and the ease of stealing and reselling them suggests a need for bicycle security as well as weather protection. A number of transit authorities provide bike racks and shelters at their stations, but BART has introduced totally enclosed bicycle lockers that can be rented on a monthly basis. BART has also developed a permit program for allowing bicycles on trains. The permit program allows BART to maintain some regulation and control over the number of bicycles and ensure proper safety procedures.

Bicycles hold promise as a connecting mode at suburban rail stations. In Japan, 15 percent of suburban rail commuters bike to their stations, while as late as 1970 bicycles had played an insignificant role.[15]

Transit/transit transfers

Many transit systems have designed key bus/rail or bus/bus interchange facilities to maximize convenience for the passenger. Integration of service is achieved by minimizing the distance between bus and rail platforms, installing clear signs, eliminating as many barriers between the two modes as possible, and ensuring that transfers take place in a weather-protected area. In the Boston area, the MBTA rapid transit station in Harvard Square connects below street level to loading platforms for buses operating in a tunnel for about a quarter of a mile. Portland, Oregon, has introduced a transit mall that brings all downtown buses along a transit-only street, thus avoiding the need to walk from one street to another to change buses.

To minimize travel times in suburban locations where it is infeasibile to introduce more frequent headways, British Columbia has introduced an approach known as the "Time Transfer Focal Point." Using this approach—which is broadly similar to the airline hub concept—buses from several suburban neighborhoods are scheduled to converge simultaneously at the main focal point of activity for the community. Passengers needing to continue their journey on other local or regional buses can transfer immediately without having to wait around. This serves to minimize total travel time between two points, but requires realistic scheduling and good time-keeping on all routes, since each vehicle is effectively functioning as part of an integrated system. The "Time Transfer" approach also requires a terminal sufficiently large to handle several buses converging at once, rather than a steady trickle of one bus at a time.

The pricing of journeys involving a transfer is problematic, since the task of issuing and controlling transfers has to be traded off against equitable treatment of passengers. In cities without transfers, riders may pay twice as much for, say, two one-mile rides as they do for one two-mile ride. This may discourage use of transit for journeys involving two or more separate vehicles, even when scheduling and physical integration have been otherwise well planned.

Most cities with rapid rail transit provide free transfers between lines meeting at the same station, but not necessarily for interchanges between subway and commuter rail. Transfers between bus and rail are sometimes free in the rail–bus direction but not vice-versa (e.g., BART–AC Transit). Bus–bus transfer policies vary from city to city. Sometimes they are free, provided the traveler does not reverse direction; sometimes there is a small supplementary charge for a transfer; and in some cities each bus used requires a new fare. In the Boston area, the MBTA's monthly pass program constitutes a unified fare structure that allows regular users to transfer between commuter rail and transit and between comparably priced bus routes.

The need for bus–bus transfers is increased when the route structure is deliberately laid out on a grid basis, since any "diagonal" journey necessarily involves traveling two sides of a triangle and changing at the apex. This grid approach is believed to offer faster travel and more extensive route coverage for the majority of travelers than does a meandering zig-zag route pattern. However, proper scheduling at transfer points, availability of benches or shelters at these points, and availability of free or low-priced transfers may be necessary ingredients to make transfers successful with consumers.

CONCLUSION

Building new transit user markets often depends on offering new services or modifying existing ones. Whether or not new or modified services are actually successful depends on how closely the service design addresses the needs of potential new customers.

For transportation planners to design a new service and then leave marketing departments with the job of "finding" new riders for the service, is hardly a formula for success. Marketing considerations must play a primary role in service design so that the resulting new operation is one that can successfully be promoted to new riders.

Notes

1. Ryan, Patrick. "Get rid of the people and the system runs fine," *Smithsonian* (September 1977): 140.

2. Frank, Warren. "Employee/consumer relations—the Centro professionals," in *Marketing Public Transportation: Policies, Strategies and Research Needs for the 1980's*, Proceedings Series, edited by R.K. Robinson and C.H. Lovelock (Chicago: American Marketing Association, 1981), p. 45.

3. Transportation Research Board. *Urban Transportation Economics*, Special Report 181, (Washington, D.C.: National Academy of Sciences, 1978), p. 192.

4. Ibid., p. 193.

5. Coffman, Larry. "The Marketing role of transit employees," in *National Transit Marketing Conference: Proceedings* (American Public Transportation Association, 1975), p. 78.

6. "A Streetcar named participation," in *International Management* (October 1976): 29.

7. Southward, Frank, and Fred Westbrook. "HOV lanes: Some evidence on their recent performance" (Oak Ridge National Laboratory, Box X, Oak Ridge, TN 37831), unpublished paper presented at Transportation Research Board Annual Meeting (January 1986), p. 2.

8. For a detailed description, see C.B. Weinberg and B.H. Weitz, "The Golden Gate corridor busway," in *Public and Nonprofit Marketing: Cases and Readings*, edited by Christopher H. Lovelock and Charles B. Weinberg (New York: John Wiley & Sons, 1984).

9. Cherlow, Jay R. "Measuring the values of travel time savings," *Journal of Consumer Research* (March 1981): 360–71.

10. See Shanna O'Hare, "High speed transit ferries on San Francisco Bay," *Transportation Quarterly* (October 1985): 553–69.

11. San Jose–Palo Alto Bus Demonstration Project Plan, UMTA Project Cal-MDG–14 (May 1972).

12. *Passenger Transport* (February 15, 1980): 7.

13. Ibid.

14. See Catherine Ross and Jay M. Stein, "Business and residential perceptions of a proposed rail station: Implications for transit planning," *Transportation Quarterly* (October 1985): 483–93.

15. *Urban Transportation Abroad* (Washington, D.C.: Council for International Urban Liaison, Fall 1983).

Part IV
Managing Demand for Transit Services

8
Pricing Strategies

In the private sector, approaches to pricing are relatively straightforward. The objectives are fairly explicit: recover all costs and make a profit. As public agencies, most transit authorities do not recover their full costs from the farebox and are not in the business of making a profit. In fact, the majority of transit organizations receive large public subsidies. Thus, pricing strategy entails a different set of objectives for the transit organization.

PRICING IN THE PUBLIC SECTOR

Transit pricing decisions often involve public debate. Arguments for and against fare increases reflect differences in political philosophy regarding the appropriate allocation of costs to taxpayers and riders (with some consideration of fiscal realities). In the United States, government regulations often require public hearings on fare increases. Political figures often speak out on fare proposals and newspapers at times editorialize on the topic.

With a high level of political involvement, it would seem that transit managers have little role in the pricing of their services. But this is not the case. Political discussion of fares is really concerned only with the total percentage of revenue to be derived from the farebox. Carefully developed pricing strategies involve much more than just setting a dollar price. An actual fare structure must be developed. Decisions must be made on how, where, and when fares are to be paid. Plans are needed for how fares should be communicated to customers and who should take responsibility for collecting payment. While transit managers do not always have full authority to establish pricing policy, they are important players in determining pricing because they set the agenda, conduct the analysis, and set the tone for public discussions. In most cities, managers have almost total discretion in designing fare structures, distribution channels, and communications strategies.

Approaches to setting price

The foundations underlying pricing strategy have been described as a tripod, with the three legs being labeled costs, competition, and market demand. The costs to be recovered set a floor to the price. The value of the product to the customer sets a ceiling. Finally, the price charged by competitors (for similar or substitute products) helps determine at what level between cost and value to set an actual price. These three forms of pricing are usually known as cost-plus (profit) pricing, value pricing, and competitor pricing.

Cost basis. For public transit agencies, the equivalent of cost-plus pricing is probably "cost-minus" (subsidy) pricing. In order to control the growth of public subsidy, some public authorities have legislatively mandated an actual cost recovery formula for transit service. For example, in Chicago, a transit service must cover 50 percent of its costs from the farebox. The remaining funds are met through public subsidy. The cost recovery formula sets a floor for the price of transit service.

Most transit authorities live with some form of cost recovery pricing, whether or not an actual formula is publicly articulated. There are limits to public subsidy as evidenced by the fact that "free" public transit has not gained popular support. In most instances, there appears to be a wide political consensus that some user fees are appropriate for public transit. Cost recovery is a mechanism for setting the lowest price that the public will tolerate in subsidizing transit service.

With cost pricing, there is a problem of how to determine and allocate costs within an existing organization. Cost-based pricing was traditionally used in regulating public utilities such as privately owned bus operations and commuter railroad services. Cost-based pricing decisions in a regulated environment tend to be influenced by accountants and lawyers who are not usually sensitive to issues of market-based pricing.

For public transportation, at issue is whether costs should be limited to operating expense or include capital expenses, which are often heavily subsidized by the federal government. A further question is how to allocate costs within a given operation. Should each route be able to hold its own or do some local routes, which serve as feeder routes for trunkline services, merit a lower recovery ratio? Should peak hour services be required to carry additional costs given the marginal costs of operating extra services? Should a zone fare system based on distance be developed?

By itself, cost-pricing does not provide adequate criteria for determining fares. A generalized cost recovery ratio for a transit system may be an appropriate method for government to articulate goals for a transit system as a whole. However, given the complexities of costing and pricing services, the actual structuring of fares is a task for transit analysts and managers relying on other analytic approaches.

Value pricing. Services and products can be priced on the basis of value to the customer rather than on the seller's costs. The costs associated with painting the Mona Lisa would probably be only a few dollars even at today's prices, but no one would dream of pricing this work of art on a cost-plus basis.

For public transportation users, value is often analyzed as a tradeoff of time-spent versus money-saved. How much additional cost in time is a potential transit user willing to incur in order to obtain the benefit of saving a certain amount of money? Economic models have been developed that determine the relationship between time and money expenditures for urban travel. Since different market segments value their time differently, mode choice tradeoffs will vary by group. A high-paid executive will value time very highly and therefore pay a high price for the fastest possible service (e.g., using a helicopter from a major airport to a downtown location). Clerical staff, on the other hand, are willing to spend a certain amount of time in order to obtain monetary savings due to their limited discretionary income. Thus, value analysis needs to incorporate market segmentation in determining price.

It is important to consider the interrelationship of quality of service issues and pricing in determining the strength of market demand for transit. Consumers can be as sensitive to the quantity and quality of service as they are to price. Value pricing helps estimate consumer response to service costs and benefits and sets the ceiling transit authorities can charge without eroding ridership.

Competitive pricing. A great deal of pricing of all products and services is based on determining what the competition charges. Since most public transportation operations have monopoly status, there is no direct competition. However, there is considerable generic competition. People can often choose to drive their own cars. For transit, competitive pricing analysis can focus on the marginal (out-of-pocket) costs such as gasoline, parking, and tolls; or consider the overall costs of automobile ownership. Since most consumers tend to consider only the marginal costs of automobile use, this is probably the more appropriate basis for competitive price analysis. Overall automobile costs, however, are relevant for developing targeted promotional programs. For example, where a family has a second car that is used solely for commuting purposes, it may be useful to consider the full costs of ownership.

WHY CHARGE FOR TRANSIT SERVICES?

Under certain circumstances, it may be appropriate to offer free transportation. Examples include school bus service (where the goal is to provide safe and reasonably convenient access to school for all children), parking and car rental shuttles (where the price of riding the shuttle is bundled in the costs of parking or car rental), and airport shuttles, designed to minimize congestion. However, in most situations today, transit riders are asked to pay for their travel.

In addition to the need to recover costs from users, there are other reasons for selling transit service rather than giving it away. Charging a fare may make passengers more aware of the value of the services supplied. When the Denver RTD offered free travel outside of rush hours, one of the problems it suffered was an increase in vandalism. This was partly due to the access offered to young people but also to the attitude engendered by the service's being free.[1]

There are also internal organizational reasons for selling transit. If services are sold, the responsible department can be treated as a revenue center rather than just as a cost center, so that both input and output can be measured in monetary terms. The manager of a revenue center thus becomes responsible for operating in such a way that revenues cover a predefined portion of costs. When services are sold, the resulting revenue figures are a useful measure of the quantity of services supplied by the organization. Unless an organization has appropriate output measures, it's hard to evaluate either efficiency or effectiveness.

Subsidized transit

Subsidy of public transit operations by taxpayers is a compromise between views that it should be free and that transit users should pay all of their own costs of service. Historically, operating subsidies for public transit developed as a method of stabilizing fares (and often improving service) to reverse the declining ridership.[2] (The federal support for capital improvements, such as new subway systems, rehabilitation of older systems, and new vehicles, is a somewhat different issue. Federal capital support was motivated by the fact that local authorities did not have the financial resources to make major capital investments.) financial resources to make major capital investments.)

Arguments in favor of operating subsidies are based on two policy considerations. The first is that transit service should be subsidized as a basis of welfare policy—large numbers of poor people use transit. However, it can be argued that there are more efficient methods of providing income redistribution than subsidizing transit operations. A study of 101 urban communities found that federal operating subsidies were "negatively correlated with percentage of low income families. This suggests that probably federal operating assistance is channeled more toward affluent communities."[3]

If transit use is considered to be an appropriate area for welfare subsidy, it can probably be provided more efficiently through user-side programs (e.g., a transit equivalent to the food stamp program) rather than through operational support. For instance, perhaps transit should be priced to the level that commuters are willing to pay, but social service organizations (or, if necessary, the transit agency) can provide subsidies for those in need.

The second policy consideration in favor of transit subsidies is that low prices are needed to entice automobile users to leave their cars and use transit. Some economists argue that it would be more efficient to have automobile users pay the full cost of the congestion that they produce by, say, charging tolls on expressways during rush hours, than by providing subsidy to transit.[4]

It is probably correct that congestion pricing of the roadways would result in greater transit ridership and alleviate some traffic problems. However, congestion pricing does not have political support in the United States. Rather than pay rush hour tolls or fees, automobile users would rather pay taxes to transit agencies to keep bus and train riders from making already congested urban expressways more congested. Thus, automobile users are able to drive for "free" any time of day or night—albeit slowly during commute hours. This is the logic behind the political consensus that has developed in favor of transit subsidies over congestion pricing.

Marketing's role in cost control

Transit subsidies are a form of third party payment for service. As with other uses of third party payments (e.g., health insurance), guaranteeing efficient use of funds is a difficult task. Managers are not as accountable for controlling costs because third party payments can shield an organization from the market pressure of decreasing consumer demand resulting from escalating prices being fueled by uncontrolled costs. In a competitive, nonsubsidized operation, cost control is critical to implementing pricing strategies as well as to the ability of the organization to generate an acceptable profit. Failure to do so results in dissatisfied shareholders and ultimately a bankrupt organization.

While transit agencies are not held accountable to shareholders, they often receive vigorous oversight from political bodies that authorize taxpayer expenditures. Transit funding crises in the early 1980s were dramatized by a transit shutdown in Boston and massive service reductions and fare increases in Chicago. These crises were, in part, the result over a period of years of huge budget increases exceeding the inflation index.

The public felt it was getting worse, not better, service for its money. Transit authority issues became highly politicized.

From a marketing point of view, it is important that transit agencies present themselves to the public as efficient organizations or risk loss of support for public financing. The resolution of the crisis in Boston occurred with the passage of "Management Rights" legislation, which limited use of overtime and featherbedding union agreements. In Chicago, restraints were placed on labor contracts by the legislature and a 50 percent cost-recovery formula was mandated. While inflexible use of cost recovery formulas can limit the use of promotional fares, the formulas can be effective. According to Ronald J. Hartman, head of the Maryland MTA, "For us, it has imposed discipline. We are a leaner organization."[5]

The varying objectives of transit pricing

There are a number of objectives that can be sought in pricing transportation services. Objectives for pricing transit include profit seeking, revenue enhancement, cost covering, maximizing ridership, and managing demand. It is important to realize that these objectives can be in conflict with each other. For example, attempting to generate the largest number of passengers may not maximize the revenues.

In practice, pricing strategies cannot be developed with the single-minded aim of satisfying just one objective. Realistically, each of the five objectives plays a role in developing a pricing strategy, although the comparative importance of each may vary over time and from one situation to another.

Profits. Most transit organizations are not in the business of setting prices that will generate a profit. However, there are instances where a transit operator will price certain services to yield a profit that will help cross-subsidize other services. For example, premium express bus services for commuters and bus charters are operations that can be priced high enough at times so that they might actually generate a profit for the organization (at least in terms of their marginal cost of operation).

Revenue enhancement. Often a goal for a transit organization is to maximize revenue from the farebox, even if it does not produce a profit. A revenue seeking organization will attempt to set fares at a maximum level without producing such a large drop in ridership as to negate the impact of the fare increase. In times of fiscal austerity, transit authorities are pressured to adopt revenue enhancing strategies.

Cost-coverage. Transit authorities are coming under increasing pressure to implement cost-covering approaches so that fares cover a certain percentage of operating expenses. With a significant growth of public subsidy for transit in the 1970s, proponents of cost-covering believe that it is important that the user should pay a fair share of transit costs. In addition, cost-covering approaches attempt to ensure that subsidy dollars are being wisely spent and not being wasted on marginal services with low ridership.

There is certain justification to the view that cost-covering objectives can make transit management more accountable for improving the efficiency of transit by forcing managers to hold down costs.

Maximizing of ridership. The goal of passenger-oriented pricing is to maximize the number of passengers. Various industries in the private sector have seen profits eroded as companies engage in price wars in order to increase market share (percentage of consumers using a given company). While transit organizations do want to increase ridership, wholesale discounting of prices can result in significant loss of potential revenue and/or overburdening the system during peak periods—where capacity may be constrained. Thus, it is important for transit authorities to recognize differing ability to pay and differing dependence on transit among various market segments, and to price accordingly.

Pricing and demand management

Airline services are similar to public transit in that they are highly susceptible to shifts in demand over time. An empty seat is a lost sale. A fully booked aircraft may cause would-be passengers to be turned away. Thus, airlines have developed demand-management pricing of their services. Fares differ based on season, day of week, and even time of day. Airlines offer discount, off-peak fares to encourage ridership while pricing peak services at a premium because the market for premium fares (the business traveler) is willing to pay a higher fare.

Demand-management pricing—whether off-peak discounts or peak-period surcharges—has been used in various industries to meet one or more of three goals. First, demand-management pricing can help to redistribute demand from the peak to the off-peak. Second, off-peak discounting can be used to generate new demand in time periods when an organization has extra capacity. And third, peak load pricing can be used to generate increased revenue from peak users who may be less sensitive to price increases.

Since adding capacity to handle incremental peak demand is quite expensive, higher peak prices can be rationalized on an accounting basis as well as on a marketing analysis. But, demand-management pricing for transit must be designed with careful analysis and consideration of objectives.

Redistributing the peak. In an attempt to redistribute demand, the Massachusetts Bay Transportation Authority (MBTA) sought to decrease crowding at peak hours and increase it at midday by offering a 60 percent fare discount between 10 a.m. and 2 p.m. Although the MBTA attracted some new riders during these times, management eventually discontinued the experiment because only a small percentage of rush-hour commuters switched to travel during off-peak hours. The problem, it became evident, was not that the discount lacked appeal, but simply that most people traveling to and from work lacked control over their hours of employment. The moral? Understand the factors determining the timing of demand before trying to change it. Thus demand-management pricing cannot accomplish for transit the goal of shifting demand from peak to off-peak periods. Subsequently, the MBTA developed a marketing program to encourage employers to adopt variable work hours as a demand management program (which is discussed in Chapter 9).

Improving cost recovery with peak surcharges. A more successful case of demand-management pricing is in Washington, D.C., where Metro adopted peak pricing for its new rail system. On Metro rail, a peak surcharge is added to all fares during the morning and evening rush hours. While the surcharge may not have an effect on managing demand, Metro has identified a market (commuters) who can afford to pay and will pay a higher fare for the high quality rail service at a time of day when roads are congested and parking is constrained. In essence, commuters in Washington cross-subsidize more price sensitive off-peak users. From an operations point of view, the peak service is quite expensive due to high utilization of equipment and labor over a relatively short period of time. Thus, demand-management pricing at Metro has incorporated operational, revenue, cost, and passenger objectives.

Increase demand for off-peak services. Another use of demand-management pricing is to reduce fare in the off-peak in order to increase ridership. Discounting off-peak prices can be advantageous to the transit authority. Adding passengers to an empty train or bus costs almost nothing, and thus may be profitable—even when fares are heavily discounted. Conversely, adding extra discounted passengers to an already full train results in overcrowding—which discourages other full fare passengers from using the system—or costs the transit authority money by having to add additional capacity. While time-of-day discounting was not successful in Boston, day-of-week discounting has had better success in other cities. For example, in Chicago a targeted fare decrease on Sundays of 44 percent produced a 100 percent increase in Sunday ridership.[6]

A nationwide study of time-of-day pricing found that the most prevalent reason for demand-management pricing was to encourage ridership to shift from peak to off-peak:

Unfortunately, there was little empirical evidence to suggest that time-of-day fare programs to date have accomplished just that, although in most cases the proportion of total ridership during off-peak periods rose. Off-peak users were found to be more sensitive to differential fare changes than peak riders . . . Cost recovery rates did increase significantly for most peak surcharge programs . . . The most successful programs have been those which collect fares on the basis of run direction (rather than exact time) and which aggressively marketed their programs.[7]

DETERMINING PRICE ELASTICITY

The concept of elasticity is used to determine the impact of fare changes on ridership. For transit use, elasticity relates the percentage change in ridership to the percentage change in fare. When a small change in fares has a big impact on ridership, demand is said to be "price elastic." In the reverse situation, when a change in price has little effect on ridership, demand is described as "price inelastic."

Historically, transit ridership has been quite sensitive to fare increases (price elastic). A landmark study by Simpson and Curtin in 1968 determined that on average, a 10 percent change in fares will produce a 3 percent loss of ridership, referred to as an elasticity of -0.3.[8] While fare increases, on average, benefit the transit authority with increasing revenue, the fare change does produce a ridership loss. Subsequent studies of fare increases have found that price elasticities, on average, have remained constant through the 1970s and early 1980s.[9] Systemwide fare reductions in Toronto and Atlanta demonstrated price elasticity to fare reductions to be comparable to fare increases: generating new ridership, but at considerable revenue loss.[10]

Disaggregate elasticities

Relying on aggregate analysis of fare changes is perhaps too simple. Some differences in fare elasticity exist between different market segments. There is some indication that considerable differences exist between peak riders and off-peak users. For example, a study of a fare increase by the Southeastern Michigan Transportation Authority found that "transit trip making in the off-peak period appears to be nearly twice as sensitive as that in the peak period."[11] Shoppers and the elderly are also more price sensitive than commuters. Those with a choice of travel modes are twice as likely to abandon transit when faced with a fare increase than are commuters, captive riders, the poor, and students.[12]

The problem that many transit authorities face when pricing fares is that the bulk of ridership consists of commuters. If commuters are half as price sensitive as off-peak users but constitute more than half the ridership, then a relatively smaller percentage loss can translate into a very large ridership loss in absolute numbers. Thus, transit authorities can find themselves in a paradox. The best approach to raising fares, facing the twin objectives of maximizing revenue and minimizing aggregate ridership loss, may be to bias fare subsidies in favor of commuters. (But this approach only further worsens the ratio of peak to off-peak travel.)

Service elasticities

At times, transit authorities may shy away from a fare increase, due to loss of ridership, and contemplate reductions in service instead. However, service elasticities can be far greater than price elasticities. A study in Chicago found that a service reduction of 2.2 percent produced a 2.2 percent drop in ridership. This 1.0 service elasticity indicates consumer sensitivity to a reduction in service at over three times that of fare increase. The authors of the Chicago study concluded: "While it is more costly to pay a higher fare, the elimination of a train can be more serious than the burden of an additional expense. It can be argued that the rider response may be to postpone the trip so that another train can be used, but that is frequently not practical."[13]

The UMTA *Manual for Planning and Implementing a Fare Change* suggests the importance of balancing fares and service levels:

There is a tendency to think of the fare level only in terms of what it will do to the financial condition of the transit agency. Seldom, if ever, do transit managers plan fare changes in conjunction with service changes to meet ridership needs. . . . Money spent holding fares down might produce more ridership and revenue if it were spent maintaining or increasing services. . . . The principal problem with transit planning today is that fare and service-level decisions are seldom jointly planned, even though fares and service levels are intrinsically related. In addition, less traditional fare and service concepts are seldom given serious consideration when major policy changes are under review.[14]

FARE STRUCTURE

There are two basic approaches to charging for individual transit trips. One is to charge one fee for entry into the system, as is the case in the New York subway system, and riders travel short or long distances for the same price. Another approach is to charge a relatively low entry fee to gain access to the transit system and then to add mileage supplements or incremental zoned fares. London Transport implemented a popular "core area" base fare, which resulted in an initial reduction in fares for short trips, but increased fares to outlying areas.

In the United States, San Francisco's BART and Washington's Metro, relying on expensive fare card technology, use zone-based fares. Numerous bus systems use zone based fares and charge more for longer trips.

In Boston, the MBTA has implemented a unified zone-based fare structure, based on mileage, which applies to all modes of public transit—bus, rapid transit, and commuter rail. A passenger traveling by a suburban express bus will pay the same fare as a commuter rail user providing that the trips are equivalent in mileage.

Discount fare strategies

Urban transit systems are positioned in the marketplace as the low cost transportation carrier. A number of transit authorities have at times fulfilled that role by charging all riders the lowest possible fare. Yet, farebox revenue can be maximized without losing ridership by developing a targeted discount fare strategy. By understanding the needs, behavior, and ability to pay of different market segments, transit authorities can develop different fares for different groups.

Price segmentation strategies

In economic terms, multiple fare categories is a form of "price discrimination" because the different fares do not reflect a proportional difference in marginal cost to the operator. The different fares may reflect the ability of different groups to pay for transit or the value of the transit trip to different market segments. For price discrimination to work, certain conditions must exist:

- The market must be segmentable and the segments must show a different price sensitivity.
- There should be no chance of the members of one segment, having paid the lower price, turning around and selling their ticket to another segment.
- There should be little chance of competition underselling when pricing high in one segment.
- The cost of segmenting and policing the market should not exceed the extra revenue derived.
- The customer should not become confused or upset by the use of multiple fares.

Different segments within the traveling public not only vary in terms of their travel needs (and the benefits they seek) but also in terms of when they travel and their ability to pay. For example, Golden Gate Transit in Northern California offers a number of premium express bus routes and ferry services from the suburbs to downtown San Francisco. Golden Gate has found that many suburban commuters are looking for speed and comfort when commuting to work, but are not as price sensitive as many urban residents. This group wants a premium service and is willing to pay a higher fare for quality.

A contrasting example is the 50 percent discount fares offered to the elderly in the Boston area by the MBTA. The use of the discount fare is restricted to off-peak periods because of capacity constraints during the rush hour. The restriction on use helps shape the timing of travel by discount travelers in order to fill up trains and buses in the off-peak hours when capacity is available.

Promotional prices

Discounting can also be used for promotional purposes when markets are highly segmented. London Transport has introduced special fares and passes for visitors and tourists to London. Visitor passes, which often come with a map, have been promoted internationally in cooperation with local tourist authorities. Another use of promotional discounting is to distribute free coupons in a neighborhood to encourage trial use of a new bus route or even an existing route. In any situation, the discount should be targeted and have a clearly defined objective prior to introduction.

A key criterion for any promotional program is that the fares should be simple to use for the consumer and simple to administer for the transit authority. For example, it would hardly be beneficial to introduce a pricing program that made it easy for a small but visible minority of riders to evade fare payment. Use of an honor system for fare payment can simplify use for the consumer and administration for the operator. But, while successful in Amsterdam and some other European cities, an honor system did not work when attempted in Portland, Oregon. (In contrast, American operators in large urban areas are reluctant to have bus drivers attempt to strictly enforce fare payment when faced with unruly riders on late night bus runs.)

Fare prepayment: The use of transit passes

A transit authority has to make a number of key decisions about fare collection:

Who should collect payment?

When should fares be paid?

Where should fares be paid?

How should fares be paid?

The "Who, When, Where, and How" of fare collection comes into play when considering the adoption of a fare prepayment program. While technology is having a major effect on cash payments in many transit systems, it is having little impact on the marketing of transit. Off-peak pricing, as an example, is just as feasible with exact fare vacuum machines as by hand methods. By comparison, changes in technology and the social and political climate are having a pronounced effect on the role that fare prepayment can have on marketing transit.

The use of punch cards to facilitate prepayment of fares has existed for about as long as public transit itself. The use of such "passes" reached a peak in 1935–1945 and then began a steady decline until the late 1960s. During the early 1970s a major revival of interest in fare prepayment occurred and a number of fare repayment systems are now in use. They vary by defining maximum number of trips (fixed or unlimited) and by limiting use to a certain length of time (day, week, month). Exhibit 8–1 outlines a classification of prepayment approaches.

Exhibit 8–1
Classification of Prepayment Passes

		Maximum number of trips	
		FIXED	**UNLIMITED**
Duration of instrument	**UNLIMITED**	A. **Trip pass** —Punch card, magnetic card, ticket book, etc. —"good for 10 trips"	B. **Non-expiring passes** —employees —senior citizens **Credit cards**
	FIXED	C. **Fixed duration/fixed number of trips** —"10 trips this week" —"2 trips per day"	D. **Fixed duration passes** —daily, weekly, monthly

Growing use of prepayment

Increased interest in fare prepayment reflects the impact of new technology, consumer convenience, social welfare considerations, and public policy. Each of these is discussed briefly below:

New Technology. The advent of a number of sophisticated technologies—magnetic card recording, self-indented wires, and light pattern readers—has opened up the opportunity for automatic passes. These passes do not require staffing at transit stations to monitor a pass gate, since they are used to operate automatic turnstiles. More importantly, they can provide an opportunity for an accurate count of the number of pass-riders on the system. Therefore they offer the potential benefit of increased productivity and control. However, pass reading equipment for buses is still at the research and development phase.[15]

Consumer convenience. The advent of exact fare requirements created an inconvenience for the consumer. A pass that removes the need for exact change has therefore acquired a major benefit—convenience. There is also convenience for the transit authority in that fares are collected in advance, regardless of subsequent ridership levels by passholders during the period of validity.

Social welfare. The growing awareness of the importance of mobility to the under-privileged, especially the elderly, has produced a large number of pass programs dedicated to free or reduced price travel. Fares can be paid for by a third party without inconvenience for the transit organization and without social stigma for the individual.

Public policy. With energy conservation goals and air quality mandates, transit gained support as a solution to excessive use of the automobile. From a policy perspective, transit is seen as more than just a service for the under-privileged and passes have become a mechanism for marketing transit.

Pass program design

In general, pass programs must be designed with simplicity of consumer use in mind. The more restrictive a ticketing program, the more the passenger needs to understand exactly what can and cannot be done. If the pricing program has been developed logically, it should be reasonably easy to communicate to the traveler. Conversely, if it is impossible to explain easily use of the ticket or pass, then the pricing strategy is probably confused.

Objectives. The introduction of passes requires the same careful analysis of objectives required for any pricing program. Is the goal profit seeking, revenue seeking, cost covering, operations oriented, and/or passenger oriented? Many prepayment programs are meeting more than one objective—for example, increasing ridership and producing time savings during the boarding of buses.

The objectives of a fare prepayment program should be carefully articulated. If the objective is to increase revenue, than an actual ridership gain would be needed to offset any decline in revenue per rider. If the objective is to obtain a profit, then the increase in ridership must also offset any costs of the pass program.

Unfortunately, "operators do not usually go through the formal process of setting up objectives for prepayment plans. . . . The common approach, rather, is to 'try it and see what happens.' "[16] The objectives for pass programs are, at times, only implicit: perhaps the program should increase ridership while not decreasing revenue or significantly increasing costs. Some are based on a belief that "bulk purchase" should be rewarded by some kind of discount.

In Ottawa, a bus pass was introduced with an objective of "providing subsidy benefits to regular users while allowing full-cost pricing of irregular usage."[17] The problem with this approach is that daily commuters are less price sensitive than occasional off peak users. In addition, it is more expensive to provide peak hour service than it is to provide off-peak service. By analyzing peak demand and capacity, it might make more sense to give only small promotional discounts to encourage prepayment by daily commuters and to allow those commuters to obtain significant financial savings on the weekend—when there is excess capacity.

For fare prepayment programs, objectives should incorporate market segmentation analysis based on usage. Fare prepayment can be used to maintain or increase riding by current regular users; increase riding by infrequent users; and/or encourage use by nonriders. Another objective of a pass program could be to increase ridership by socially disadvantaged groups, such as the elderly. Exhibit 8–2 outlines how objectives for a pass program can vary by market segment and in terms of whether the transit authority's goal is to increase ridership or simply to maintain existing ridership.

Exhibit 8–2
Objectives Matrix for Pass Programs

	CURRENT REGULAR RIDERS	CURRENT IRREGULAR RIDERS	CURRENT NON-RIDERS	SOCIALLY DEPRIVED
INCREASED RIDERSHIP	A. Get a regular rider to travel off-peak or more often. These people are regular commuters.	B. Get someone who is currently splitting their travel between modes to use *all* transit.	C. Bring about a mode switch or generate trips.	D. Increase the mobility of the "transit dependent."
MAINTAIN RIDERSHIP	E. Avoid losing a regular user because of a traumatic experience: fare increase, system failure.	F. Stop someone who is definitely *not* transit dependent from going totally to another mode.	G. Not applicable.	H. Maintain the mobility of the "transit dependent."

Program features. The objectives sought by the transit authority should guide the design of the pass program and aid in deciding which types of passes (outlined in Exhibit 8–1) should be promoted to the public.

Market segmentation analysis can be used in developing more than one "pass product." In Bridgeport, Connecticut, transit planners have introduced and priced two products that meet the needs of two different groups. The first product is a low priced "fare cutter card" targeted to lower income users. The card provides unlimited travel but requires a

$0.25 payment for each trip. The second product is a more expensive commuter pass that does not require an additional fare but that can only be used during the rush hour.[18]

Transit pass products can also be developed for use on more than one carrier. On the San Francisco Peninsula, the introduction of a joint bus–train pass allowed riders to buy one pass for riding suburban commuter rail trains and connecting bus services in downtown San Francisco and in residential suburban communities. Within one year, ridership on commuter trains increased 9.4 percent with 47.2 percent of riders buying the pass.[19]

A UMTA study of fare prepayment addressed the problem of the price sensitive off-peak user and recommended the development of a new "pass product":

Day passes have significant but largely undiscovered advantages related to providing passenger convenience, encouraging off-peak travel, and meeting the needs of low-income passengers. They can be sold by the driver, even in exact fare systems, and therefore do not require the passenger to make a special trip to a prepayment outlet. Day passes not only enable people to consolidate several trips into a single day at a low price, but offer a convenient means for commuters to pay for round trips.[20]

Promotion of a fare prepayment program also must consider the objectives of the program and market segments that are being targeted. For example, if a pass program is attempting to obtain new riders, then advertising within the system (on buses, in train stations, etc.) would not make sense. However, advertising on the outside of buses could be used for promotional purposes targeting nonriders.

Pricing issues

Conflict over objectives often occurs within transit authorities over the pricing of pass programs. Marketing managers like to see the passes priced low to encourage greater use of transit. Financial managers tend to be concerned over potential loss of revenue. From a consumer perspective, there are two benefits of purchasing a pass: financial savings and convenience. While convenience is a major benefit, some monetary savings must be offered before convenience becomes relevant in a prepayment program.

In general, a fixed time period/unlimited travel pass may have little effect on revenue if properly priced: Loss of revenue from discounted travel provided to current riders will be compensated for by revenue increases produced by new transit ridership. Thus pass programs can be designed to meet the objective of increasing ridership, but not necessarily increasing revenue. For example, in Boston, transit pass holders are allowed to take a guest on the transit system for free on Sundays. With additional discounts for children, this promotion encourages families to use transit service as a group at a time when the transit authority has extra capacity. While revenues and costs remain constant, increased ridership is being promoted.

An important benefit of pass programs in large urban areas with multiple transit modes and perhaps multiple operators is a move to unified, integrated fare structures. For the consumer, paying multiple fares for a trip that may necessitate use of more than one mode or carrier can only serve as a deterrent to transit use. In Boston, the MBTA has developed a unified fare structure that sets rates based on mileage traveled—without discrimination between modes and with certain transfer privileges. In the San Francisco area, a joint transit pass has been introduced that combines use of AC Transit's bus network and BART's rail system.

Another benefit of pass programs is that they have been helpful in mitigating the effects of fare increases. During fare increases in Boston in the early 1980s, overall ridership proved to be price elastic (as one would anticipate) except that monthly pass use did not drop even though pass prices increased proportionately (after a two month promotional discount).

Probably the most important long-term benefit to transit authorities is that pass programs can be designed with distribution systems so that third parties such as employers and retail organizations can sell the passes. A distribution system involving employers opens the door for subsidy of transit passes as an employee fringe benefit—a subject discussed in Chapter 9.

CONCLUSION

Pricing is a key component of the marketing mix for transit services. While much attention focuses on aggregate price elasticity during fare increases, pricing decisions provide a rationale to relate fares to service levels. Further, promotional programs can be used to increase ridership and even revenue.

Even with public involvement, transit authority managers have a great deal of latitude in pricing transit services. Public debate implicitly concerns the amount of revenue to be achieved from the farebox. The development of detailed fare structures is a complex question for managers and involves the development of clear pricing objectives and considerable use market segmentation analysis.

It is important to recognize that not only are different people willing to pay different amounts for different services, but that people differ on the amount that they will pay for the same service. Market segmentation is the tool for identifying distinct target markets and pricing services accordingly.

NOTES

1. "Free fares: Will it work?" *Metropolitan* (May 1979).

2. For a recent case study of fare stabilization used to save a transit service, see "Southern Pacific fare stabilization program" in *Transportation Systems Management: Implementation and Impacts: Case Studies*. DOT-I-82-59, prepared for UMTA (New York: Urbitran Assoc., March 1982).

3. Vaziri, Manouchehr. "Consideration of special user groups in regular transit operation and finance" (Dept. of Civil Engineering, Univ. of Kentucky, Lexington, KY), unpublished paper presented at Transportation Research Board Annual Meeting (January 1986), p. 11.

4. For a discussion of urban transportation pricing, see Transportation Research Board, *Urban Transportation Economics*, Special Report 181 (Washington, D.C.: National Academy of Sciences, 1978), pp. 10–65.

5. Young, David. "Farebox recovery ratio: A solution or trap?" *Mass Transit* (May 1985): 17.

6. Pikarsky, Milton, and Daphne Christensen. *Urban Transportation Policy and Management* (Lexington, Mass.: Lexington Books, 1976), p. 172.

7. Cervero, Robert. "Experience with time-of-day transit pricing in the United States," Dept. of City of Regional Planning, Univ. of California–Berkeley, unpublished paper presented at Transportation Research Board Annual Meeting (1985) (abstract).

8. For a discussion of price elasticity, see Urban Mass Transportation Administration, *Pricing: Transit Marketing Management Handbook* (1976), pp. 6–13.

9. Boyle, Daniel K. *Transportation Analysis: Report #44*, August 1984 (New York State Department of Transportation, Albany, N.Y. 12232). Also see Lago Mayworm and X. McEnroe, *Patronage Impacts of Changes in Transit Fares and Services*, prepared for UMTA (Bethesda, MD: Ecosometrics, Inc., 1980).

10. Pikarsky and Christensen, *Urban Transportation*, op. cit., p. 172.

11. Damm-Luhr, David L. "Assessment of a transit fare increase: The case of the Southeastern Michigan Transportation Authority," in *Trends in Transit Marketing and Fare Policy*, Transportation Research Record 972 (Transportation Research Board, 1984).

12. Lago, Armando, and Patrick Mayworm, quoted in David Young, "Fares/riders: Ups & Downs," *Mass Transit* (June 1983): 14.

13. Soot, S., and H.H. Stenson. *Transit Information and Transit Knowledge: The Chicago Experience*, NTIS #PB83-2626565-9 prepared for UMTA (Chicago: Urban Transportation Center, Univ. of Illinois at Chicago, May 1983), p. 22.

14. *A Manual for Planning and Implementing a Fare Change*, UMTA-MD-06-0093-85-1, prepared for UMTA (Ecosometrics, Inc., August 1984), pp. 3–4.

15. Markowitz, Joel. "Prospects for differential transit pricing in the U.S." (Metropolitan Transportation Commission, 101 8th St., Oakland, CA), unpublished paper presented at the Transportation Research Board Annual Meeting (January 1986), p. 22.

16. Urban Mass Transportation Administration, *Transit Fare Prepayment* (Washington, D.C.: Office of Services and Methods Demonstration, 1976), p. 124.

17. Bureau of Management Consulting (September 1977).

18. Oram, Richard, et al. "The fare cutter card: A revenue-efficient and mar-ket-segmented approach to transit pass pricing," in *Transit Management and Services*, Transportation Research Record 947 (Transportation Research Board, 1983), p. 28–33.

19. Slater, Geoff. "The Peninsula pass: Joint transit pricing in the San Francisco Area" (Metropolitan Transportation Commission, 101 8th St., Oakland, CA), unpublished paper presented at the Transportation Research Board Annual Meeting (January 1986), p. 27–28.

20. Hershey, W.R., et al. *Transit Fare Prepayment*, prepared for UMTA Office of Transit Management (Ann Arbor: Huron River Group, August 1976), xiv.

9
Working with Third Parties

In previous chapters we have discussed transit marketing primarily in terms of two-party interactions—the transit agency promoting its services directly to existing or potential riders. In contrast, this chapter focuses on marketing transit through use of "third parties": intermediary organizations that benefit from transit service and are capable of influencing consumer behavior.

Why should transit authorities work with third parties?

A third party may be an employer capable of encouraging employees to use public transit by selling monthly transit passes to employees, perhaps discounted as an employee benefit. Other types of third parties who may help transit authorities are government service organizations, such as libraries, which may be willing to display and distribute bus schedules, or a post office, which may sell transit passes to the public at large. Additionally, certain retail organizations may cooperate in a joint promotion with a transit agency or even sell transit passes to the public (for a small fee).

Leverage. A major benefit of working with "third parties" is that the transit organization can significantly leverage its own resources by obtaining assistance, at negligible cost, from participating groups. For example, companies that sell transit passes to their employees provide the transit agency with a distribution system at virtually no cost. In essence, the company administrator responsible for selling the passes becomes a sales representative for the transit authority but is paid by the participating company.

Credibility. Another important benefit to transit authorities of obtaining cooperation from other organizations is that third parties may have more credibility with consumers than the organization that is trying to make a "sale." For example, outside of the transportation industry, one often encounters restaurants and movie theaters displaying favorable reviews from local newspapers and television stations. The consumer tends to receive these critiques by "objective" third parties favorably. When the third party happens to be an employer, the message can be interpreted as an endorsement with a certain amount of "friendly persuasion." The annual United Way fundraising campaign for charities is an example of voluntary cooperation of employers (and participating employees) helping local community services. It is a highly successful method of raising large amounts of funds for good causes at low administrative cost—due to the donation of staff time, a distribution system, and the implied endorsement of participating employers.

Marketing to third parties. Obtaining cooperation of third parties requires some understanding of industrial marketing strategies and techniques. A sales approach to an organization is quite different from that targeted to an individual consumer. Marketing staff need to identify and work with decision makers as well as those responsible for implementation. It is also often necessary to secure support from groups such as local chambers of commerce to provide validation of a transit agency's outreach activity to private businesses.

In the case of employer transportation programs, effective industrial sales require an understanding and consideration of the targeted organization's problems and needs (as well as those of specific manager and department). It may be helpful to offer businesses a product line of programs rather than simply one program. Different organizations have different problems, needs, and biases. By having a product line—which can include transit passes (subsidized or not), variable work hours, ridesharing and parking management programs—corporate managers can choose which program, or combination of programs, best meet their needs. Transit marketing personnel can play the role of "consultants" assisting organizations to custom design a transportation program to meet their needs.

FACTORS MOTIVATING THIRD PARTIES TO WORK WITH TRANSIT AUTHORITIES

Three factors are likely to motivate a third party organization to cooperate with a public transit agency, although the relative importance of each factor will vary from situation to situation. First, a cooperative program is seen as benefiting employees or clients. Second, the program is perceived as being of benefit to the community. Third—and often most important—the program is viewed by management as benefiting the organization itself. In brief, enlightened self-interest probably best describes the rationale for much public–private cooperation.

An example of enlightened self–interest's motivating cooperation occurred when the energy crises of the 1970s galvanized interest in employer cooperation with public transit agencies. Employees were facing dramatically increasing gasoline prices and, at times, long lines at gas stations. A significant problem existed for many communities and the nation as a whole.

The first company in the United States to participate in a transit pass program—the John Hancock Mutual Life Insurance Company in Boston—did so after the 1973/74 gasoline shortages. Corporate executives decided that public transportation played an important role in the company's future in Boston. In order to "do something" to show a commitment to transit, the company agreed to participate in an experiment of offering monthly transit passes by payroll deduction. The sequel: ten years later, 500 companies in Boston were selling passes to their employees, although the original motivation of coping with an energy crunch has long since disappeared.

Another factor likely to motivate some managers is what their peers are doing in other organizations. For example, managers are likely to be influenced if a similar organization sells transit passes to its employees and that program is perceived as successful. This is difficult for the transit sales representatives who are trying to make their first sell. Yet independent endorsement can be as persuasive in industrial marketing situations as in consumer marketing. (See Exhibit 9–1 of endorsements obtained by the Baltimore Regional Planning Commission.)

Examples of third-party cooperation

Organizations likely to cooperate with a transit authority are those that receive some benefits from public transportation.

Employers. An employer whose plant or offices are served by transit recognizes that many employees rely on transit to get to work. These employees benefit from the transit service (which makes the job accessible and saves them the expense of owning and operating a car for commuting purposes). The employer meantime does not have to be concerned about the costs and hassle of providing additional parking. Resources that might otherwise have to be tied up in parking lots or structures can instead be invested more usefully elsewhere.

Further, a rationale of "helping our people" with a view to maintaining good relationships with employees may motivate many employers to participate in distributing transit passes. In a national survey, 72.8 percent of companies involved in employee transportation cited "the desire to provide an employee benefit" as a major motivation.[1]

Retailers. Particularly in downtown areas, retail stores benefit from transit because public transportation brings a market of consumers to their door steps. Without transit service, these customers might not

Exhibit 9–1
Corporate Endorsements in Maryland of Employer Programs

"Variable work hours benefits employees and management at vir-
tually no cost to the company."
Frank Mitchell, Employee Policies Analyst
Baltimore Gas & Electric

"Employees who use the [subsidized] bus pass love it—it's a benefit
they see every day. They feel 'the company cares about me.' "
Judy Baker, Asst. Vice President
Chesapeake Life Insurance Company

"Dollar for dollar, it [the subsidized pass program] is the best benefit
we have."
Joseph J. Avis, Director of Human Resources
The Riggs National Bank

"The vanpool program has resulted in improved attendance, morale
and productivity. What's more, all talk of a new parking deck has
ceased."
Walter Dennison, Administrative Services Supervisor
Bechtel Corporation

"In addition to saving considerable garage space, the vanpool pro-
gram has evolved into a low-cost employee benefit."
R. N. Holmber, Director, Marketing Administration
Commercial Credit

Source: Hidden Business Costs of Employee Commuting, Regional Planning
Council, Baltimore, MD.

patronize the stores at all because of parking problems or lack of access by
car.

Real estate developers. These represent another category of private sector
beneficiaries of transit. Of particular importance to cities with rail systems is the fact that rapid transit stations tend to increase the values of
nearby land and buildings. Joint or cooperative development is often
possible between transit systems and private real estate interests.

Libraries, schools and other public agencies. Since transit is a public service,
it is also possible to obtain cooperation from organizations that do not
directly benefit from transit but, like transit agencies, are also involved in
providing public services. For example, public libraries are often willing
to display timetables and distribute them free of charge to visitors. Public
schools in some areas have cooperated with transit agencies in providing
students with transit education programs. The schools and libraries may
not receive any benefit from transit, per se, but it is understood that their
clients—children and library users—do benefit from their cooperation.

SPREADING RUSH HOUR DEMAND

A serious problem faced in marketing transit service is matching the timing of demand to service availability. Transit systems have the dilemma of managing both excess capacity and excess demand—which occur at different times of the day. Travel demand during the rush hour determines the number of vehicles and personnel needed by a transit authority—but outside peak periods, productivity is low. During off-peak periods, equipment either lies idle or runs half empty, and many transit employees have time on their hands. If travel demands could be distributed evenly throughout the day, less staff and fewer vehicles would be needed to transport the same total number of passengers.

The other side of the peaking problem is the difficulty of promoting transit service to commuters if buses and trains are at 100 percent capacity during the rush hour. While capacity could be increased to handle new demand, it becomes extremely expensive to add an additional unit of service that may only be needed for perhaps two hours each day. Even use of part-time drivers (while helpful) does not really address a capacity surplus that often exists in the hour before and after the "rush hour." These are the time periods when commuters are most likely to use the system if they are able to shift their working hours.

While most transit systems have additional capacity off-peak, it has been difficult to shift excess rush hour demand to fill the available supply. Looking to the consumer to redistribute transit demand outside the peak has proven to be ineffective. Offering discounts in the off-peak to motivate morning and evening commuters to change commuting times has not worked (as described in the discussion of peak-load pricing in Chapter 8). Transit agencies have found that the timing of demand for their services is, in most cases, out of the control of the transit user. The timing of peak demand for transit is determined by a third party—the employer. Therefore, marketing strategies to redistribute peak demand need to focus on employers.

Variable work hour programs

Interest in variable work hours—variations from the traditional "9 to 5" working hours—has increased dramatically for two reasons. First, the need for demand-management techniques has increased in many urban areas as peak travel has outstripped capacity for both public transportation and road systems. Second, variable work hours offer a number of non-transportation benefits to employees and, most importantly, to employers.

The two major variable work hour programs are staggered work hours and "flexitime." Each results in a shift of employees' working hours to earlier or later time blocks during the work day, thereby spreading peak travel demand.

Staggered work hours is the more conservative approach. It may involve either an entire organization, or a group of employees (such as a department), or an individual employee. In each instance, work hours are changed to a new time frame and this newly defined schedule is then adhered to. *Flexitime* allows employees a greater degree of freedom in varying work hours each day, so long as the requisite number of hours are worked each week or pay period.

Both staggered work hours and flexitime help spread peak transportation demand. However, the programs offering more individual choice allow employees to adjust their work hours to meet the schedules of transit routes with less frequent service.

Marketing programs to shift peak demand by promoting use of variable work hours have been successful in New York City, Newark, Philadelphia, Toronto, Madison (Wisconsin), and Riverside (California)[2] as well as in Boston and San Francisco. In New York, the Port Authority of New York and New Jersey developed an active promotional campaign (see Exhibit 9–2). In Boston, the MBTA began promoting variable work hour programs to employers after the failure of its "dime-time" pricing promotion. (This was designed to spread travel demand to the off-peak by reducing the then–25 cents fare to just 10 cents between 10:00 a.m. and 2:00 p.m.). The MBTA obtained the cooperation of the area Chamber of Commerce in sponsoring conferences and workshops for employers explaining the benefits of variable work hours and providing information for personnel managers on how to introduce the programs in their organizations (see Exhibit 9–3). As a result, the MBTA has been able to redistribute peak loading demand at key downtown subway stations by 20 percent.

Demonstrating the benefits

The key to successful marketing of variable work hours has been to demonstrate the benefit of these programs to the employer and employees—not just the benefits to the transit organization. Fortunately, a good deal of research in the human resources field has clearly documented benefits for participating employees and organizations. Benefits include increased productivity, the elimination of punctuality as an issue, less personal business conducted on company time, less absenteeism, reduced personnel turnover, additional recruiting leverage, and lower unit labor costs. Half or more of all user companies experience economic gains; few experience net losses.[3]

For the employee, benefits often include less time spent commuting, increased job satisfaction, and more time for leisure, personal business, and family activities. In an analysis of the flexitime experience at the First National Bank of Maryland, it was noted:

Exhibit 9–2
Poster to Promote Use of Staggered Work Hours

Source: Courtesy of the Port Authority of New York & New Jersey.

One other major benefit from the system was the creation of a more adult atmosphere. No longer did employees have to ask for time off for doctor or dentist appointments. Missed rides, traffic jams, or late baby sitters no longer brought the pressure and frustration as they had with the traditional nine-to-five schedule. Without question, employees responded in a positive manner when given some control over their lives.[4]

Indicative of most corporate experience, a survey at the First National Bank of Maryland indicated that 90 percent of the employees and 100 percent of the supervisors wished to continue with flexible work hours.[5] Well over 90 percent of all organizations that have started flexitime programs have continued them.[6]

Employer distribution channels for passes and information

Employers can also be asked to assist transit authorities by encouraging transit use among their own employees. Companies can be a very effective distribution channel for transit information and for the sale of transit passes.

A study in Santa Clara County, California, showed that employees prefer to get information about transit rates and schedules from their employer.[7] Providing up-to-date transit information on a periodic basis to employers for distribution to employees is a relatively easy and low cost marketing activity for a transit authority. Compared to the other methods of distributing the same information, this approach is considerably more efficient. It does, however, impose an additional discipline since information given to such third parties must be timely and accurate if the ongoing relationship is not to be upset.

A number of transit authorities have developed monthly pass programs and some have sold passes to employers for resale to employees, often by payroll deduction. For the consumer, the sale of passes adds some of the psychological benefits of a "membership" relationship between the consumer and the transit agency. It replaces numerous small discrete purchases with one monthly transaction. If sold through payroll deduction or at the work site, it adds a significant measure of convenience by eliminating the need to travel to a sales outlet.

Retail outlets may also be willing to sell monthly transit passes at minimal cost to the transit authority. The retailer provides a public service, assists current customers, and obtains a flow of potential new customers into the store. In a number of cities, banks, post offices, and merchants (as well as employers) sell monthly transit passes.

While staffing a corporate sales division with a couple of professionals and support staff may sound expensive to a marketing director, the payoffs can be considerable. In Boston, for example, the MBTA pass program staff have been able to generate $30 million annually in pass

Exhibit 9–3

Employer's Guide

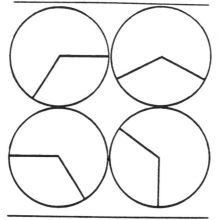

Breaking the 9-5 Habit:

Employer's Guide to the Design and Implementation of a Variable Work Hours Program

Produced under contract
MASSACHUSETTS BAY TRANSPORTATION AUTHORITY

revenue for the authority through the sale of passes at 500 employers and retail outlets—all at no direct cost to the authority. Pass sales account for over one-third of all fare revenues for the MBTA.

Subsidizing transit passes as an employee benefit

Some companies in nineteen cities also subsidize the purchase price of the passes as a fringe benefit. Tax law changes by Congress in 1984 provide that up to $15 per month of a transit pass can be provided by employers as a tax-free fringe benefit.[8] A rationale for Congressional action was that free and subsidized employee parking is a tax-free fringe benefit and something needed to be done to correct the tax bias in favor of driving over transit use. Prior attempts to eliminate the tax benefits for free parking were unsuccessful. (At the state level, California allows employees to deduct up to $7.00 per month on tax returns for transit passes.[9])

The provision of free parking by employers has historically provided employees with a powerful incentive for commuting alone by car. This incentive is heightened when no comparable incentives are provided for use of public transportation or ridesharing. Some organizations now provide equal commuting benefits to all employees. Chesapeake Life in Maryland, for example, provides each employee with an $18 per month transportation benefit, which can be applied toward a transit pass or toward the price of parking. As noted earlier, the employer may benefit from not having to expand parking facilities and being able to invest parking expansion funds more profitably elsewhere. In some instances, a combination of increased parking fees, transit subsidies, and encouragement of carpools and vanpools may even allow an employer to reduce the amount of land presently taken up by parking lots.

Subsidizing transit passes has other financial benefits, too. Employees receive the actual dollar value of the transit subsidy, up to $15 per month, without having to pay tax on it while the company can write off the subsidy as an expense. An equivalent payment by a company to an employee as a wage increase would be diminished by withholding to the federal government for social security and for taxes. Thus, for the same cost to the company, an employee receives "more" from a tax-free fringe benefit such as a transit pass than from an equivalent pay increase.

Transit subsidy programs offered by employers in Denver, Fort Worth, and San Francisco have resulted in a 5 percent increase in transit use with a 50 percent subsidy and a 10 percent increase with a 100 percent subsidy.[10] Another benefit to transit authorities of employee transit subsidy is that employer participation in fare payments can help mitigate the impact of fare increases because the fares are already discounted and the employer absorbs part of the cost of the fare increase. Businesses, in turn, would rather provide user-side subsidies to their employees than make special purpose tax payments directly to a public transit authority.

Retailer subsidy of transit fares

Payment of customers' parking expenses by validating their parking checks has long been used by retailers as a device to encourage patronage by car drivers. The same approach can also be used to attract transit users. Instead of paying parking fees for the customer, the retailer can offer to pay the transit fares.

Possible approaches include reimbursing the customer for the trip to the retailer (which requires some proof of transit use) and giving customers who purchase more than a certain amount of merchandise a token or coupon valid for the return journey. Retailers can also sell tokens or passes at a small discount to the public or to customers who purchase a minimum dollar value of merchandise. In Chicago, the CTA was able to develop a cooperative program in the late 1970s with a major supermarket to sell ten tokens for the price of nine at a number of local outlets and with a local appliance chain to provide return transit fare to customers.

Joint promotions

An established pass program provides a distribution system for reaching a well defined market of consumers who may be attractive to local retailers. A number of transit authorities have provided merchants with access to pass holders as part of joint promotional efforts.

A typical joint promotion will involve a retailer's offering a discount on merchandise to transit passholders in exchange for the transit authority's publicizing the discount at low or no cost to the retailer. The benefit to the retailer is low cost advertising to a targeted market. In addition, the pass holders represent a clearly identified group of people with a number of things in common. This allows for a better targeting of promotions.

The benefit to the transit authority is that merchant discounts to pass-holders increase the potential value of a transit pass to the consumer. Seattle Metro has had over 180 organizations providing discounts to passholders. Participants have included performing arts groups, retail stores, restaurants, fitness centers, and sports events.[11]

In Los Angeles, joint promotions have been provided to purchasers of Sunday unlimited travel passes. Purchasers of the Sunday tickets have been provided coupon books with discounts at the Los Angeles Zoo, the NBC Studio tour, the Queen Mary tour, outdoor recreation centers, and Wendy's Restaurants.[12]

In Boston, the MBTA has obtained discounts for passholders at a number of major museums and attractions as well as from retailers. In Massachusetts, transit users who purchase 11 passes per year also receive a 10 percent discount on their automobile insurance (up to $75). The theory for the discount is that automobile owners who use public transit to commute to work drive fewer miles and therefore have less exposure to automobile accidents.

In planning for special events, Ticketron reservation systems can be used for advance purchase of tickets for both events and for public transit. In 1984, the Olympics in Los Angeles and a Tall Ships Festival in Rochester, New York, both successfully relied on Ticketron for advance purchase of special bus passes in conjunction with event tickets. A strategy relying on Ticketron is applicable for one-time regional or national events where reservations are needed, where transportation capacity is limited, and where there is a premium price for premium service.[13]

WORKING WITH PUBLIC AUTHORITIES

Transit authorities need not focus solely on private sector organizations when looking for cooperation in improving transit services. The construction of urban transit malls in cities such as Portland (Oregon), Vancouver (B.C.), Minneapolis, and Long Beach (California), are examples of transit's playing a vital role in efforts to improve downtown business areas.[14] While involvement of local business is important to business district revitalization programs, the influx of public funds by local government agencies is critical to improving public facilities.

Transit agencies receive significant benefits of looking for assistance of both public and private organizations. In Ottawa, Ontario, the introduction of bus lanes on select streets, coupled with flexible working hours and a hike in parking charges resulted in reduced bus travel times and a 42 percent increase in annual trips per capita while car travel decreased 15 percent.[15]

Public/private joint ventures

Cooperation between the public and private sectors is a concept that is receiving considerable attention in transportation and other public service areas. Transit agencies can benefit from cooperating with private and other public organizations in projects designed to improve traffic in urban areas. In Hartford, Connecticut, a public/private sector collaborative planning effort developed a program that covered a range of traffic, parking, and pedestrian improvements as well as transit actions such as increased parking enforcement at bus stops, bus stop consolidation, and increased use of flexitime and staggered work hours.[16] In Los Angeles and Seattle, developers are required to implement ridesharing programs (including transit marketing) in return for receiving permits.[17]

BROADENING EMPLOYER INVOLVEMENT IN EMPLOYEE COMMUTING

A growing number of employers are taking a broadened view of employee commuting and instituting programs that include elements such as:

- Selling and/or subsidizing transit passes for employees;
- Offering variable work hours;
- Facilitating ridesharing (carpooling and vanpooling);
- Promoting increased use of public transit;
- Implementing parking management programs, including increases in parking fees and reservation of close-in spaces for vanpools and carpools.

This section describes the rationale for employer involvement in employee commuting.[18]

The problem: escalating cost of commuting

Hidden business expenses: The costs of commuting are a hidden business expense, reflected in personnel problems manifested as tardiness, absenteeism, and early departures toward the end of the work day as well as lower employee morale and productivity. These costs may be reduced (although probably not eliminated) by paying attention to employees' travel needs and the alternatives currently available to them, identifying possible solutions, and introducing new programs.

Cost to employees: The cost of driving to work in the mid–1980s can run from $900 to over $2,300 per year (depending on distance traveled and type of car). For every employee who works in downtown areas where parking is limited, an additional cash expense may be daily or monthly parking fees. In downtown Baltimore, for example, monthly parking fees in 1982 ranged from $45 to $90. This means that each employee must earn from $1,100 to $3,000 before taxes to pay for commuting expenses. These costs can consume as much as 10 percent of an employee's household income.

Each year, 15 percent of the labor force must replace a car and experience the "sticker shock" of prices ranging from $6,000 to $10,000 for a typical new car—with financing and monthly payments at perhaps twice the rate paid on the previous car. For employees replacing cars, the costs of commuting are rising rapidly—even with stable gas prices.

In sum, the total costs of commuting can significantly reduce an employee's discretionary income and the net value of the monthly paycheck.

Cost of congestion: When employees commute in congested rush hour traffic, they often encounter delays and lengthened trips. Rush hour commuting can add anywhere from a few minutes to nearly an hour each day to work trips in Maryland. The cost of delays is borne by both the employee and the employer. A traffic delay produces a tardy and harassed employee. If a worker must start leaving home earlier to be sure of arriving at work on time, then the total work day has been lengthened without financial benefit to either the employee or the employer.

Cost of providing parking: The cost of parking is an often unrecognized overhead expense for many businesses. Free parking is the one transportation benefit that many suburban firms provide their employees. However, it is an expensive benefit. The amortized cost of one open air parking space can be as high as $1,200 per year, reflecting land costs, taxes, insurance, construction and maintenance, security, and lighting.

Even in congested urban areas, employers sometimes provide free or heavily subsidized parking in a parking garages where the net annual costs amount to several thousand dollars per space.

The opportunity cost of utilizing land for parking spaces can be even higher. For example, a growing business may be able to use a portion of an existing parking lot to expand its facility even while increasing the number of employees—rather than purchase additional land or move to new quarters elsewhere. The impact of a ridesharing program that could free parking spaces for expansion would be worth millions of dollars to a company contemplating a new site.

Companies that provide unlimited free parking unintentionally create an incentive for employees to drive alone to work. The consequence is that the value of free parking as an employee benefit is reduced or even negated by the expenses of driving alone to work.

Cost to the community: Economic growth depends upon an efficient transportation network. Yet, for the duration of the 1980s, transportation investment will probably be less than in previous years. Traffic conditions are likely to worsen as the economy grows, until the deterioration slows further economic development.

An increase in congestion means slower traffic, which also means increased air pollution and gasoline consumption. In addition, congestion decreases the efficiency of the public transit system, another expense borne by taxpayers.

The transportation solution of the past, new road construction, is becoming less realistic given the shortage of tax dollars at both the state and federal level. New gasoline taxes are targeted primarily at repairing existing facilities.

A further cost to the community (and often a source of deteriorating relations with local employers) comes from use of scarce on-street parking by employees.

CONCLUSION

National political attention in the 1980s has focused on developing "public/private cooperation" and "privatization" of public agencies. For public transit services, privatization seems unrealistic since most transit agencies were privately held until they approached bankruptcy.

Yet opportunities do exist for public transit agencies to develop cooperative programs with the private sector. This chapter has illustrated that there are considerable benefits for transit agencies in actively seeking the involvement of employers, retailers, and other third parties in promoting public transportation.

NOTES

1. Weber, Nathan. *Transporting Employees: The New Corporate Programs*, Research Bulletin (New York: Conference Board, 1983), p. 15. Three quarters of respondents also cited energy concerns. Almost all companies reported more than one primary reason.

2. Selinger, Carl S. "Managing transportation demand by alternative work schedule techniques," in *Transportation Systems Management*, Transportation Research Board Special Report 172, (Washington, D.C.: National Academy of Sciences, 1977), p. 68.

3. Nollen, Stanley D. "What is happening to flexitime, flexitour, gliding time, the variable work day? And permanent part-time employment? And the four day week?" *Across the Board* (April 1980): 10.

4. Cottrell, Charles A. and J. Mark Walker. "Flexible work days: Philosophy and bank implementation," *Journal of Retail Banking* (December 1979): 80.

5. Ibid., p. 79.

6. Nollen, "What is happening," op. cit., p. 10.

7. Crain & Associates. *Santa Clara County Solo Driver Commuters: A Market Research Study Report Summary*, April, 1984, cited in *Traffic Mitigation Reference Guide: A Review of Options Available to the Public and Private Sectors* (Oakland, CA: Metropolitan Transportation Commission, December 1984), p. 23.

8. Tax Reform Act of 1984, P.L. 98–369, effective January 1, 1985; 26 U.S. Code, Sections 132(a) and (e); *House of Representatives Report* No. 432, 98th Congress, 2d Sess. 1603, reprinted in 1984 U.S. Code Cong. & Admin. News: 533–34. *House Report* states: "To illustrate, benefits which generally are excluded from income and employment taxes as de minimus fringes (without regard to the aggregation rule) include . . . monthly transit passes provided at a discount not exceeding $15. . . . "

9. S.B. 320 (1982) as cited in *Quarterly Bulletin* (Bethesda, MD: Ecosometrics, Spring/Summer 1984): 11.

10. *Air Quality and Vanpool Programs*, U.S. Environmental Protection Agency, Document EPA 400/2–78–002a, cited in *Traffic Mitigation Reference Guide* p. 24.

11. *Urban Transport News*, 12, No. 19 (September 17, 1984): 145.

12. *Passenger Transport* (October 19, 1979): 4.

13. Thomas, John E. "A special event parking and transit pass system using Ticketron: The Rochester, N.Y. Tall Ships experience," Bureau of Planning, City of Rochester, unpublished paper presented to the Transportation Research Board Annual Meeting (January 1985), p. 1.

14. Hebert, Ray. "Long Beach Mall: Front seat for transit," *Mass Transit* (January 1983): 25.

15. *Mass Transit* (April 1983): 12.

16. Connecticut Department of Transportation, *The Downtown Hartford Transportation Project: Public/Private Collaboration on Transportation Improvements* (Cambridge, MA: Cambridge Systematics, July 1983).

17. Roche, Patrick, and Richard Wilson. "Ridesharing requirements in Los Angeles: Achieving private sector commitments" (Community Redevelopment Agency of Los Angeles), unpublished paper presented to the Transportation Research Board Annual Meeting (January 1986), p. 2.

18. This section is based on *The Hidden Costs of Employee Commuting*, prepared under contract by Gordon Lewin to the Regional Planning Council, Baltimore, MD, 1982.

10

Developing a Communications Program

INFORMING, PERSUADING, AND REMINDING THE PUBLIC

Many people make the mistake of equating *communications* and *marketing*, instead of recognizing that the former is simply a very important ingredient in the overall "marketing mix."

Communication may take place through impersonal channels (such as TV advertising or printed information) or on a person to person basis (as, for example, when a person telephones a transit information office or a traveler receives advice and instructions from a bus driver).

Studying *transit marketing* clarifies that there are three roles for communication: to inform, to persuade, and to remind. People cannot be expected to use a service they do not know about; additionally, they may be unable to use a service properly without instructions on how to use it. This is an important consideration when seeking to improve productivity through consumer cooperation.

Even when people know that a service exists, they may need encouragement to try it or to use it in a different way, especially if this involves changing established habits. Reasoned arguments, illustrations, and reassurances may be needed to encourage the critical first trial. Finally, people forget: just because they have been told something once does not mean that they will necessarily remember it. Hence, the need to remind people from time to time. However, it is very important that the nature and content of all messages (as well as the media through which they are transmitted) be credible and tailored to the specific audience(s) at which they are directed.

The need for targeted strategies

All too often marketing departments have limited their communications to advertising, promotion, and information aids.[1] While these areas can be important elements of a marketing department's program, communications also include media relations, publicity, community relations, complaint handling, personal selling, and all contacts by service operators with the consumer.

Of all the marketing functions, transit systems have most readily adopted communications programs—very often without a real understanding of the role and limitations of communications and in isolation from other marketing functions. Communications programs have experienced problems due to a reliance on defining the market too broadly and on utilizing communications tools too narrowly.

Too broad a definition of the market: Historically, almost all of the work done in transit communications has been addressed to the "mass market." Transit systems created advertising departments before they had marketing departments and long before anyone suggested a strategy of different messages and services for different groups. What has invariably been missing is a clear definition of who is to be reached—the target market.

Too narrow an approach to communications tools: The communications function has tended to be the responsibility of an "advertising department," or possibly the "advertising and promotion" department. But communications involve all contacts between the organization and its publics—whether a traveler telephoning for transit information or a car driver listening to a 30-second rush-hour radio spot. If the radio spot promotes easy-to-use transit service with an information "hot line," but the telephone lines are always busy and the bus stops poorly signed, then the transit authority risks developing a less favorable public image than if it had no promotion program at all. A major task in creating a communications program is to integrate all of the various channels so that their messages are collectively consistent and serve to reinforce each other. To achieve this requires clear objectives for the communications strategy and a clear idea of the target market.

Setting objectives for communications

Communications programs can be used to accomplish three tasks. First, they can build awareness of a service that may be new to the consumer or serve as a reminder of a service known but possibly forgotten. An example might be a Christmas season promotion reminding the public that families can travel for one fare on Sundays and avoid parking problems in the shopping district.

Second, communications programs can communicate specific information about a service. A newspaper insert in community papers could include a route map and schedule for a new bus route.

The third task is the most difficult, entailing creation of communications programs designed to change attitudes. The Columbus Ohio Transit Authority (COTA) developed a creative advertising campaign to change attitudes by illustrating the financial benefits of riding the bus in order to provide nonriders with an additional rationale for switching modes: "Ride to an $1,800 vacation," the ads proclaimed. "If driving costs don't get you, sky-high downtown parking will. But if you ride the bus to work downtown every day using a COTA monthly local pass, the savings can add up to more than $1,800 a year."[2] (See Exhibit 10–1.)

Only when objectives have been developed and target groups have been identified should consideration be given to designing the message and the particular communications channel to be used in conveying that message.

Promotion and advertising of transit service alone cannot guarantee changes in behavior, because many other variables can intervene between a favorable attitude and actual behavior. For example, one Canadian transit agency found that users and nonusers both had positive attitudes toward transit and were aware of service features. A subsequent advertising and promotional campaign failed to increase ridership because no additional rationale for riding was provided to nonusers.[3]

In setting objectives, it is important to understand consumer behavior and how communications can be used to affect that behavior. In addition, economic and service contraints must be borne in mind. If the service is poor and the budget restricted, then the objectives set for communications should be realistically modest.

Objectives should be set relative to specific market segments. Encouraging existing transit users to make more trips by bus or train is completely different from appealing to nonusers to start riding transit. As discussed in Chapter 2, the target group can be set in terms of frequency of usage, geographic area, or by demographic characteristics (e.g., "middle-aged women not employed outside the home"). A target group for an awareness campaign can be very large, but it is unwise to expect a communication strategy to be successful across wide-ranging groups with different needs and habits.

Evaluation. One of the major advantages of setting clear objectives and defining target groups for communication is that it simplifies subsequent evaluation. If the objective is to achieve a given level of awareness among a particular group, this awareness can and should be measured.

No communications program is complete unless it includes provision for measuring the impact of the program. Did it change attitudes among

Exhibit 10–1
Advertisement for COTA Monthly Pass

Source: Courtesy of the Central Ohio Transit Authority.

the target audience(s)? Did it increase ridership on specific routes and at specific times of day or week? Benchmark measures of ridership and attitudes should be developed before a communications program is conducted and additional research may be needed after the program to determine the results. Other relevant performance measures may include editorial coverage in the mass media, phone calls and letters from members of the public, and comments by employees.

THE COMMUNICATIONS MIX

The term "communications mix" is sometimes used to describe the array of communications tools and channels available to marketers. Just as marketers need to combine the elements of the marketing mix (including communications) to produce a marketing program, they also need to select the most appropriate ingredients for the communications program.

The elements of the communications mix fall into four broad categories:

- Personal Selling;
- Media advertising;
- Publicity and public relations;
- Promotional or information activities at the point of sale.

The distinction between personal communications and the other three elements is that the former involves representatives of the organization engaged directly in two-way communications with customers, either in person or over the telephone. The latter three elements are all one-way communications—from the marketer to the customers.

Interpersonal communications

Communications between individuals have two powerful advantages over mass media communications: 1) the message goes directly from sender to recipient, and 2) personal communications are two-directional. Personal communications include not only direct sales approaches (e.g., visits by transit salespeople to major employers to encourage them to participate in monthly pass distribution programs), but also customer contact activities such as inquiries to a telephone information line and communication between a bus driver and passengers.

Salespeople. Personal selling represents the most powerful communications channel, but also the most expensive in terms of messages conveyed per individual. The use of professional salespeople might be questioned as an inefficient method of selling 50-cent bus rides. Yet, if the personal sale results in repetitive behavior, the time invested in the sales effort can be cost effective. For example, if a car driver becomes a regular transit rider, the transit authority will receive additional annual revenue of about $250 (based on a 50-cent one-way fare). Working through intermediaries such as employers, colleges, and retailers may be the most effective sales approach. For instance, targeting potential repeat customers, the Rochester-Genesee (N.Y.) Regional Transportation Authority instituted a "Commuter Router" program for employees at cooperating local businesses. After submitting relevant information, each employee received a personalized transit information package with detailed bus route and schedule information for trips between their home and workplace.[4]

Personal selling is also cost effective when it is reserved for opinion leaders: people whose actions and statements will influence many others. Several systems have used community sales representatives to visit high frequency locations, such as shopping centers, office buildings, and major employers. In addition to setting up displays in prominent locations and answering questions about new and existing services, sales representatives have obtained employer and retailer cooperation in promoting transit use.

Customer contact personnel. It is important not to overlook the role of employees in communicating with consumers. Not all service organizations bring users into face-to-face contact with employees on a regular basis. Transit users see the bus driver all the time. Citizens needing police assistance see or speak by phone with police officers; people using a library are often in contact with a member of the library staff; patients needing medical care are tended by a doctor or a nurse; students are in contact with school teachers or administrators.

In some instances, this human contact *is* the service. The appearance, demeanor, and behavior of the professional or other employee may play a significant role in determining how consumers perceive and use the service. Often one hears somebody exclaim, "I hate the Department of Motor Vehicles, their employees are so rude!" or "Nobody at City Hall seems to give a damn when you phone for information!" or "I asked the bus driver what bus to take to get to Fifth and Main and he hadn't the faintest idea."

While such irritations sometimes reflect the behavior of an employee with an unpleasant personality, they may also result from a lack of proper employee training. In turn, inadequate training and support often reflect a lack of management understanding of the contacts that employees have with the public, the types of information that the public expects employees to be able to provide, and the frustrations that employees experience in their jobs.

Transit operations whose drivers have a reputation for courtesy, helpfulness, and the ability to answer basic questions about the system rarely developed that reputation by accident. Rather, driver training emphasizes their role as "ambassador" for the system and they are helped to familiarize themselves with details of other routes; rider complaints and compliments are promptly followed up and—where appropriate—disciplinary action taken or managerial recognition given. Proper training and provision of proper working facilities have been found to be equally important in developing effective transit information offices.

AC Transit in Oakland, California, is known for its excellent transit information office, which provides both phone information and also printed maps, brochures, and timetables. The staff go through a rigorous training program, work in pleasant offices, and have a number of mechanical and technical aids to help them in their work.

A comparative analysis in 1973 of AC Transit and the San Francisco Municipal Railway ("Muni") revealed dramatic differences in the quality of information service provided. One Muni information operator, when asked by phone for the quickest way from downtown to the Hall of Justice (courthouse) suggested, "Throw a rock through the nearest window!" However, the researchers laid much of the blame on Muni management for the lack of training, the periodic use of bus drivers for the information job, unsatisfactory working conditions, hard-to-use information materials in the offices, and unsophisticated telephone equipment, which could not stack calls.

The lesson for other public transit organizations is that monitoring consumer behavior and understanding travelers' information needs may provide useful insights into ways in which the public seeks assistance from employees and interacts with them in the performance of the service. Armed with these insights, managers will be better placed to provide the necessary training and support facilities required for responsive service.

Complaint handling. Personal communications is also a central aspect of complaint handling and resolution. Few transit organizations approach this task with a positive attitude, yet it is one of the few times when a transit system is in direct contact with its riders. Analysis of complaints can highlight real problem areas, provided sufficient detail is obtained. The attitude of the person taking the complaint can save a user from abandoning transit after a bad experience. Conversely, a message of friendliness in advertising can be destroyed in one second by a surly complaint handler. The same holds true for telephone information systems, which can be both a source of information and an important communications channel.

Word-of-mouth advertising. Just as satisfied customers may tell several people about a good experience with an organization or its products, so an unhappy consumer is likely to tell a number of friends, family members, and co-workers about an unpleasant experience.

All service organizations are highly susceptible to the power of personal endorsement—or bad-mouthing. The recommendation of a fellow consumer to use or to avoid a specific product or service is one of the most important factors in consumer decision making. Unfortunately, research studies show that consumers tell more people about their bad experiences than about their positive ones! In industry, a number of companies have established consumer "800-number toll-free hot lines" so that they hear about complaints and can attempt to assist the customer. Recognizing this problem, the Southeastern Michigan Transportation Authority (SEMTA) has an "800" toll-free complaint hot line that is promoted with the slogan "We Want to Hear Your Complaint Before Your Neighbors Do." (See Exhibit 10–2.)

Exhibit 10–2
Advertisement produced by SEMTA

**We Want To Hear Your Complaint
Before Your Neighbors Do.**

*NO SOONER
SAID
THAN
DONE!!*

σ SEMTƎ 1·800·462·5161

Source: Courtesy of the Southeastern Michigan Transportation Authority.

Impersonal communications

Although personal selling is a powerful method of communications, it is also costly and time consuming. Much information can be delivered far more cheaply through impersonal sources, particularly when the objective is to generate initial awareness.

Communications channels. The principal impersonal communications channels for transit are broadcast and print advertising, direct mail, outdoor advertising, signs, and printed information aids. It is important to distinguish between mass communications channels for transit controlled by the marketer (paid advertising and direct mail) and those controlled by the media (press releases, public relations events and, to a lesser extent, public service advertising).

The use of the mass media for transit advertising tends to limit the possibilities for targeting of communication. While the message can certainly be targeted at a specific group, the cost of reaching that target group may be substantial due to the high wastage level: advertising costs tend to reflect the total audience receiving the message, even if many are likely to ignore it. Billboards, the press and local radio, and direct mail are all more selective than TV. Exhibit 10–3 summarizes some of the key characteristics of each medium.

Use of market segmentation analysis is key to development of effective communications programs, since cost-effective promotions require careful targeting. Direct mail, billboards, and community newspapers provide an opportunity to target markets geographically. Except for billboards, print media are more effective than broadcasting for transmit-

Exhibit 10–3
Consumer Information Elements

System Map

A comprehensive and accurate system map should be compiled by each transit system. In the larger, regionalized systems, a schematic map featuring routes and key landmarks is essential for an overall view of the system. Detailed route-alignment information should be available to supplement the larger systemwide maps. Periodic reissuance of the system map should be keyed to the frequency of route changes.

Timetable Information

Each transit system should have timetables that include a schematic map of each route and its daily schedule. A compendium of timetables should be considered for the entire transit system. The timetables should be simple and readable. Timetable information should be issued twice a year and disseminated by vehicle drivers, at information kiosks and intermodal transfer points, and by mail.

Information Signs at Stops

An information sign should be provided at each transit stop; it should carry the system logo and list the routes that serve the stop. Route schedule and fare information should be available to patrons at each inbound stop and at outbound stops that are major transfer locations. Major transfer and intermodal points require systemwide information kiosks and staffed information centers. Transit stops at major activity centers, such as tourist sites or large intersections, should be named (on large visible signs).

Destination signs

The transit vehicle's destination should be clearly identified on roller (or electronic) signs at the front and side. Consideration should be given to a rear destination sign as well. Destination signs should be large and understandable to the transit patrons. If possible, the route destination signs should be color coded and information describing the route should be provided.

Employees

Every transit employee who is in contact with the public should be totally familiar with the transit system and able to properly answer any questions about it or refer travelers to another source of information.

Excerpted from Transporation Research Board Report, *European Transit Market Programs and Consumer Information Aids*, Urban Mass Transportation Administration (May 1978).

ting messages containing a great deal of factual information (such as new bus routes and schedules).

Credibility and leverage can often be gained by undertaking joint promotions with organizations at locations served by transit. Retailers may be glad to work with the transit agency in an effort to boost their business, particularly if car access is difficult for all or some of their patrons. To encourage shoppers to use transit, the Southern California RTD developed a "Bus 2 Us" promotional campaign for retailers. The RTD developed the concept—based on a slogan on a California vehicle license plate—and encouraged its use by retailers located along bus lines.

Depending upon the demographics of an urban area, it may be important to develop promotional programs with materials in more than one language, if there is a significant number of foreign-language residents. If an urban area has a large number of foreign visitors, a targeted tourist brochure in major languages may also be warranted. A number of transit authorities already recognize visitors as an important market segment and produce a tourist brochure or cooperate with local convention and tourist authorities in seeing that their visitor brochures include public transportation information.

Public information

Information aids are a critical component of any communications program for a transit agency. Information aids include signs such as bus stop and station markings, and route system maps, timetables, and signs on the transit vehicles themselves. A study of European transit marketing programs concluded that these elements—combined with knowledgeable and helpful employees— "have the greatest potential for improving the attractiveness of a transit system."[5] Without accurate and easy-to-use information sources, it is quite difficult to increase transit ridership.

Printed information. While awareness of a transit system may be high, potential riders need detailed information on routes, schedules, and fares. Unfortunately, the preparation of information aids is not always assigned to the marketing department, where it realistically belongs. Final products are all too often little more than bus driver assignment sheets printed (badly) as a money-saving alternative to properly designed and produced transit schedules. The need for high quality, modern graphics in all information aids is paramount.[6] Exhibit 10–4 provides examples of both well prepared and poorly designed information aids. A good timetable and map should be easy to read at a glance by the rider. A good route map will often rely on a schematic presentation. Bus stop signs with route and perhaps schedule information (or a telephone number to call) are far preferable to a "Bus Stop—No Parking" sign.

Even a quality schedule and map can be difficult to use. A UMTA-funded study of urban residents in Seattle, Dallas, and Columbus (Ohio) found that even with information available, 46 percent of people in a transit exercise could not correctly get departure times from an "ideal" schedule and map.[7] A comparable study in Chicago with similar results concluded that "at the root of the problem is the lack of knowledge among urban residents about the basic geography of the metropolitan

Exhibit 10–4a
Example of a Good Insert Map

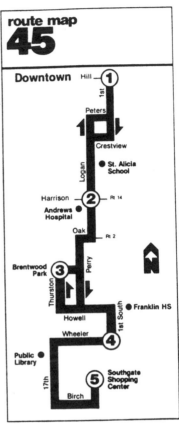

Example of a Bad Insert Map

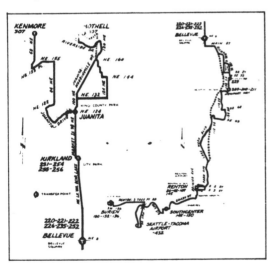

Exhibit 10–4b
Example of a Bad Time Block

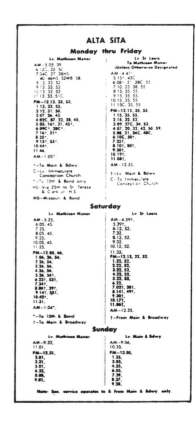

Example of a Good Time Block

Weekday departures							
Downtown			Southgate				Downtown
①	②	④	⑤	④	③	②	①
1st & Hill	Logan & Harrison	1st South & Wheeler	S'gate Shopping Center	1st South & Wheeler	Brent-wood Park	Logan & Harrison	1st & Hill
7:20	7:30	7:45	7:55	8:05	8:15	8:30	8:40
8:40	8:50	9:05	9:15	9:25	9:35	9:50	10:00
10:00	10:10	10:25	10:35	10:45	10:55	11:10	11:20
11:20	11:30	11:45	1:55	12:05	12:15	12:30	12:40
12:40	12:50	1:05	1:15	1:25	1:35	1:50	2:00
2:00	2:10	2:25	2:35	2:45	2:55	3:10	3:20
3:20	3:30	3:45	3:55	4:05	4:15	4:30	4:40
4:40	4:50	5:05	5:15	5:25	5:35	5:50	6:00
6:00	6:10	6:25	6:35	6:45	6:55	7:10a	

Exhibit 10–4c
Example of a Bad Bus Stop Sign.

Example of a Good Bus Stop Sign.

Source: Courtesy of the Iowa Department of Transportation.

area. Progress here requires long term public education remedies, perhaps starting in elementary school."[8]

Many transit authorities already run safety programs in conjunction with local school systems. In St. Louis and Philadelphia, transit agencies have introduced programs with local schools to teach children how to use public transportation.[9] Teaching skills such as reading transit maps and bus schedules can benefit not only a transit authority in the long run but can also assist elementary school teachers by providing practical examples of certain basic classroom fundamentals. (In addition, elementary school students are an excellent distribution channel for circulating information to their parents!)

Of critical importance in developing materials is the integration of information aids into the message being conveyed through other channels. If the mass media are promoting a modern and efficient system, then the schedule cards must reflect the same characteristics. It is also important that visual elements of graphics, colors, and information content be consistent for all products.[10] Fort Worth and Los Angeles are communities that have developed bus sign programs that include a schematic of the route and timetable information on each bus stop sign.[11] A fully-integrated consumer information system at Seattle Metro resulted in a 10 percent increase in ridership.[12]

Distribution channels for information aids must be handled with the same care as the production of materials. It is one thing to print schedules, it is another to place them in the hands of a targeted market. One transit system in Pennsylvania printed maps and schedules in a new format and distributed them throughout the system, door to door, and in local newspapers in one suburban community. The net result was a 4 percent increase in ridership in the targeted area—while ridership declined elsewhere in the system.[13]

Even regular transit riders familiar with service in their community may not be aware of service elsewhere in an urban area or services provided by other transportation providers. A study conducted in Chicago found that

Even riders familiar with the transfer point do not know how to ride public transit to a suburban destination selected for its ease of access. More difficult destinations surely would have produced even poorer results. The implication of this is that district boundaries can act as barriers to transit interaction. Even though transit districts frequently promote cross district travel by providing free or low cost transfers, information about the "other" district is frequently not readily available.[14]

In response to this problem, regional paperback guidebooks to all forms of public transportation have been successfully produced for both the Boston and San Francisco areas.[15] The guides are sold retail through bookstores and newsstands. Each guide features directions to important and popular destinations throughout the region as well as listing transit services by community and urban neighborhood. One feature of the guide *Car-Free in Boston* is that maps of key transfer points clearly indicate exactly where the stops for different bus routes are located (see Exhibit 10–5). The guide is produced by a citizens' group.

Telephone information systems. The telephone has become an important information source for consumers, especially for travel purposes. The airline industry has found telephone information to be an important component of the marketing mix for air travel due to the need for advanced planning and reservations for most flights.

Many transit systems have developed telephone information systems on an ad hoc basis. As late as the mid–1970s, all too many transit authorities tended to rely on former bus drivers (at senior bus driver pay scales) to staff poorly designed telephone information desks equipped with conventional telephones. Due to low productivity (the result of poor design) and understaffing (partly the result of high labor cost), consumers attempting to obtain transit information would face long waits for information—or a continuous busy signal when calling the transit authority. Since the telephone system may be the consumer's first contact with a carrier, a poor experience on the telephone is likely to make it the last.

Several changes have occurred at a number of transit authorities that have introduced new technology and implemented management strategies to produce more efficient telephone services. Automatic call distributor (ACD) systems place calls in a queue on a first call-first serve basis and distribute calls to the next available agent. Computerized, microfiche, or simply well-designed manual systems can also help increase the quality and productivity of telephone agents. To control costs, some systems train and employ part-time agents or entry level clerks (instead of former bus drivers), and/or contract out service to a private firm.[16]

Another management approach to operating transit information systems efficiently is to control demand for services. The problem that transit authorities face with telephone inquiries is similar to that faced by telephone company "directory assistance" lines: Strong consumer preference exists for obtaining free information and organizations do not want to discourage usage of their service by discouraging access to information.

A transit authority may attempt to subtly "de-market" the telephone line by not printing the telephone number on, say, every bus stop sign in order to discourage unnecessary use of the telephone. An effective distribution of printed materials (at low unit cost) can provide the consumers with needed information so that they do not have to call the transit authority. Telephone operators can also offer to mail free maps

Exhibit 10–5
Map from *Car-Free in Boston*

Watertown Sq.-Newton Corner

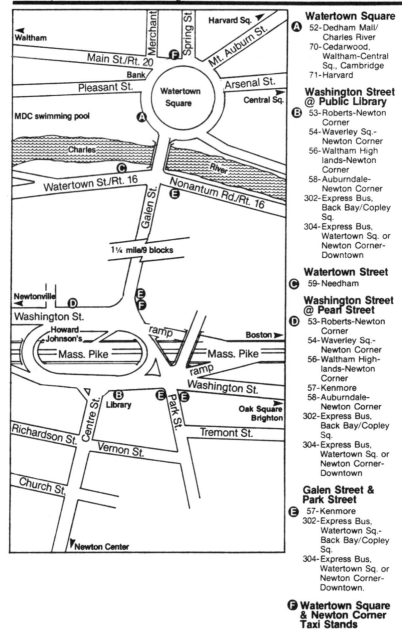

Watertown Square

Ⓐ 52- Dedham Mall/
     Charles River
   70- Cedarwood,
     Waltham-Central
     Sq., Cambridge
   71- Harvard

**Washington Street
@ Public Library**

Ⓑ 53- Roberts-Newton
     Corner
   54- Waverley Sq.-
     Newton Corner
   56- Waltham High-
     lands-Newton
     Corner
   58- Auburndale-
     Newton Corner
   302- Express Bus,
     Back Bay/Copley
     Sq.
   304- Express Bus,
     Watertown Sq. or
     Newton Corner-
     Downtown

Watertown Street

Ⓒ 59- Needham

**Washington Street
@ Pearl Street**

Ⓓ 53- Roberts-Newton
     Corner
   54- Waverley Sq.-
     Newton Corner
   56- Waltham High-
     lands-Newton
     Corner
   57- Kenmore
   58- Auburndale-
     Newton Corner
   302- Express Bus,
     Back Bay/Copley
     Sq.
   304- Express Bus,
     Watertown Sq. or
     Newton Corner-
     Downtown

**Galen Street &
Park Street**

Ⓔ 57- Kenmore
   302- Express Bus,
     Watertown Sq.-
     Back Bay/Copley
     Sq.
   304- Express Bus,
     Watertown Sq. or
     Newton Corner-
     Downtown.

Ⓕ **Watertown Square
& Newton Corner
Taxi Stands**

Source: Courtesy of the Association for Public Transportation, Inc.

and relevant schedules to callers to help curtail the need for repeat calls by the same individual.

Given that transit routing is far more complex than using a telephone book and that the public has limited ability and/or patience to interpret maps and schedules, well-managed telephone information systems are going to be an important element of the communications mix. For future planning, transit authorities may want to review opportunities to computerize the information systems, tie into existing personal computer networks, and provide service through two-way cable systems.

Public relations

Media and community relations are particularly tricky issues for transit authorities. Because they are public agencies, transit organizations often face the scrutiny of the news media. Large transit organizations often have at least one person responsible for handling inquiries from the press.

Further complicating matters is the fact that in many urban areas, transit authorities operate in a highly politicized environment. While political debate of a transit authority regarding, say, budget items, does not immediately affect ridership, transit management should be concerned about "negative" press and its long-term impact on ridership and funding. Due to the political nature of much press coverage, it is perhaps better to assign press and PR functions to individuals directly responsible to, and in touch with, the organization's chairman and/or general manager. Since press functions tend to be very short-range in scope, the marketing department may be better off devoting its energy to medium and long-range programs to increase ridership and support for transit.

Community relations can also involve working in a political environment. A good community relations function is not as reactive as working with the press, and therefore it is an appropriate function for a marketing department. Community relations involves meeting with neighborhoods and civic organizations on issues ranging from new construction and bus route planning to consumer complaints and fare increases. As a community relations function, the MBTA in Boston publishes a regular newsletter for riders (see Exhibit 10–6). Given the overlap with local politics, it is important that community relations staff have some access to the general manager; otherwise they are likely to be perceived as "flak catchers" by constituent groups.

Promotional activities. Transit systems can generate favorable publicity for themselves by cooperating in special events in their local community. In Boston, the MBTA has offered free night service on New Year's Eve for many years. Services run until early in the morning in order to accommodate participants in the annual "First Night" downtown and to assist the Governor's anti-drunk driving program. Frequently transit agencies

Exhibit 10–6
MBTA Newsletter for Riders

FREE

T

Rider

Your guide to the ⓣ!

Green Line expects busy winter

Meet the bus operators

Mark your ballot for a name!

Senior citizens ride for less

Win your free ⓣ Pass

January/February 1986

Source: Reproduced by permission of MBTA, James F. O'Leary, General Manager

have developed cross-promotions with merchants served by public transportation. In some instances, tradeoff agreements can be reached with media organizations, wherein the transit authority provides free advertising on, say, its vehicles in exchange for free advertising of its services on a television or radio station.

Making communications decisions

Other than behaving in an ethical way, what do we mean by "good communications decisions"? There are two criteria. One is that the communications program achieves the specific objectives, in terms of measurable results, that management intended for it. Second is that the program makes efficient use of the transit organization's resources (including management and staff time) in achieving the desired results.

Effective, efficient communication strategies require that communication objectives be linked explicitly to broader marketing objectives and that communications budgets be set in the context of the overall marketing budget and the value of the goals to be achieved. Knowing how communications work and being aware of the wide array of communications tools available are important prerequisites to sound decision making.

Budgeting. A transit agency's communications budget must be established with reference to the tasks that are to be performed and the value to the organization of the desired outcomes. Alternative ways of spending the budget must be carefully evaluated. Finally, research inputs will probably be needed at four levels:

1. To develop the campaign objectives.
2. To set budgets.
3. To pretest the effectiveness of the planned program.
4. To evaluate the impact of the program by measuring key variables (attitudes, ridership) both before and after the campaign.

Changing communication needs

The balancing of goals, positioning of messages, and distribution of materials must reflect the current situation and available budget. The marketing needs of the organization may need to be changed over time.

Consider, for instance, the case of a newly constructed rapid transit system. When the system first opens, management can probably rely on widespread publicity from stories in the mass media to build awareness, but it may need to augment this with an informational advertising campaign giving people specific details on using the new service and letting them know how to obtain further information. Perhaps a direct-mail campaign may also be conducted in the corridors served by the rapid transit lines to distribute maps and schedules. As time passes and public knowledge of the system improves, special promotions may be used to boost ridership during off-peak hours.

Sales representatives may also be hired to work with large employers, retailers, and other groups to develop public transportation packages tailored to the needs of specific market segments. In the unlikely event of a strike shutting down the system, effective use of public relations may help to minimize unfavorable publicity and to ensure that the mass media provide accurate information about transportation alternatives. When the dispute has been resolved and the system re-opens, a new advertising campaign will be needed to restore public confidence and rebuild ridership.

CONCLUSION

Developing a communications program involves far more than deciding on the message of an advertising campaign. Communications programs are the ultimate output of a marketing department. Therefore, they must be carefully derived from the marketing strategy and consumer analysis developed by the transit organization.

NOTES

1. Deslauriers, Brian. "A survey of informational, advertising and promotional activities of Ontario transit systems and attitudes of transit officials" (Ontario Ministry of Transportation and Communications, June 1977).

2. "Columbus 10 years later: How to succeed in transit by really trying," *Mass Transit* (May 1984): 34.

3. Ontario Ministry of Transportation and Communications, Project Planning Branch. *Kingston Transit Community Information and Marketing Program* (1976).

4. "Schedules personalized for Rochester riders," *Passenger Transport* (March 21, 1980).

5. Transportation Research Board. *European Transit Marketing Programs and Consumer-Information Aids* (Urban Mass Transportation Administration, May 1978), p. 32.

6. For a full discussion of graphic components, see Urban Mass Transportation Administration, *User Information Aids: Transit Marketing Management Handbook* (Washington, D.C.: Office of Transit Management, November 1975).

7. Battelle Memorial Institute. *Transit User Information Aids: An Evaluation of Consumer Attitudes*, prepared for Urban Mass Transportation Administration, Office of Transit Management (1976).

8. Soot, Siim, and Stenson, H. H. *Transit Information and Transit Knowledge: The Chicago Experience* (Urban Mass Transportation Administration, May 1983) (abstract).

9. "Children learn value of public transportation," *Passenger Transport* (April 4, 1980): 5; and "Today's children are tomorrow's commuters: Transit needs to

reach into grade school classrooms," *Passenger Transport* (October 3, 1980): 44–45.

10. Transportation Research Board. *European Transit*; op. cit., p. 32.

11. "Fort Worth answers, 'When's the bus due?' " *Passenger Transport* (April 6, 1979): 12; and "Bus stop signs make getting information easy," *Passenger Transport* (January 18, 1980): 12.

12. Larry L. Coffman. "Information services, advertising and other communication programs," in *Marketing Public Transportation: Policies, Strategies, and Research Needs for the 1980's*, R. K. Robinson and C. H. Lovelock, eds. (American Marketing Association, Proceedings Series, 1981), p. 64.

13. Carnegie-Mellon University Transportation Research Institute. *Allegheny County Transit Study* (1968).

14. Soot and Stenson. *Transit Information*, op. cit., p. 39.

15. *Car-Free in Boston & All Massachusetts: A User's Guide to Public Transportation* (Association for Public Transportation, Inc., P.O. Box 192, Cambridge, MA 02238) and *Regional Transit Guide* (Metropolitan Transportation Commission, 101 8th St., Oakland, CA).

16. For more information on telephone information systems, see Marc Cutler, "The impact of technology and labor management strategies on efficiency of telephone information services," unpublished paper presented at Transportation Research Board Annual Meeting, 1985 (Dynatrend, 21 Cabot Road, Woburn, MA 01801) and Walter Diewald, "An examination of transit telephone information systems," in *Trends in Transit Marketing and Fare Policy*, Transportation Research Record, #972 (Transportation Research Board, Washington, D.C.).

Part V
The Role of Marketing

11

Building a Marketing Orientation

The creation of marketing departments within transit authorities is a relatively recent development. As late as 1973, a survey found that fewer than 50 percent of a sample of U.S. and Canadian transit systems had marketing departments.[1] Only one third of the transit systems surveyed had even a minimal marketing plan. Most of the plans at that time were prepared by an advertising agency and emphasized promotion and advertising.

There is a general lack of agreement as to what is meant by marketing in a transit context. Some people use the term *marketing* to justify expansion of the planning function, others hope promotion and consumer education will build ridership served by existing lines, and still others argue that a marketing orientation should lead to the creation of new services based on a profit-seeking viewpoint.

In many operations, managers take the attitude that if their organizations are well run according to a set of internally-generated performance standards, then customers will automatically use the service.[2] Such an attitude leaves little room for the development of strong marketing function.

WHERE DOES MARKETING FIT IN?

Our view, emphasized throughout this book, is that marketing is concerned with anything that affects the customers' decision to use (or not use) public transportation in preference to other modes, as well as their level of satisfaction (or dissatisfaction) with transit service. The goal of marketing is to increase ridership and rider satisfaction within the financial constraints established by the general manager and board of directors. The bottom line is social profits, not financial profits.

Exhibit 11–1 summarizes each of the various elements of transit service and identifies which departments tend to be responsible for them. In the typical transit organization, all of the various responsibilities are generally assigned to other than marketing personnel—whether these are product features (such as vehicle specifications and operations), pricing, or distribution decisions concerning routing and scheduling.

In this chapter we discuss the difference between the role of a marketing department and the task of the marketing function within the overall organization. Although it is probably unrealistic (and not necessarily desirable) to give marketing managers responsibility for activities that fall within the province of operations and human resources, a good argument can be made for encouraging marketing inputs into such activities. A marketing goal for the transit organization should be that all decisions are made with reference to their impact on customers. Managers and employees in each department should seek to leverage the marketing effectiveness of their actions and thereby stimulate creation of a strong transit marketing function that crosses departmental lines.

Exhibit 11–1
Responsibilities for Transit Management

Activity	Departmental Responsibility in Typical Transit Agency
Routing	Operations, planning
Scheduling	Operations, planning
Vehicle specifications (new purchases)	Purchasing, operations
Vehicle specifications (refurbishing)	Maintenance, purchasing
Security	Transit and/or city police
Vehicle operation	Operations
Driver selection and training	Personnel, operations
Fare levels	Accounting, treasurer, Budget Office, Board of Directors
Fare collection systems	Treasurer's Office, operations, purchasing
Stations, terminals, waiting areas	Construction, planning
Public information	Marketing, operations
Advertising	Marketing
Community relations	Marketing, public affairs
Pass program	Marketing, Treasurer's Office

Centralization vs. dispersion of marketing tasks

In 1975 the UMTA published a volume of the *Transit Marketing Management Handbook* focusing on the "Marketing Organization."[3] The study reviewed the development of marketing departments within the transit industry and found that rarely were all the transit marketing activities to be found in one organizational unit. The consultants to the study recommended the formation of a centralized marketing department organized along functional lines (as outlined in Exhibit 11–1).

The argument for a centralized functional organization was based on the assumptions that transit services are homogeneous, the market is relatively localized, and resources are limited. The advantage of this structure, beyond simplicity, was that the marketing manager clearly had the ultimate responsibility for the development of the marketing plan and had the resources needed to develop such a plan. Unless these conditions were met, a meaningful marketing plan would be substantially more difficult to develop.

In contrast with this "ideal" model, marketing functions tend to be scattered in the real world of transit organizations. For example, service development—the key activity for improving transit effectiveness in the marketplace—is usually an adjunct to an operations unit or a planning group. In larger systems, public relations or community affairs is often linked to legislative affairs or governmental relations and reports to the general manager. Market research, as often as not, reports to the planning group.

The purpose of this chapter is to discuss why it is so difficult to have strong marketing departments in transit and whether this absence is a real problem. We will use the term "marketing function" to describe the full array of marketing activities in a transit authority, regardless of whether they are centralized in one department or dispersed within the organization. The chapter concludes with a discussion of approaches to improving the influence of the marketing function without resorting to a centralized marketing unit.

THE ORGANIZATIONAL PROBLEMS OF MARKETING

It is important to stress that the problems of transit marketing are not unique to transit agencies. Many organizations within the service sector of the economy are faced with similar issues. Marketing has not traditionally played a major role in the management of most services. To be sure, managers of such businesses have often performed marketing tasks, ranging from pricing strategies to introduction of new services, but such actions were rarely planned, coordinated, and implemented by professional marketing managers with a strong orientation toward cus-

Figure 11–1

Recommended Marketing Organization and Functions for Larger Public Transit Systems (From *Transit Marketing Management Handbook: Marketing Organizations.*)

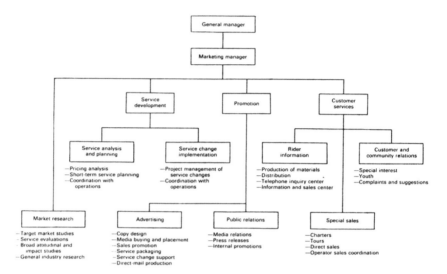

tomer needs, market trends, and competitive analysis. As likely as not, they were taken by managers with responsibilities in such areas as operations, finance, and economic analysis.

There has been little perception of the inefficiency resulting from lack of overall marketing integration, market targeting, or competitive positioning. Even if these inefficiencies are perceived at all, they have been outweighed by the importance of running the organization in an operationally efficient way.

Contrasting services and manufacturing organizations

This situation stands in sharp contrast with the approach that prevails in manufacturing firms, especially those in the business of selling consumer goods. Since the post-World War II period, marketing has been a dominant management function in consumer goods firms, offering strategic direction as well as tactical expertise.

The absence of any real competition in many areas of the service sector—including transit—has meant that there was little perceived need for a marketing function. This led to the historic domination of the operations function, since undoubtedly operations creates the product and without a good operations department, there certainly cannot be a satisfactory product.

In a service organization, there is greater interdependence of various functions as compared to a manufacturing firm. With manufactured products, there is a clear separation between production and consumption. A physical good can be produced in one location, sold in a second, and consumed or used in a third. Hence, there is normally no need for "production" to have any involvement with the firm's customers. Marketing plays a linking role in such firms, providing the manufacturing division with customer-oriented guidelines for product specifications, estimates of the extent and timing of demand, and feedback on marketplace performance. Marketing is also responsible for developing distribution strategies—through company-owned outlets or retail intermediaries—to deliver the product to prospective purchasers.

In a service company or institution—and especially a transit organization—the service is consumed as it is produced. Thus there has to be direct contact between production (operations) and the consumer. No inventories can be stockpiled to insulate productive capacity from the fluctuations of demand. Many service operations are literally a "factory in the field,"[4] which customers enter at the specific point in time that they need the service. Transit vehicles and station facilities are the "factories" that create the transit product.

The simultaneous nature of production and consumption in a service organization creates a major problem for marketing management. Unlike the marketer of consumer goods, the service marketing manager cannot wait to take responsibility for the product until after it leaves the factory. Instead, the marketing function is closely interrelated with, and dependent on, managers responsible for the human resource and operations functions. Based on the explicit link between production and consumption, a decision made in one management area can very often affect the other two areas. The interrelationship of management functions becomes quite apparent, for example, when addressing how to control the customer–product contact.

Customer contact

Differences in consumer needs usually mean that the customer-contact system must allow room for individual initiative within the constraints of meeting consistent service standards. Operational requirements must be balanced against responsiveness to customers. For example, is it wise to prohibit drivers (whose primary function is safe operation of their vehicles) from asking passengers if they can provide change for the occasional rider who doesn't have the exact fare? Adopting a marketing orientation does not automatically result in requiring bus drivers to make change for thoughtless riders who carry only $20 bills. However, occasionally helping a passenger in difficulty may create a more human image for the transit system, especially when the problem occurs in full view of other customers. Letters describing positive experiences of riders on AC Transit (reprinted in Exhibit 11–2) illustrate the importance to the consumer of quality contact with employees.

Clearly, service personnel should be allowed some discretion in dealing with difficult or unusual circumstances. Ralph Waldo Emerson's observation that "a foolish consistency is the hobgoblin of little minds" seems particularly appropriate in this context. In designing an organizational structure to ensure a quality customer-contact function, managers must consider their transit system's special characteristics and perspectives of operations, marketing, and personnel.

Exhibit 11–2
Rider and Driver Interactions on AC Transit, Oakland, California

I still say that AC Transit drivers are the nicest ones in the country, but I want to commend a very special driver, *Deborah Lanier*.

I rode on an 82 bus with her, and she greeted everyone with a happy 'hello'; and, as each departed, she would say, "Watch your step," etc. Everyone thanked her for her beautiful attitude. She made each rider feel important. Besides that, she's an excellent driver.

K. S.
San Leandro

In downtown Oakland, shopping for a trip, I bought much needed shoes—two pair, expensive because [they are] orthopedic. In my haste to get off a bus to make a connection, I somehow left the shoes. I had no money to replace them.

Calling your Lost and Found—miracle of miracles—the bus driver [had] turned them in, and I had them the next day before I took off.

I want you to know I am grateful to the bus driver (*Robert L. Edwards*) and all of you.

V. D.
Albany

I wish to recommend a young driver of a #51 bus (*M.A. Nulno*).

When he noticed me struggling with the high steps (I am old and slow), trying to board, he left his driver's seat and came quickly to help me. The same happened when I left the bus. He also called out the names of the stops.

Such courtesy is rare these days.

Mrs. G. H. L.
Berkeley

On Sunday, February 17, the Alameda Fire Department responded to the Posey Tube for a reported AC bus on fire.

On arrival, it was noted that—due to the quick professional actions by AC driver *Arletha Ward* of stopping her bus, removing her passengers to a safe area, calling for help and then using a dry chemical fire extinguisher—she had thereby terminated a possible difficult emergency situation.

It is a privilege to me to write this letter saying "Thank You" for a job well done.

H. B. Z
Assistant Fire Chief
City of Alameda

I'm writing to compliment one of your drivers, *Mary Ann O'Roarke*.

Her manner was all business, but jocular and helpful—none of the discharged hostility that can make a bus ride miserable. There were a variety of types of people on the bus that day—some potentially difficult—but they were a snap for her to handle, and handle respectfully and pleasantly.

P. C.
East Bay

Reprinted from AC Transit, *Transit Times*: "Our 'Stockholders' Write." Alameda Contra Costa County Transit District. Selected issues, 1985. By permission.

Conflict between marketing and operations

Almost invariably the marketing function finds itself in conflict with operations. Often the marketers are seeking change and the operations people are urging caution. The marketers tend to be revenue and passenger oriented and see only the revenue or ridership potential of a new idea. Operations personnel, by comparison, tend to be cost and efficiency oriented; they are more concerned initially with the short-term costs of any new idea or service concept. This kind of conflict is exacerbated by the difference in the time horizon between the two departments, with operations typically having a much shorter time horizon than marketing.

A different conflict arises at times when there are serious cost pressures on the organization. The intuitive approach of operations is to cut employees and services in an attempt to meet a reduced budget allocation. The marketing response is usually to view the problem as a shortfall in the revenues needed to cover fixed costs and therefore to advocate better, not worse, service to boost ridership.

The complexity of operating problems faced by transit managers may overshadow other issues. Unfortunately, excessive focus on operational issues is likely to accelerate the decline of a transit system, as a result of cutting costs without reference to their potential impact on revenues.

For instance, a common cost-cutting strategy is to eliminate lightly used services on the grounds that they incur heavy losses. However, a traveler on a local feeder service may also be using a well-patronized interurban route and abandon both services in favor of car travel if the feeder is eliminated. Likewise, commuters may occasionally take a late evening bus or train if they have to work late at the office—an event that cannot always be predicted in advance. If that service is withdrawn, they lose the "safety net" it represents and are stranded. Their need for flexibility may lead them to give up using public transit altogether and to drive their own cars instead.

When an operations orientation is dominant, both major policies and minor operating procedures are established in ways that increase the internal efficiency of the system yet inconvenience customers and thus diminish revenues.

The marketing "Catch-22"

Being relatively new to almost every transit organization, the marketing function must attempt to prove its value. However, managers responsible for marketing activities often find themselves in a kind of "Catch-22." To establish the influence it needs, the marketing function must achieve recognized success. However, marketing managers have virtually no direct control over the key factors needed to generate that success, particularly when faced with an antagonistic operations department. Without the ability to influence such things as quality of service, marketing personnel are likely either to give up and become totally passive or to make the decision to focus on advertising, over which they generally do have full control.

Balancing operational efficiency and marketing responsiveness

A well-run, efficient operation is a prerequisite for success in providing a transit service. However the pursuit of efficiency must not be allowed to become totally dominant, lest it result in a mindset that regards passengers as a hindrance to the provision of efficient service!

On the other hand, over-emphasizing customer needs and concerns is likely to result in runaway costs. The search for total customer satisfaction would lead to a proliferation of services, vehicles, schedules, and features tailored to meet the preferences of smaller and smaller market segments. A transit agency cannot aspire to offer limousine service at subway prices. Obviously a balance is needed between operations and marketing.

If a centralized marketing department is missing from a transit organization then can it be assumed that marketing has been short-changed in favor of operations? In a consumer goods company, the answer would certainly be "yes"—the marketing department and the marketing function are synonymous.

Paradoxically, the creation of a marketing department in the service organization can often—at least initially—be counterproductive. The emergence of such a department may be perceived as a threat. If line operations managers feel threatened by a marketing department, they can probably sidetrack or sabotage marketing initiatives. The mere existence of a marketing department can lead to the attitude, "Well, at least *we* don't have to worry about marketing anymore." It is more important to develop a strong marketing function within the organization than it is to create a powerful marketing department.

STRENGTHENING THE MARKETING FUNCTION

To improve the balance between operations efficiency and marketing responsiveness, the transit agency's board of directors and top management team must learn to differentiate between the *marketing department* and the *marketing function*. What is implicitly required is to create a greater awareness of marketing within operations and human resource management areas.

No transit authority can develop a strong marketing orientation unless the chief executive (or general manager) and board members hold a clear commitment to marketing themselves. The general manager must be able to coordinate the different functional perspectives of operations, human resources, and marketing personnel and to resolve such conflicts as emerge between them.

With transit services, the "general manager role" exists at both the upper echelons of the organization and in the field where services are delivered to customers. The managers out in the field—in different bus and trolley divisions, rapid transit lines, and ferry terminals—are controlling each of the elements with which the customer must interact. They control the tangible aspects of the organization, such as vehicles, stations, and information centers, where the services are produced, distributed and consumed. Line managers are the people who must make the tradeoffs between the conflicting needs of marketing, operations, and personnel. Unfortunately, these line managers very often see nothing but the day-to-day demands of the operation. The need for a marketing orientation is ignored in establishing and maintaining operational standards.

There are a number of ways in which service firms are seeking to improve the influence of the marketing function, many of which are applicable to transit organizations. What follows is a description of some key approaches and is based upon research undertaken in a number of different service industries.[5]

Interfunctional transfers

To ensure a broader perspective, managers can be transferred from one functional department to another. The transfer of a carefully selected operations manager to a marketing position has a two-way benefit. First, other marketing personnel become aware of the problems faced by those responsible for transit operations. And second, marketing obtains credibility from the presence of an operations manager working on marketing tasks. This situation should enhance marketing's influence in the long run. When that individual returns to an operations position, it may be much easier to achieve customer-oriented changes in operational procedures with the aid of a sympathetic manager who understands both perspectives. Transfers of personnel in the opposite direction, from marketing to operations, are also likely to improve understanding of both perspectives, but the payoff will probably take longer to achieve since marketing is the newer and less influential function.

Creation of task forces

Another approach involves creating a task force for a specific project—such as planning the introduction of rapid transit service on a new extension. The general manager should select individuals from each functional area, with special emphasis being placed on their capability for understanding others' viewpoints. From operations, field managers are needed—personnel who are practical and understand how to deal with people, rather than being totally systems- and technology-oriented. From marketing, the general manager should select individuals who have an orientation toward operating systems and making them work.

A task force offers a way of integrating functional viewpoints into an environment that is somewhat insulated from the pressures and distractions of day-to-day management activities. Participants are in a position to create a microcosm of the organization, to focus attention on the task at hand. As one task force leader remarked about his fellow participants: "The most important thing is that people in the task force were a *team*: they were not marketing or operations or construction people."[6]

Properly planned and managed, the task force environment provides a forum for discussion and resolution of many of the problems likely to occur during the development and introduction of an innovative service. There needs, of course, to be an external mechanism for settling any disputes that members of the task force cannot resolve among themselves. In transit, there is likely to be a need for external resolution of problems that have political or budgetary implications.

In those instances where a marketing manager is assigned the leadership role on a task force, the commitment of top management to this individual must be explicit, since such an appointment flies in the face of the traditional seniority of operations.

New tasks and new people

Bringing about organizational change in a transit authority requires that new relationships be developed, jobs redefined, priorities restructured, and existing patterns of thought and behavior modified—often sharply. There are two schools of thought on reorganization. One involves taking the existing players and redirecting them. The other calls for replacing certain players with new people.

The extent to which the second approach is feasible depends not merely on institutional policies and procedures, but also on the availability of an appropriate pool of new people—either outside or inside the transit agency. Larger organizations obviously have a bigger pool of people on whom to draw; they have managers and specialists in other divisions or regions who have not been "contaminated" by close exposure to the activity in question, yet are sufficiently knowledgeable about the organization that they can quickly be productive on a new project. One difficulty is the still limited availability of skilled marketing managers in any kind of service organization, let alone transit. Accordingly, some small and medium size transit systems have obtained additional management expertise on a contractual basis through private management firms.[7]

DEVELOPING A MARKETING ORIENTATION IN THE FIELD

One of the key problems facing the development of a marketing function in a transit organization is the need to produce some form of consumer orientation in those people who are in day-to-day contact with travelers. Other service industries have successfully adopted a number of approaches that are also appropriate for public transportation, such as decentralization, internal marketing, and control through formal procedures manuals. These approaches are most often used in combination rather than separately. Each has its own advantages and disadvantages.

Decentralization

One reason why field managers may lack a consumer orientation is that, as part of the operations function, they have traditionally been subject to evaluation on cost-based criteria rather than on revenue criteria. When operations are in a cost-centered environment, managers and staff are likely to be driven inward to focus on their operation rather than outward to reach toward their customers.

Decentralization of revenue responsibility represents one solution to resolve this problem. Outside the transit industry, the most impressive example comes from banking. The field manager in banking is the branch manager, who has traditionally been responsible only for costs and for security, but not for generating revenues. One major East Coast bank made branch managers responsible for profit as far as possible and rewarded them accordingly. While some managers could not cope with the change, a number began analyzing their market and initiated steps to bring in new business to the bank.

Within larger transit systems, opportunities may exist for creating regional divisions (perhaps based on major bus depots) or modal divisions based upon local buses, express buses, rapid transit, commuter rail, and ferry services. A major barrier, historically, to acceptance of operating improvements has been fear of increased costs, but if these improvements result in increased revenues, then managers may see the extra costs as a necessary and worthwhile investment.

Internal marketing

Service innovations targeted at existing and potential customers must be designed with customer needs and concerns in mind. This requires a strong orientation toward the marketplace. But there is also an *internal* marketplace, in the sense that innovations usually affect service employees, too. Sometimes innovations involve just minor changes in operating procedures; and other times, they may require major procedural changes, and retraining or displacement of employees. This poses a need for internal marketing, which may be as important for success as externally focused efforts.[8]

Gaining acceptance of transit service innovations among management and staff members is a human relations problem. Formation of a task force is one way of moving the project off the drawing board and into the development phase. Yet final implementation requires that members of the task force interact with operating personnel in the field. Winning the cooperation of operating managers in the field requires that they, too, be represented on the task force.

As an example of an internal marketing approach in another industry, consider the introduction of a recent major innovation—the automatic teller machine—into a large branch bank network. Taking an internal marketing point of view, management decided to introduce the service in just one region and to test it first at two specific branches. The vice president for that region estimated that for some 15 months he spent between 60 and 75 percent of his time on internal marketing—winning employee acceptance of a new way of doing business. This level of commitment to a new service is vital if it is to be introduced fully and well.

Another variant of internal marketing can be seen in the orientation of many fast food firms toward training. Training in manual tasks has been supplemented by efforts to develop appropriate attitudes among field staff, particularly toward their customers. The necessary education often includes sophisticated training films whose message content (directed specifically at employees) has been developed with as much care as any advertisement seen by the customers.

Control by procedures manuals

One of the most common documents found in most service firms is the procedures manual, which lays down detailed procedures and systems for virtually every operating task. This manual is the operations department's standard control document.

When a service organization finds itself faced with the need to adopt a stronger consumer orientation, one of the ways to achieve this is through the medium of its procedures manual. The manual can be expanded to include procedures for interacting with customers. In the unionized environment typified by many transit agencies such approaches are more difficult to implement. However, many union locals have, in fact, been quite supportive of operating procedures designed to improve the quality of their members' interactions with the general public. Transit managers should remember that the unions themselves constitute an important internal marketing target, and that most unionized employees would rather be perceived as heroes than as villains by their customers.

CONCLUSION

The introduction of a strong marketing orientation into transit organizations is something that has been implicitly assumed throughout this book. Without such an orientation, many of the policies we have advocated could not be implemented. The purpose of this chapter has been to consider how to introduce such an orientation at both the head office and in the field.

The introduction of a marketing orientation in an operations dominated environment is never simple. Within transit service organizations, there are a number of problems with adopting and implementing customer-oriented strategies and procedures. Transit marketers have to be much more aware of and involved with operations and human resources than do marketing managers in manufacturing firms. Care is needed to avoid unconstructive conflict with longer-established and more powerful functions. The introduction of a new department or new management activity will nearly always be seen as a threat by "old timers."

Field managers who have general management responsibility, yet only middle management authority, pose additional problems for transit marketers. Managers and supervisors in stations, terminals, and on the street can greatly influence the service received by the traveler. They must also make tradeoffs between marketing and operational issues. For example, a bus garage manager who is worried about a potential bus shortage will probably send vehicles into service that should otherwise be cleaned or repaired. Unfortunately, because of reporting lines, traditions, and job pressures, field managers and supervisors tend to be excessively oriented to the day-to-day demands of operations—at the expense of issues important to the consumer.

There is no simple solution to this problem. The introduction of a strong marketing department can often be counterproductive. We recommend an approach of developing a strong marketing function throughout the transit organization rather than forcing a centralized department on a reluctant or even hostile group of managers. To compensate for the loss of integration characterized by a central department, we suggest the use of task forces, interfunctional transfers, and outside expertise. In the long run, it may prove appropriate to centralize certain marketing tasks and to coordinate others out of a single office. However, this is not necessarily the best way to build a strong customer orientation in the first instance.

Creating and strengthening the marketing function in transit agencies is never easy, especially in heavily unionized environments. However, approaches used in other the service industries demonstrate that a customer orientation can, in fact, become an organizational reality.

NOTES

1. Mundy, Ray A., David W. Cravens, and Robert B. Woodruff. *The Potential for Marketing Management Applications in Public Transportation Planning* (Knoxville, TN: University of Tennessee, 1974).

2. Urban Mass Transportation Administration. *Transit Marketing Management Handbook* (1975).

3. Urban Mass Transportation Administration. *Transit Marketing Management Handbook: Marketing Organization* (November 1975).

4. Levitt, Theodore. "Production line approach to service," *Harvard Business Review* 50 (1972): 41.

5. See Eric Langeard, John E. G. Bateson, Christopher Lovelock, and Pierre Eiglier, *Services Marketing: New Insights from Customers and Managers* (Cambridge MA: Marketing Science Institute, 1981), pp. 87–95.

6. Brook, Harvey, Lance Liebman, and Corrine Schelling. *Public Private Partnerships: New Opportunities for Meeting Social Needs*, published for American Academy of Arts and Sciences (Cambridge, MA: Ballinger Publishing Co., 1984), p. 100.

7. See Christopher H. Lovelock, *Services Marketing* (Englewood Cliffs, NJ: Prentice-Hall, Inc., 1984), pp. 346–47.

8. Langeard et al., *Services Marketing*, op. cit., pp. 66–80.

Appendix A

Santa Monica (California) Municipal Bus Lines Marketing Plan

TABLE OF CONTENTS

INTRODUCTION

This marketing plan has been developed as part of Santa Monica Municipal Bus Lines' marketing study. The plan is based upon primary research information regarding SMMBL's current and potential markets.

The objectives of this document are as follows:

1. to determine the potential markets for SMMBL services

The preparation of this report was financed in part through a grant from the United States Department of Transportation under the provisions of Section 8 of the Urban Mass Transportation Act of 1964, as amended. This material is in the public domain.

2. to outline the proposed strategies and programs
3. to determine the appropriate media
4. to provide media schedules
5. to describe an appropriate method of evaluation.

The information in the first three sections of the plan—Market Segmentation, Media Analysis, and Perceptions & Attitudes of Non-Riders—reflect the salient findings from SMMBL's March, 1985 telephone survey, conducted by Transcom with the assistance of MSI International. The complete description and analysis of the survey findings are contained in a separate report.

The sections following describe the SMMBL marketing program, including strategies, media, and schedules. The final section outlines the evaluation method.

This marketing plan covers the period through October 31, 1985, by contractual agreement between SMMBL and Transcom Inc.

MARKET SEGMENTATION

The SMMBL market research was designed to identify and describe "potential riders" from among other non-rider groups.

Non-riders who said that they are "very likely" to try riding SMMBL in the next six months comprise a potential rider group, as compared with those who said they are "not at all likely" to ride. In addition, non-riders who said they had "actually thought about taking the Santa Monica bus" also comprise a potential rider group, as compared with those who had not thought about taking the bus in the past six months.

Twelve percent (12%) of all non-rider respondents in the sample said they are "very likely" to ride the Santa Monica bus in the next six months. Twenty-six percent (26%) said they are "somewhat likely"; 59% said they are "not at all likely" to try riding; and 3% had no opinion.

Twenty percent (20%) of non-riders said they thought about riding the bus in the past six months. Eighty percent (80%) had not considered using the bus for a specific reason and time during the past six months.

Having some knowledge of the bus system has a positive effect on whether a respondent considers himself or herself "very likely" to try riding. Of those who have some knowledge of the SMMBL system (those who could identify the bus route they live near versus those who could not), 43% said they are "very likely" or "somewhat likely" to ride, compared with only 27% with little or no knowledge of the bus system who said the same.

Those who are "very likely" to ride are twice as likely to live in a household with someone who already rides SMMBL. Of those who are "very likely" to ride, 20% live with a rider. Among those who don't live with an SMMBL bus rider, only 9% said they are "very likely" to try riding.

One-third (33%) of those who considered riding in the past six months live with an SMMBL rider, compared with one-quarter (24%) of those who did not consider riding sometime during the past six months.

Students are more likely than other groups to say they are "very likely" to ride": 16% of students vs. 10% of employed persons and 13% of the homemaker/retired group said they are "very likely" to ride in the next six months.

Thirty percent (30%) of student non-riders said they considered riding during the previous six months, while 19% of employed people considered it, and only 13% of the homemaker/retired group did so.

More people in the 16–24 age group are "very likely" to ride in the next six months: 18% of this age group are "very likely" to try riding (compared with 13% of the 25–35 group, 5% of the 36–49 group, and 13% of those 50 and over).

Fifteen percent (15%) of Hispanic people said they are "very likely" to ride vs. 10% of those from other race groups.

Thirteen percent (13%) of Hispanics said they had actually considered riding at a specific time during the past six months, compared with 23% of those in all other races. Thus, while more Hispanics said they are "very likely" to try riding in the next six months, fewer said they had actually considered riding during the past six months. Regardless of this comparison, the Hispanic population should be considered as a potential market of some significance for SMMBL services.

The study identified three market segments as having the most market potential:

1. students
2. age group 16–24
3. Hispanics

These three market segments should be considered as groups having a greater potential than others for riding SMMBL. While careful attention to *all* people in SMMBL's service area should be paid and while information about SMMBL will be seen by everyone, where the opportunity exists to slant motivational messages toward one group or another, these groups should have first consideration.

MEDIA ANALYSIS

Newspaper

The following table shows the newspapers that survey respondents read most often:

	All *Riders*	*All* *Non-riders*
Los Angeles Times	51%	57%
Santa Monica Outlook	18	11
Los Angeles Herald Examiner	5	5
La Opinión	11	15
Other	5	3
None/no answer	11	10

The following table shows the newspapers most often read for each of SMMBL's target market sub-groups:

(1) those who considered riding SMMBL in the past six months at a specific time for a specific purpose

(2) those who said they are very likely or somewhat likely to try riding in the next six months

(3) Hispanics

(4) Age 16–24.

	Non-riders									
	Considered riding		Likely to ride		Race		Age			
Newspaper	Considered riding	Did not consider	Very/ somewhat likely	Not likely	Hispanic	All other	16–24	25–35	36–49	50+
LA Times	70%	54%	41%	69%	31%	73%	57%	55%	62%	60%
Santa Monica Outlook	8	12	12	11	7	13	7	5	15	21
LA Herald Examiner	5	5	1	6	3	6	7	5	3	4
LA Opinión	8	17	28	5	42	0	21	19	15	2

The above information indicates for members of each market segment shown, which newspaper respondents read "most often". It appears that messages placed in the LA Times, Santa Monica Outlook, and La Opinión (a newspaper printed in the Spanish language) would reach potential rider groups. The Los Angeles Times has special Westside editions, on Thursdays and Sundays. Ads in these three papers might reach 86% of those non-riders who actulaly considered riding, 81% of those who are "very likely" or "somewhat likely" to give SMMBL an initial trial, and the highest proportions of other groups.

Radio

While the radio market is highly fragmented in the Los Angeles area, with 2–3% of the market going to each of more than 30 radio stations, the research identified six stations which reach a significant proportion of SMMBL's target markets. These stations are shown in the following table:

Age 16–24		Students		Hispanics	
KIIS 102.7 FM	21%	KIIS 102.7 FM	16%	KTNQ 1020 AM	17%
KLOS 95.5 FM	11	KLOS 95.5 FM	11	KLVE 107.5 FM	14
KMET 94.7 FM	7	KMET 94.7 FM	11	KIIS 102.7 FM	7
KTNQ 1020 AM	7	KOST 103.5 FM	8		
Total	46%		46%		38%

With six radio stations, SMMBL could reach nearly half of the 16–24 age group and half of the student market. SMMBL could reach 4 in 10 Hispanics.

While production costs for radio can be minimized, the cost for purchasing air time can be extravagant.

One reason that radio time is very expensive to purchase is the extensive area that is served by radio. Rotating time spots cost between $300 and $700 each (:60). The most desirable time spots can cost between $1,100 and $1,300 for each :60 spot.

Unfortunately, the cost for a minimum buy of 10–12 spots per week, per radio station is approximately $5,000.

Thus, for six stations, SMMBL could easily spend $30,000 to rotate 2–3 spots per day. The recall rate—people remembering that they heard your ad—in this case, with only a one week minimum buy, would be exceedingly low.

Therefore, Transcom feels that purchasing radio time for SMMBL messages would not be prudent. However, since SMMBL has an advertising trade agreement with KSRF 103.1 FM, the opportunity exists to update radio scripts to the current ad campaigns.

PERCEPTIONS AND ATTITUDES OF NON-RIDERS

Overall, respondents have a very high opinion of the Santa Monica Municipal Bus Lines. Ninety percent (90%) of riders give the system an "excellent" or "good" rating. Two-thirds of non-riders had an opinion and one-third had no opinion of SMMBL. Of those who had an opinion, 81% said the system is "excellent" or "good".

The general image that non-riders have of transit, however, is that it is for those with no car or those who don't drive. Two-thirds (64%) of non-riders have this perception.

The only group with a slightly different image of transit is the 16–24 group. Just over half (54%) agreed that transit is "mostly for people who don't have a car and can't drive". This group is more likely to feel that transit is for everyone, a travel mode of choice, rather than of necessity.

One misconception among non-riders that SMMBL can work to correct is the feeling that service is not direct. Both riders and non-riders rated various aspects of SMMBL service. One aspect was "direct service with no transfers". While only 30% of non-riders said SMMBL service is "good" regarding this aspect, people who ought to know, the riders, gave this aspect of service a "good" rating 64% of the time—more than twice as often.

Non-riders gave SMMBL a "good" rating 46% of the time regarding reliability and on-time service. Riders gave SMMBL a "good" rating 70% of the time on this aspect of service.

Regarding frequent service during the rush hours, 37% of non-riders gave SMMBL a "good" rating, while 59% of riders said the same. Hispanic non-riders rated the rush hour frequency as "good" only 29% of the time.

Non-riders predictably tend to have a large proportion of "don't know" or "no opinion" responses to a survey regarding aspects of bus service, such as those cited above.

The following table indicates the perceptions and attitudes that non-riders, particularly those in the potential rider groups, have about bus riding and SMMBL.

These attitudes can be used to develop motivational messages to encourage new ridership on The Big Blue Bus. These attitudes can also be used to identify misconceptions about the service which could be corrected by disseminating the appropriate information about SMMBL:

	Non-riders Who Agree with Statement			
Statements	*Total*	*16–24*	*Students*	*Hispanics*
If they could reduce the time it takes to travel by bus then I would think about using the bus.	66%	79%	81%	85%
If I had an idea of when the bus comes by maybe I would consider riding it.	65	71	68	85
I might take the bus if I had more information about the places it goes.	61	75	65	78
If I understood Santa Monica Bus Lines services better I would probably ride the bus.	57	71	62	82
Even if Santa Monica Bus Lines could offer service as quick and convenient as a car, *I would not ride the bus.*	42	36	41	43

The above table indicates that the top three aspects of service that would motivate the potential rider groups [of non-riders] are fast travel time, schedule information, and destination information. We have already seen that the majority of non-riders have very different perceptions about aspects of the service than riders who have experience with the system.

It follows, then, that maybe if non-riders were provided with information about (1) where the bus goes—directly; (2) the travel times to those places; and (3) how often the bus runs, that SMMBL could take advantage of opportunities to increase ridership among those non-rider groups that show a predisposition to messages of this sort. The following table supports these ideas:

| | Non-riders Who Said These Aspects of Service are "Very Important" | | | |
Factors in Choice Between Car and Bus	Total	16–24	Students	Hispanic
If you know when the bus will come	79%	89%	81%	78%
Having the flexibility to go *where* you want	78	79	81	75
If you know where the bus travels	77	75	78	81
The flexibility to go *when* you want	75	79	89	76
Whether the buses usually run on-time	75	79	73	69
Whether the buses run often enough	71	68	73	72

The factors shown on the previous table indicate a high level of interest among non-riders in various aspects of the SMMBL service. This interest and the direction it's taking, along with the following rating, show that there exists a unique opportunity at this time for SMMBL to attract new riders.

While there is a high level of interest in SMMBL shown by non-riders, this group seems to feel that there is not enough transit information easily available. Only one-third (34%) rate the "availability of transit information" as "good". Only 29% of Hispanics rate this aspect of service as "good".

Thus, while those who have used timetables find them relatively easy to use, and those who have used the bus stop schedule information or telephone information find that helpful, non-riders feel that, overall, there is not enough riding information available.

The following marketing programs that are proposed for SMMBL seek to provide the information that non-riders, particularly those with the propensity to give SMMBL an initial trial, would need to try riding.

MARKETING PROGRAMS TO INCREASE RIDERSHIP

Objectives of Programs

1. To generate awareness and encourage the use of the SMMBL transit services.

2. To provide the riding information that non-riders, particularly the potential rider groups, would need to try riding The Big Blue Bus.

3. To provide information in a simple and interesting manner.

Target groups

1. Residents of the SMMBL service area.
2. Youth ages 16–24.
3. Students.
4. Hispanics.

Target market

The City of Santa Monica and other areas in the SMMBL service district.

Campaign dates

June through October, 1985.

MARKETING APPROACH

SMMBL is in the business of providing transportation for people within a 36 square mile area. The car is undoubtedly transit's biggest single competitor: of SMMBL non-riders, 85% have a driver's license and only 5% live in households where no one owns a car.

However, since SMMBL has had few opportunities in the past to provide consistent public messages about its services, the campaign planned for 1985 should establish an identity for SMMBL on its own, rather than positioning SMMBL against the automobile.

Since three-quarters of the potential rider market agree that a greater availability of transit information would encourage them to ride, the information provided in the ads should make it seem easy to find information about riding. In particular, since 74% of non-riders said they would use the telephone for riding information, the phone number should be emphasized in messages.

Ads to position SMMBL and its riding information as immediately available ("It's HERE, available for you quick and easy."), almost as if SMMBL finds you, you don't have to find SMMBL, should show that personalized riding information can be found easily. "It's easy to get information. It's easy to ride."

At the same time that the newspaper ads will be projecting an "easy to find, easy to ride" image, the riding information will be arriving at the homes via direct mail—reinforcing the "easily and immediately accessible" image.

MEDIA RECOMMENDATIONS

1. *Newspapers* are recommended as they provide excellent coverage of the SMMBL service district and afford sufficient space to provide infor-

mation about the service. In addition, campus newspapers offer the opportunity to communicate with the student market.

2. *Direct mail* is recommended as it provides a way to disseminate riding information that is specifically suited to residents along the bus routes. Proposed for the mailing are the following:

- How to Ride brochure
- system map
- timetable appropriate for the household
- letter from SMMBL

3. *Exterior transit cards* are recommended as they would provide a consistent daily reach to the current riders and to the potential new riders.

4. *A brochure* to detail specific riding information for new riders and potential riders is recommended as follows:

How to Ride brochure: The "How to Ride" brochure will be in English and in Spanish. Both versions will be distributed through direct mail and also be available at the current SMMBL timetable locations. The Spanish brochure will also be an insert in the newsletter which the Santa Monica Latino Resource Organization distributes to 3,000 Spanish homes on the Westside, to libraries, and to stores.

5. *A slide show* for community groups that describes SMMBL and its services is a recommended way to reach businesses, residents, and others in the SMMBL service area.

[Authors' note: The proposed advertising schedule called for newspaper advertising to run in late June in the *Los Angeles Times, Evening Outlook*, and *La Opinión*, and during the first week of October in UCLA's *Daily Bruin*. Exterior transit cards were to be featured from late June through the second week of August. A slide show was to be presented from mid-October onwards, while a proposed brochure would be distributed by direct mail in late June and thence through the end of the year at SMMBL timetable locations.]

Appendix B
Toronto Transit Commission Marketing Plan, 1986

BACKGROUND

Over the next decade and beyond, the TTC will experience ever-increasing demands on its resources. Many of the demands, such as social and demographic changes felt over the last decade, will intensify and new requirements resulting from changing external factors will appear. Many of these major trends such as stable population growth, employment growth, decline in the high transit use of the female labour force, stable or slightly declining real wages, increased mobility demands of Metro residents, increased road congestion, a changing labour force, the safety perception of transit, etc. will intensify the pressure to improve the level and quality of service.

In pursuit of this goal of accommodating an increasing ridership demand while at the same time reducing the unit costs of operating the system, the TTC must aggressively pursue all opportunities for productivity improvements.

To respond to these trends, the Marketing and Community Relations Plan for 1985 continued to emphasize off-peak ridership through a variety of promotional/advertising programs directed at increasing ridership while minimizing TTC vehicle and manpower requirements.

It is intended once again to provide major off-peak emphasis in 1986 based on the success of existing programs and the results of a major off-peak market segmentation study undertaken to better define potential target markets. The 1986 Plan will also ensure the continued maintenance of peak ridership through the promotion of the economy of the TTC by encouraging auto users to seriously consider the various costs associated with owning and operating a car when compared to taking the TTC.

Mission statement

The Marketing and Community Relations Department is responsible for the promotion of the TTC, the generation of both transportation and non-transportation revenues to help offset operating costs and the provision of information and service to its customers to ensure that the needs of TTC riders are met.

Departmental goals

1. To maximize awareness of the TTC and promote ridership within available resources;
2. To ensure the public understanding of the TTC and the importance of its role in the community;
3. To optimize public satisfaction with the TTC;
4. To maximize non-transportation revenue;
5. To provide market information as an aid to improving the decision-making process; and,
6. To disseminate information to the public generally and to employees.

Key opportunities

The key opportunities in 1986 consist of:

- Increasing frequency of use primarily in the off-peak periods by the following categories:

    TTC 'captive' riders

    Mainly TTC use, but some car

    Mainly car use, but some TTC
- Increasing dual usage of car/TTC to increase TTC ridership.
- Promoting rider and employee participation in maintaining a clean, safe and functional transit environment.
- Continuing the investigation of new markets such as visitors to Metro Toronto to increase transportation revenues.
- Continuing to perfect the processing of customer complaints/enquiries through the centralized customer communications system.
- Undertaking localized research and promotion of routes capable of growth to improve ridership.
- Investigating the use of paid advertising to reduce or offset the cost of producing information material to TTC riders and employees.
- Ensuring the appropriate capital expenditure by Trans Ad to maximize non-transportation revenues to the Commission.

- Investigating the cost effectiveness of expanding the provision of on-street information to TTC customers.
- Pursuing bulk sales of TTC fare media to Metro companies and encouraging the use of Variable Work Hours.
- Implementing a computerized telephone information service (TimeLine) for the full TTC system.
- Continuing the co-operative activities undertaken in 1985 with the Attractions Council of the Metro Toronto Convention and Visitors Association to increase off-peak ridership.
- Continuing to capitalize on the increasing value and attractiveness of subway retail space through the implementation of the Leasing Plan.
- Analyzing and adjusting Guide functions as appropriate, to maximize the effectiveness of Guides, e.g. sales, marketing community work, surveys, etc.
- Continuing to exploit the Novelty/Memorabilia market through the provision of TTC-related items.

MARKETING PROGRAM OBJECTIVES AND STRATEGIES—1986

Objective. To increase off-peak ridership by a net 1% in 1986. This would result in an estimated 4.37 million rides, with a corresponding net revenue of $3.1 million.

Strategy. Promote use of the TTC in off-peak periods by encouraging use for shopping and to attend a variety of entertainment destinations.

Conduct area-specific research and promotion of routes capable of growth, primarily in the off-peak periods.

Objective. To maintain peak ridership.

Strategy. Promote the benefits of the TTC versus the car by illustrating car operating costs, parking costs, etc.

Objective. To increase non-transportation transit advertising revenue from approximately $5.2 million in 1985 to approximately $5.55 million in 1986, an increase of 6.7%.

Strategy. Identify and develop additional revenue-producing initiatives.

Ensure maximization of transit advertising revenue between the Commission and Trans-Ad, primarily through our involvement in the capital investment process.

Objective. To increase the modal share of trips taken by the Visitors market through the provision of Visitors Passes, from 3.8% in 1985, to 5.8% in 1986.

Strategy. Promote sale of Visitor's Passes to convention planners and conference organizers.

Objective. To present the TTC as a modern, clean, safe transit system.
Strategy. All promotion/information material will present the TTC as a modern clean, safe transit system.

Objective. To encourage use of the TTC by providing important travel information to the public.
Strategy. Encourage use of TTC by providing information to the public, while reducing the cost of the information through paid advertising.

Objective. To maximize the effectiveness of Guides.
Strategy. Analyze the duties of the Guides to determine the best staff allocation by function, e.g. sales, community work, etc.

REVIEW OF MARKETING PROGRAM OBJECTIVES AND ACTIVITIES FOR 1985

Objective. To increase off-peak ridership.
Activity. As in 1984, a greater emphasis was directed to the general promotion of off-peak travel. The Toronto's Entertainment Network campaign was repeated in the spring, with commercial updating occurring for the fall period.

A co-op promotion was undertaken between the TTC, Metro Toronto Convention and Visitors Association to increase the public awareness and use of the TTC's Sunday/Holiday Pass and discounts offered by participating attractions.

With the expansion of special transit services to all Blue Jays and Argos home games in 1985 a promotional program was developed highlighting the 'Stadium Express Service'. Information was provided to the public through newsprint, transit advertising, Blue Jay radio broadcasts, Stadium scoreboard, news releases, etc. A final report on the year's program is to be prepared shortly.

Objective. To maintain the current level of peak ridership.
Activity. The intent of the program was to:

1. Retain present riders by reminding them of the costs involved in car ownership and usage;
2. To forestall families contemplating the purchase of a second car; and,
3. To encourage drivers to use their car less and the TTC more.

As in past years, the TTC 'Test' newsprint format was revised and strengthened in 1985 through the use of testimonials. This economy approach has been strongly supported as documented in various research studies.

Objective. To increase non-transportation-related revenue such as transit advertising and leasing, from $6,400,000 in 1984 to $7,390,000 in 1985, an increase of 15.5%.

Activity. Staff, working closely with Trans Ad, the system advertising contractor, increased TTC transit advertising revenue from $4.6 million in 1984 to $5.2 million in 1985, an increase of 13%. Leasing revenues are covered in the Leasing Section.

Objective. To maximize efficiency for sale of fare media via Guides, currently accounting for over $6,000,000 annually.

Activity. During 1985, TTC Guides sold over $6.5 million in TTC fare media and provided information to customers at busy downtown locations and at major Metropolitan Toronto companies. In addition, the Guides assisted various TTC departments with community visits, display staffing, surveys and special duties. The Guides also assist in the control and issuing of TTC Student I.D. cards for students unable to obtain their photo during the annual school visitation program.

Objective. To maintain the awareness of the benefits of Variable Work Hours within the community.

Activity. Staff continued to contact employers and employees, as well as promoting Variable Work Hours for Metro employees through transit advertising in the Fall of 1985.

Other activities: Visitors market

One aspect of the 1985 program was the re-issuing of a revised edition of the successful brochure - "Exciting Toronto by TTC". The production of this attractive, high-quality information piece with over eighty of Metropolitan Toronto's most popular entertainment sites, cultural attractions, historical landmarks, etc. was shared jointly by the TTC and the Metro Toronto Convention and Visitors Association. A total of 250,000 brochures were distributed through subway collector's booths, the TTC Information Centre, Metro Toronto Convention and Visitors Association information kiosks, major hotels, motels and attractions.

In addition, 'visitor display' and 'pass' information material was developed and actually promoted to major planners during the special planning sessions set up by the Metropolitan Toronto Convention and Visitors Association.

With major activity undertaken in this area, pass sales in 1985 have amounted to $110,000, up from $5,500 in 1984.

Provision of information aids

To encourage use of the TTC, information related to services, fares, products, etc. was provided in printed form in 1985 via newsprint advertisements, direct mail, Ride Guides, Rider News, pocket timetables, laminated schedules, pole cards, in-transit advertising such as "Our Riders Write" poster series, etc.

A redesigned pocket timetable was developed in 1985 resulting in improved readability and understanding of the information by the customer. This review will also result in internal production savings through the use of various computer applications of the initial schedule information. It is planned to make this available to the public in mid–1986.

A special TTC Task Force was formed in the Fall of 1985 to investigate the feasibility of providing on-street information at TTC stops. The Task Force will review the possibility of a test application on a number of CIS Routes in 1986.

Marketing and Community Relations staff are co-ordinating a review of the expansion Metro-wide of the 'TimeLine' automated telephone system.

Investigations continued into alternative forms of providing consumer information such as the use of videotex terminals.

In addition, the TTC's Transit Information telephone service handled approximately 2,474,961 enquiries via the telephone and the TTC's Info Booths.

COMMUNITY RELATIONS, PROGRAMS, OBJECTIVE: 1986

Objective. To respond to complaints and inquiries from the public within five working days of receipt of communication.

Strategy. Continue Centralized Customer Communications system and endeavour to improve five-working days acknowledgement/response rate from 86% to 90%, to ensure public satisfaction.

Objective. To increase public exposure to TTC Community Relations activities by 10%.

Strategy. Increase TTC/community interface via TTC Info-Bus, displays, participation in local public events and meetings, distribution of TTC A-V material in community, etc.

Objective. To increase public/employee awareness and understanding of TTC policies and procedures with the aim of improving customer relations.

Strategy. Continue to provide information on TTC policies and procedures to customers and employees via various internal and external media.

Objective. To contribute to the maintenance of the TTC's world-wide position of esteem in the transit industry.

Strategy. Co-ordinate arrangements for all system tours and visitors'/TTC officials' meetings, as well as producing TTC materials - printed, audio-visual, etc. - for use by/at various transit association (APTA/CUTA/UITP) etc. meetings and functions.

Objective. To contribute to TTC non-transportation revenue.

Strategy. Continue the sale of existing postcards, develop additional ones; develop TTC calendar for 1987; continue to co-ordinate and arrange billing of advertising and production companies for filming on TTC property; etc.

REVIEW OF COMMUNITY RELATIONS PROGRAM OBJECTIVES AND ACTIVITIES FOR 1985

Objective. To respond to complaints and inquiries from the public within five working days of receipt of communications.

Activity. The six-month test of the Centralized Customer Communications System was completed in April, 1985. The system subsequently was made permanent and, in the year since its inception (October 1984 to October 1985), 825 responses have been co-ordinated on behalf of Commission and Senior officials. Approximately 86% of the necessary acknowledgements/responses were prepared within the five-day turn-around time.

Objective. To increase exposure to TTC Community Relations activities by 5%.

Activity. The TTC Info-Bus was scheduled in the Community for approximately 100 days, including the CNE, and was visited by 75,000 people. Free-standing TTC displays were viewed by an additional estimated 40,000 people. The TTC/CNE display, including Info-Bus, which was promoted through newsprint and transit advertising, was viewed by 106,000 persons. In addition, TTC Guides participated in nine Safety and Security mall visits which, according to Safety and Security estimates, were visited by 33,000 people. The TTC A-V presentation, "Moving People", was shown in the community on fourteen occasions. Public exposure was further heightened through co-ordination of the Annual Subway Musicians' Auditions (media coverage), the TTC involvement in the Family Service Great Celebrity All-Star Auction and in providing TTC familiarization training as part of the Metropolitan Toronto Convention and Visitors Association's program for counsellors.

Objective. To increase public/employee awareness and understanding of TTC policies and procedures with the aim of improving passenger relations.

Activity. A new A-V presentation - "Responding to the Public" - was produced to explain the dynamics of complaint handling to employees. An internal poster series on common complaints and how to handle them was also started for Operating employees. The Coupler carried feature articles each month on the work and responsibilities of all TTC Branches/Departments, as well as a special message re the importance of courtesy from the Chief General Manager in the May issue. This was a follow-up to an earlier letter (April) sent to all TTC employees by the Chief General Manager. The Transportation Department - specifically the Manager - visited all TTC Divisions throughout the year to discuss concerns, suggestions, policies, procedures, etc. with employees. As part of the "Customer Relations/System Cleanliness" program, a new poster series with the theme "We Want You To Know More About Us" was launched for the public in the transit system in October. An "Award of Excellence" employee recognition program was introduced for Transportation Department employees. The "Our Riders Write" poster series was expanded, and a new A-V presentation on TTC Safety and Security procedures/facilities was also produced for community and employee use.

Objective. To increase by 5% customer and employee awareness of their roles in helping to keep the system clean.

Activity. An "Award of Excellence" employee recognition program was introduced in the Plant and Equipment Departments for employees involved in subway station and vehicle cleaning respectively. The June 1985 Coupler carried an article on system cleanliness for employees and was a follow-up to a letter sent to all TTC employees by Mr. A. H. Savage which also covered the subject of system cleanliness. A new transit vehicle and station poster, emphasizing the customers' role in keeping the system clean, began running in the system in the Fall. Related "cleanliness" messages were also included in the "Our Riders Write" poster series and the monthly "Rider News" pamphlet. Pre-research with customers was carried out in late 1984. Post research will be conducted by early 1986.

Objective. To contribute to the maintenance of the TTC's world-wide position of esteem in the transit industry.

Activity. Co-ordinated visit, tour and meeting arrangements for approximately 400 visitors to the TTC, with many congratulatory letters subsequently received. Prepared materials, e.g. new A-V presentations, printed info, and provided staff and displays for APTA and CUTA Conferences held in Toronto. Provided TTC display material to TT Consultants for use at UITP overseas trade show. Co-ordinated TTC presentation at the Urban Land Institute Conference. Co-ordinated 1985 TTC APTA nominations.

Other Activity: Student I.D.

In 1985 a new contractor was selected to provide Student I.D. Photographs for the 1985/86 school year.

The school visitation program was carried out between September 5 to October with approximately 550 schools being visited.

During this period 158,000 cards were issued. In addition, a central facility at 33 Bloor Street East is available to provide photo ID's to students who were missed at school or who have lost or misplaced their cards.

LEASING SECTION OBJECTIVES FOR 1986

Objective. To increase leasing revenue from approximately $2.115 million in 1985 to approximately $2.26 million in 1986, an increase of 6.9%.

Strategies. Co-ordinate the implementation of the Leasing Plan. Phase 1, "Personal Services", has been leased representing 7,500 square feet of the 45,000-square foot plan. Phase II, the remainder of the plan, has been scheduled to go out for proposals in early 1986.

A study and analysis of the potential market for TTC memorabilia and novelty items has been completed, with positive results. Phase 1 of the novelty program, which involves the sale of items using the 'Stadium Express' logo to TTC employees and external retail market, is scheduled to commence in April 1986. Phase 2 "Third Party Licencing", is planned to commence in June '86 subject to the results of the Phase 1 program.

REVIEW OF LEASING SECTION OBJECTIVES AND ACTIVITIES FOR 1985

Objective. Implementation of the Leasing Plan.

Activity. Phase I of the Leasing Plan has been leased, generating an annual guarantee of approximately $314,000 with a potential for approximately $600,000 per annum based on percentage rent.

Co-ordination and administration of Phase I implementation and construction.

Objective. Evaluate potential market for TTC novelty items, as well as the development of a plan incorporating promotion, sale, and distribution.

Activity. Market analysis has been completed, indicating potential for TTC novelties. A business plan had been developed incorporating two phases. Phase I involves the marketing of specific items to TTC employees only. Phase II will incorporate a third party licensing program for all TTC novelty items.

RESEARCH SECTION OBJECTIVES FOR 1986

Objective. To identify trends in attitudes or rider behaviour which have implications for programs and policies.

Strategy. As in previous years, a general survey will be conducted in the Fall of 1986. This survey will monitor riding attitudes toward the TTC. This research is important for identifying areas in need of remedial action, and for providing the Department and the Commission with background information for the development of a wide range of programs.

In addition, the section will provide numerous statistical reports on complaint trends. It is expected that the demand for this information will increase in 1986.

Communications research will also be conducted on all potential television commercials to determine public response, and to identify any barriers to effectiveness.

Objective. To identify markets and products with potential for the TTC.

Strategy. Research will be conducted to identify markets for potential expansion. The analysis will provide an estimate of the necessary investment and expected return so that an informed decision can be made as to its potential.

Candidates are direct bulk sales of fare media to commercial users, the relocation market, etc.

It was through an initiative such as this that the potential of the visitor's pass was identified.

Objective. To provide estimates of the cost-effectiveness or cost-benefit of various programs and policies.

Strategy. The major emphasis in 1986 will be on quantification of the benefits of printed information. The research will draw on previously collected data on effectiveness, supplemented by additional information on distribution patterns. A cost-effectiveness model, previously developed for this purpose, will be refined and expanded.

An evaluation will also be conducted on the activities of the Guides Section. This research, begun in 1985, will look at the impact of the Guides on queue lengths and waiting times at Collectors' Booths, at their role in promoting bulk sales to commercial users, and at their role in general community relations activities.

The program also allows for evaluation activities with regard to TimeLine and new on-street information installations planned for 1986.

REVIEW OF RESEARCH SECTION OBJECTIVES AND ACTIVITIES FOR 1985

Objective. To identify trends in attitudes or rider behaviour which have implications for programs and policies.

Activity. The 1985 Attitude Survey was expanded considerably in its analysis to look in greater depth at a variety of issues such as car ownership and specific market segments.

Research was also conducted regarding the pricing of commuter parking. Recommendations were made as to specific differential pricing levels on a lot-by-lot basis.

Objective. To identify markets and products with potential for the TTC.

Activity. In 1985, a major project was undertaken to identify market segments for the purposes of off-peak promotion. As a result, major advertising emphasis will be directed to the TTC 'captive' and TTC 'choice' car markets in 1986.

In the area of new consumer information initiatives, a package of information was developed for "Teleguide", a network of more than 800 publicly accessible information terminals. The information explained the basics of the TTC, including fares and route structure, and provided specifics on CNE access. A module also provided a "car-cost computer" to allow the user to calculate savings if TTC is used rather than the car. The units were included as part of the TTC's CNE display and the information remained on the Teleguide network for public use. The system is used largely by visitors to the city with increasing use by local residents due to the large amount of information available about local entertainment, the stock market, etc.

Objective. To provide estimates of the cost-effectiveness or cost-benefit of various programs and policies.

Activity. Evaluation projects for 1985 included a survey of Coupler readership and a survey of CNE display visitors.

Other projects were conducted on the Sunday/Holiday pass and War Veterans concession fares.

The section continued to carry out weekly surveys of Metropass riders as well as various special ridership surveys for the Planning Department.

Programs and Material Budgets for 1986

	1986 Budget	1985 Budget	Percent Increase/ (decrease)
Marketing			
1. General Traffic Building (peak and off-peak)	$1,090,000	$1,080,000	
2. Specific off-peak Programs			
(A) Stadium Express	40,000	60,000	
(B) Variable Work Hours	10,000	10,000	
(C) Transit Destinations	59,000	210,000	
3. TTC Timeline	30,000	—	
4. Student Promotion	—	30,000	
5. Visitors Market	—	20,000	
6. Promotion of poor performing routes	19,400	—	
7. Met Ticket Pass Promotion	—	10,000	
8. Fare Increase	30,000	20,000	
9. Metropass Promotion	—	30,000	
10. Scarborough RT	—	50,000	
Total—Marketing	$1,278,400	$1,520,000	(15.9%)
Community Relations			
1. Info Bus	$20,000	$20,000	
2. A-V Presentations	18,000	7,000	
3. Customer Relations/System cleanliness	30,000	85,000	
4. Displays (general)	15,000	5,000	
5. Displays (CNE)	10,000	50,000	
6. Display (counting devices)	21,500	—	
7. Network 2011	7,500	—	
8. Harbourfront LRT	7,500	—	
9. Post Cards/Calendar	10,000	—	
10. Publications, Miscellaneous	—	—	
a. Transit in Toronto	10,000	10,000	
b. Transit Dev. Connection	25,000	—	
c. Pocket Timetables Units	12,000	—	
d. A-V Technology Transfer	12,000	—	
Total—Community relations	$198,500	$187,000	6.1%
Consumer Information			
1. Service Changes/User Aids	$135,500	$110,000	
2. Ride Guides	90,000	70,000	
3. Rider News	24,000	22,000	

4. Consumer Information	20,000	15,000	
5. On-Street Information Test	60,000	—	
6. Exciting Toronto by TTC	40,000	40,000	
7. Tenders/Miscellaneous	—	10,000	
Total—Consumer Information	$369,500	$267,000	38.4%

Research

1. Creative Research	$30,000	$28,000	
2. Spring Tracking Study	30,000	33,000	
3. Fall Tracking Study	35,000	38,000	
4. System Cleanliness/Customer Relations	15,000	—	
5. Timeline	20,000	—	
6. Printed Material "Cost-Effectiveness"	20,000	—	
7. On-street Information	20,000	—	
8. Security	27,000	—	
9. Guides	14,900	—	
10. Off-peak Market Segmentation	—	28,000	
11. Consumer Information	—	10,000	
12. Tourist Market	—	10,000	
13. Met Ticket/Pass	—	8,500	
14. Novelties	—	5,000	
15. Community Relations	—	10,000	
16. Complaints	—	10,000	
Total—Research	$211,900	$180,500	17.4%
Total	$2,058,300	$2,154,500	(4.5%)

Revenue Return *Non-transportation*	*1986* *Projected*	*1985* *Actual*	*Percent* *Increase/* *(decrease)*
1. Transit Advertising	$5,550,000	$5,200,000	6.7%
2. Leasing	2,260,000	2,115,000	6.9%
3. TTC Novelty/Memorabilia	30,000	20,000	50.0%
Total	$7,840,000	$7,335,000	6.9%

Revenue Return
Transportation

1. Visitors Pass Sales	$ 100,000	$ 110,000	(9.1%)
2. Guides	$6,890,000	$6,561,000	5.0%
Total	6,990,000	6,671,000	4.8%

Index

About the Authors

CHRISTOPHER H. LOVELOCK, a leading authority on management in the service sector, is active as an author, teacher, and consultant. Previously he was a professor at the Harvard Business School for eleven years and has also taught at Stanford and the University of California at Berkeley. His business experience includes two years as an advertising executive in London and another two years in corporate planning in Montreal.

A native of Great Britain, Lovelock graduated from the University of Edinburgh with an M.A. in Economics and a B.Com. degree. He subsequently obtained an MBA from Harvard and a Ph.D. from Stanford, writing his doctoral dissertation on marketing urban public transportation.

Lovelock is author or coauthor of nine other books, focusing on marketing in public and nonprofit organizations and in service businesses. He lives with his family in Cambridge, Massachusetts.

GORDON LEWIN is principal in the firm of Gordon Lewin & Associates, consultants specializing in marketing and planning for the transportation community. He holds a B.A. in Urban Studies from Earlham College and an M.S. in Engineering–Urban Planning from Stanford University. He has taught transportation and environmental courses at Boston University, Stanford, and Central Connecticut State College. A native of Chicago, Lewin has been a resident of Cambridge, Massachusetts, since 1975 where he lives with his wife, Hilary Rowen, and their son, David.

GEORGE S. DAY is the Magna International Professor of Business Strategy at the University of Toronto. He has a B.A.Sc. (from the University of British Columbia), an MBA (from the University of Western Ontario) and a Ph.D. (from Columbia University). He has taught on numerous executive programs in Canada, the United States, Europe, and Asia. Present consulting clients include General Electric, General Motors, and Libbey-Owens-Ford on a variety of assignments related to the development of competitive business strategies and new venture programs. His most recent book is *Strategic Market Planning: The Pursuit of Competitive Advantage* (West Publishing).

JOHN E. G. BATESON is senior lecturer in marketing at the London Business School in England. He holds a B.Sc. from Imperial College of Science and Technology, an M.Sc. from the University of London, and a DBA from Harvard University. His full-time business experience includes positions as a marketing service manager with Pye Limited, and as a brand manager with Lever Brothers. Dr. Bateson's consulting and research interests focus on the management of service firms, especially issues in marketing management and consumer behavior. He has published works in many marketing journals.